Sports Heroes, Fallen Idols

Sports Heroes, Fallen Idols

STANLEY H. TEITELBAUM

UNIVERSITY OF NEBRASKA PRESS
LINCOLN AND LONDON

Library of Congress
Cataloging-in-Publication Data

Teitelbaum, Stanley H.
Sports heroes, fallen idols /
Stanley H. Teitelbaum.
p.   cm.
Includes index.
ISBN-13: 978-0-8032-4445-0
(cloth: alk. paper)
ISBN-10: 0-8032-4445-2
(cloth: alk. paper)
1. Athletes—United States—
Psychology—Case studies.
2. Sports—Social aspects—
United States—Case studies.
I. Title.
GV706.4.T43   2005
796'.01—dc22
2005002501

Printed by Thomson-Shore, Inc.

To Sylvia, for all the
ways you are there

Contents

Acknowledgments

The impetus for this book came from my lifelong love of both sports and psychology.

I wish to thank Basil Kane for his encouragement and direction of this work and Sara Springsteen of the University of Nebraska Press for her enthusiasm about the project. Rob Taylor, Chris Steinke, and Sandra Johnson provided valuable input along the way, and Alice Bennett supplied a central focus to the book.

The following family members were especially helpful in keeping me on track: Leighsa King for her sustained interest in the material and for connecting me with key resources; Lawrence Teitelbaum for his shared interest in the world of sports and maintaining a perpetual hot stove league dialogue; John King and Diane Teitelbaum for their ongoing support; and Jake Ross Teitelbaum for being an inspirational hero himself.

I owe appreciation to Ned Babbitt and Phil Harmon for their valuable critiques of sections of the book and to Peter Buirski, Alan Melowsky, Laura Stein, Al Pollock, and Joe Feldman for their useful suggestions. George Kaplan and Bob Grossman are long-standing cheerleaders who stirred me forward.

I am grateful to Sue Macy, who acquainted me with the importance of female sports icons and their travails, and to Harry Carson, who provided his keen insights into the psyche of professional athletes.

The entire staff at the Teaneck, New Jersey, public library and Victor Estrellado at the Hackensack, New Jersey, library were assiduous in locating resource material. Yoni Shenkman and Josh Lukin were relentless in researching obscure information that was indispensable for the flow of this book.

Connie Stroboulis was consistently reliable in preparing the manuscript.

I also owe a debt of gratitude to Ted Miller for his guidance on publishing and to Martin Cohen and Alicia Steger for their creative ideas about reaching a wider audience.

Most of all, I am deeply thankful to Sylvia Teitelbaum for being a constructive critic throughout the writing and for helping me maintain the perseverance and focus essential to completing this work.

Introduction

This book is about sports stars who fall from the pinnacle where they have been perched. It is about gifted athletes who lose it: lose their perspective, lose their balance, lose their appropriateness. The glory, adulation, and wealth they have acquired do not necessarily protect them from personal lapses that compromise their image and sometimes even their lives. Some by-products of fame can encourage athletes' destructive behavior toward themselves or others.

A hero-hungry public craves a connection to sports icons; the media help create heroes whose image is larger than life and who are expected to be perfect; and athletes often buy into their exalted image and develop a powerful sense of entitlement. The combination of these factors creates a climate in which there is little room to stumble.

Under pressure from their inner demons or as an outgrowth of a distorted self-image that encourages them to believe they have a free pass to do whatever they want, some of our sports heroes behave in ways that have profound and damaging consequences. Abuse of women and other violence including sexual assaults and murder have become commonplace reflections of their destructiveness toward others. Gambling, substance abuse, alcoholism, and drug-related crimes highlight the self-destructiveness of some of our most cherished stars. Under the glare of the modern media spotlight, we are frequently forced to recognize our heroes as flawed. In some cases this occurs while an athlete is at the height of his career; sometimes the luster becomes tarnished later or even posthumously.

We tend to anoint our sports heroes as gods because we need the feeling of specialness we get from affiliation with outstanding athletes. We need to perceive them as wonderful, through a tinted lens that enhances their grandeur. And we need for them not to disillusion us. Thus we often invent supermen, though our heroes are frequently imperfect. Many come from dysfunctional or traumatic backgrounds, and they are not always equipped to handle the stress of stardom. Professional athletes may develop unrealistic views of themselves, and maladaptive behavior often emerges off the field in conjunction with their distorted self-image. Many star athletes have been catered to for their talent since early childhood, and they have been conditioned to think special treatment is their due. Hubris and an attitude of entitlement and grandiosity become central dimensions of their psyches. They may consider themselves above the rules of society and believe they will not be held accountable for their moral or legal transgressions. They also tend to be unprepared for life after retirement from sports, when they no longer occupy the limelight.

Major gambling scandals, the bête noire of sports, have blemished heroes in baseball, football, and basketball. Careers have been truncated and images sullied. The public is generally captivated by these scandals, fascinated by our heroes' amorality as well as by a need to believe in their goodness.

In spite of the advantages sports heroes enjoy, many jeopardize their own careers. In recent years unprecedented numbers of star athletes have fallen from grace as a result of self-destructive behavior off the field. Drug-related crimes, alcohol abuse, and sexual transgressions have become everyday news. An attitude of omnipotence and invulnerability seems to underlie their poor judgment and impulsive acts. Their violence toward women is particularly alarming. Famous athletes are increasingly accused and convicted of domestic violence, assault, gang rape, and other forms of sexual abuse, and several high-profile athletes have been involved in murder cases.

Violence in sports mirrors our violent society, and I consider violent episodes between players in the four major sports leagues. I also examine the impact of mental health problems on the careers of sports heroes. Not only must those who are afflicted overcome their own denial, they must face a sports establishment that remains uninformed and unaccepting of their disorders.

I believe the issues I address are also relevant to our changing society. We live in an age when there is an erosion of morality and ethical behavior in the public sector, as witnessed by the scandals surrounding Enron, WorldCom, Tyco, and other leading American corporations. The decline of morality, in which crime, violence, and greed are widespread, is paralleled in the world of sports as many high-profile athletes have become enmeshed in immoral or illegal activities, with destructive consequences for themselves and others.

The value system of hero-hungry fans is shaped to some extent by their perception of their heroes' comportment on and off the playing field. Athletes set an example with regard to pursuing excellence, performing effectively under stress, and achieving success within defined ground rules and standards. In this way they contribute to the mores and moral fabric of our society. Identifying with our sports heroes, we relish their accomplishments and mourn their decline just the way we deal with the passages in our own life cycle. Thus they often exert a powerful influence on our lives.

Sports Heroes, Fallen Idols

1. The Need for Heroes

He understood that we would give him anything—if he
would always be the hero we required.

Richard Ben Cramer, *Joe DiMaggio: The Hero's Life*

Sports stars become heroes when they are admired for their athletic
accomplishments. We yearn to feel connected to them, want to be like
them, and enhance our self-esteem by imagining an association with
them and basking in the glow of their success. When our heroes perform well, we feel like winners. When they falter, on or off the playing
field, we distance ourselves from them. We are disappointed, resentful,
and angry, not wanting to associate with losers. The greater our investment in a hero's accomplishments and the more we define ourselves
through his achievements, the more we resent it when he lets us down.

Our need for heroes stems from early childhood. Our first heroes are
our parents, whom we view as all-knowing and all-powerful as they protect us and shepherd us through early life. Gradually, especially after we
recognize that even our parents are flawed, they are replaced by outside
heroes, often from the world of sports. Children embrace sports heroes
with a passion. This attachment provides a sense of specialness and an
optimism that we can grow up and also be successful. As writer Peggy
Noonan poignantly observes, "The young are moved by greatness. They
are inspired by it. Children need heroes. They need them to lift life, to
support a future you can be hungry for. They need them because heroes,
just by being, communicate the romantic and yet realistic idea that you
can turn your life into something great." [1]

It is normal for children to sometimes live through their heroes and
draw sustenance from the imagined connection. When I was twelve I
faced an emergency appendectomy. As I was wheeled into the operating room, feeling overwhelmed and frightened, I thought about my
baseball hero, Pete Reiser. I idolized the way he hit (I copied his batting stance), his base-stealing skills, and the way he made outstand-

ing catches even while sometimes crashing into the outfield wall. Although he had had several concussions, he always bounced back to lead the Brooklyn Dodgers to further victories. Thinking about Pete Reiser's overcoming physical adversity comforted me during my surgery, and the prospect of going to a game to see him hastened my recovery. This inner connection with my hero during this stressful period was a pivotal event in my youth.

James T. Farrell describes a similar experience in *My Baseball Diary*. In a moving chapter titled "Death of an Idol," Farrell recounts his reaction to the death of baseball star Eddie Collins. Recalling his deep attachment to Collins when he was a boy, Farrell notes, "It was as though he played ball for me. In my imagination, I lived in his career. He became my model . . . and in 1920, when the Black Sox scandal was exposed, I was proud that he was not one of the eight White Sox players accused of having thrown the 1919 World Series to the Cincinnati Reds.[2]

Thus hero-worship of sports stars seems useful in providing a sense of involvement, connection, and purposefulness. But it can be damaging if we are unprepared to realize that many of our heroes are also flawed and vulnerable. Hero hunger exists not only in the inner connection fans establish with sports stars but also in their pursuit of contact with them in real life. Sports celebrities are ubiquitously hounded for autographs, and athletes are sometimes insensitive to the intense value that adoring young fans give to such encounters. In his biography of Pete Rose, Michael Sokolove describes one such example: "His humor could also be cruel. When he was managing the Reds, a boy of about twelve approached him in the lobby of a Pittsburgh hotel. He was clutching an old Wheaties box with Rose's picture on it, which he wanted him to autograph. Rose waved him away. "No thanks," he said, "I already ate breakfast."[3]

At about the same age, a friend and I chanced to see Dixie Walker, another Dodgers star, on the street outside Ebbets Field. I mustered my courage, pulled a pencil and a crumpled piece of paper from my pocket, and timidly asked for his autograph. Walker scowled at me and indignantly shouted in his southern drawl, "I'm not gonna sign that junkie old piece of paper!" I was devastated as he turned and walked away.

Any direct contact with a sports hero can be exhilarating, and some young fans cherish the contact even when they are mistreated. In *The*

Baseball Hall of Shame 3, Bruce Nash and Allan Zullo deplore one such incident. An eleven-year-old boy approached his favorite Dodgers pitcher, Ron Perranoski, in the bull pen and asked for his autograph: "The reliever turned around and viewed the bright-eyed boy with annoyance. Can't sign during the game, he said. 'League Rules.' Then in one motion Perranoski reached in his warm up jacket, pulled out a water pistol, and squirted Scott in the face. The pitcher quickly stuck the gun back in his pocket, folded his arms, and resumed watching the game."[4]

In recalling this incident as an adult, this fan described the power of hero hunger to override abuse. He noted, "Like any kid, I was just thankful for the contact with a major leaguer—no matter what. I told Perranoski, 'thank you,' and then I wiped my face and walked away."[5]

The issue of star athletes' acknowledging the powerful influence that comes with being a role model is a controversial one. Adoring kids are prone to scrutinize their heroes' actions on and off the field and to imitate them in their own ways of being in the world.

Charles Barkley's famous statement "I'm not a role model" created substantial media attention. Barkley was refuting the assumption that the athlete's job includes exemplary behavior in his personal life. He did not want to be burdened with this pressure or responsibility, and he proclaimed that that place in children's life belongs to their parents. In a similar disavowal, Shaquille O'Neal has stated, "I don't like the word role model. Role means playing a part . . . [look to us] to be a *real* model. Don't be like us, be better than us. . . . If you see us make a mistake, don't make the same mistake."[6]

Many sports stars share Barkley's position; they do not want to invest in cultivating an image of humaneness and high- mindedness. They want to be recognized only for their performance in the playing arena. While Barkley may be technically correct, his view misses the point that being a role model simply comes with the territory, in that kids will identify with their heroes and imitate their actions. Though Barkley and others want to avoid that mantle, like it or not hero-hungry fans will drape them in it.

The availability of star-crazed women for sexual encounters makes many athletes prone to sexual promiscuity. What message does it send to kids, who yearn to imitate their idols, when Wilt Chamberlain reveals in his autobiography that he had sex with twenty thousand women, or when Steve Garvey is accused of multiple paternity incidents? Does it tarnish the image of the hero in the worshipers' eyes, or does it foster a desire to become a world-class stud? The hero's value system and ways of conducting himself have a profound effect on his devoted followers. The "bad boy" image portrayed by Allen Iverson or Dennis Rodman may create an example that glorifies nonconformity and arrogance.

In contrast, numerous sports icons are extremely mindful of their status as role models, and they accept the responsibility that comes with this position. Their commitment to compassion, concern, and integrity enhances their image in admirable ways. Professional football greats like Boomer Esiason, Kurt Warner, and Doug Flutie have candidly discussed with the media the challenges of dealing with their handicapped children. Watching these heroes be compassionate, loving, and sensitive in highly stressful real life circumstances makes us want to cultivate these qualities in ourselves. Harry Carson, another football legend, has been outspoken about the dangerous long-term effects of athletes' head injuries. His addressing such a cause wins him even deeper admiration among his longtime admirers. Sandy Koufax gained enormous prominence in 1965 when he declined to pitch in the opening game of the World Series because it conflicted with his observance of Yom Kippur, the holiest Jewish holiday. Koufax thus put his allegiance to his Jewish identity ahead of his loyalty to the Los Angeles Dodgers. His action augmented his status as a principled role model. In 2001 Shawn Green, a present-day Jewish Dodgers superstar, captured the essence of being a modern role model. Green also declined to play in a crucial late-season game in order to observe Yom Kippur. He made his decision "partly as a representative of the Jewish community, and as far as my being a role model in sports for Jewish kids, to basically say that baseball or anything isn't bigger than your religion and your roots."[7]

As adults, many fans continue to identify with sports heroes. They gain a sense of well-being when they feel connected to a successful star, a sense of being a winner rather than a loser. We tend to anoint our heroes as gods because we need the feeling of specialness that we derive from the sense of affiliation with an outstanding athlete. In his illuminating book *Why Men Watch Football*, Bob Andelman points out that spectators' involvement with football fills certain needs of the male psyche. Among them are the need to select and admire a hero, to identify with a winner, and to connect with a part of ourselves that takes us back to the more carefree days of boyhood. Andelman posits that "in watch-

The Need For Heroes

ing the game many men are meeting one or more deep-seated psychological needs. Such as the need to associate with a winner, the need to have something go right in his life . . . the need to be validated, to feel the satisfaction of victory."[8] Watching football, according to Andelman's research, can provide an escape from the pressures of work and family responsibility, counteract despair, and supply a measure of hope. This view is elaborated by psychologist Thomas Tutko, who maintains, "Heroes provide hope. They provide identity. They provide an opportunity to be a step above and beyond where you are right now."[9]

Idolizing sports heroes is an aspect of "celebrity worship syndrome," a term coined by psychologists James Houran and Lynn McCutcheon to describe an excessive fascination with the lives of the rich and the famous. These researchers contend that nearly one-third of Americans have an unhealthy interest in the lives of celebrities, which in extreme form can become an addiction.[10]

The opportunity to reminisce and extend the connection to our own days of athletic glory is also a factor in our involvement as sports spectators. Bruce Ogilvie, a renowned sports psychologist, has noted, "I think that very high on the list of reasons men watch football is to recapture and relive their early adolescent years and, through their identification and emotional participation, vicariously live out again this period in their life. For most of the men who have played football or been athletic, these sorts of vicarious satisfactions have very, very positive rewards/effects."[11]

Andelman concludes that "contemporary men are desperately searching for heroes in their lives. We're wanting for role models at a time when the ranks of positive male role models are fairly thin. So many athletes undeserving of our loyalty have been glorified by the press and glorified by Madison Ave. . . . Men search for an identification with a winner, a male figure who is effective, virile, and capable, one who knows how to get things done. Having a sports hero meets a need."[12]

The need for heroes frequently merges with a powerful emotional investment in the fortunes of a sports franchise. The hero becomes a more concentrated extension and embodiment of the cherished team. People often feel connected through their shared allegiance to the home team, especially when the local team is succeeding. Being able to chant "We're number one!" after a championship makes fans feel united and special. Many people's self-image is bolstered or depleted depending on how well their team does. The emotional investment in the fortunes of the team becomes entwined with their self-regard, and they develop a love affair with the team. When the success of the franchise becomes strongly linked with an aspect of self-image, the meaning of winning and losing may be blown out of proportion. When the team does poorly, their opinion of themselves may be correspondingly negative, and feelings of personal inferiority, inadequacy, and failure may emerge. Psychologist Robert Cialdini has noted that "winning and losing teams influence the morale of a region, a city or a college campus. A substantial segment of the community may actually have clinical features of depression when their team loses. People become 'blue' for several days, disoriented and non-productive, whereas if they win, they are pumped up and active."[13] Cialdini refers to this as "basking in reflected glory." In many cities an atmosphere of depression and failure prevails after the loss of a significant game. The fans were counting on their team to deliver a victory—to make their day—and instead they feel personally let down. A classic example is the way the fortunes of the Green Bay Packers, a small-town team, affect the emotional well-being of the people of Wisconsin. The governor, Jim Doyle, asserted that "the Packers are more than just a state team; they determine the state's mood. They throw this state into a depression if they lose. Productivity is affected. It's been like that forever."[14]

Reflecting on fans' commitment to hometown franchises, columnist Russell Baker has stated, "The home team is composed of players who year after year fight for the honor of the bleak, decaying city . . . the home team may, in fact, be one of the few things that help you to continue tolerating this pretty awful hometown."[15]

Thus, we need our heroes. We need them to be masterful, special, and worthy. We need to perceive them as wonderful, using a prism that magnifies their greatness. Fans who rise and fall with the feats of their heroes will be overly invested in not being disappointed. Even though we grow up and move on and the intense interest in sports that once consumed us wanes, a part of us nostalgically hangs on to childhood memories of a time when we were carefree, innocent, and perhaps passionately involved with our sports heroes. The intensity with which many of us cling to boyhood idols is eloquently described by Farrell: "But there is more than the lost desire for glory in boyhood memories of baseball. There is the remembrance of fun, of physical release, of days spent playing in the sun when nothing else but a base hit, a run scored, a fly ball caught mattered. . . . And I suspect that I was not singular in the way in which I looked upon baseball and dreamed of it. It was no mere game. It was an extension of my inner feelings and hopes. My favorite players were like my ambassadors to the world. . . . We never lose our boyhood. It hangs in our minds."[16]

We often see our sports heroes as supermen, and many will ultimately reveal wings made of wax as their talents wane and they tumble from the heights where we have placed them. But our heroes are human, with human imperfections, and they cannot always handle stardom.

Fans can be tolerant of declining abilities as their heroes age, and they often move on to embrace new stars who have been promoted by the media. When an aging superhero like Michael Jordan leaves retirement and returns to the game, many fans also yearn to recapture his glory and success. We hate being disillusioned. An extreme example was the Ford Bronco chase when spectators lined the Los Angeles freeway and cheered O. J. Simpson on even though he was a fugitive. A 1998 study of professional athletes by the Indiana University School of Law concluded that "for any player who makes a game-winning touchdown, basket, home run, or goal, the world is his oyster as the media and public exalt him to the level of a living god. Unfortunately, behind the pageantry and glamour of professional football, basketball, baseball, and hockey often lies an ugly reality of off-the-field criminal activity."[17] This report goes on to indicate that "the three most reported crimes committed by athletes are domestic violence, sexual assault, and drug related crimes."[18]

When off-field scandals strike their heroes, fans are often profoundly disillusioned. Under the media spotlight, we are forced, somewhat grudgingly, to recognize that many of our sports heroes are lacking. This can be painful, since we want our heroes to remain exalted. We need to keep them on the pedestal we have created. When our heroes' image becomes tainted, we often feel brought down by them.

Stars' off-field misbehavior routinely receives intense media coverage, so that every new unseemly incident by a professional or college athlete is immediately thrust in our faces. A very different situation once existed, in which the athletes were shielded from negative publicity.

Incidents such as Babe Ruth's contracting a venereal disease and Ty Cobb's impulsively shooting a mugger went undisclosed. In our current culture this protection no longer occurs, and the public is bombarded with stories about their heroes' sexual assaults, domestic violence, drug-related crimes, and other antisocial behavior.

With the advent of free agency and the escalation of sports stars' salaries, we have come to expect much more. Multimillion-dollar contracts translate into monumental expectations. Many fans unconsciously believe that if a star is being paid that much, we are justified in expecting him to produce colossal feats. We expect our sports heroes to cushion the sadness of what is missing in our lives or compensate for our own lost glory. In chronicling the career of David Cone, Roger Angell observed, "I hadn't understood how quickly we fans can turn our backs when our old heroes go south. This wasn't what we wanted from them, this bumbling and struggling. Get away—don't you know why we're here? Show us how to win again—get out there and be great!"[19]

When athletes falter because personal frailties interrupt and sidetrack their path to the Hall of Fame, we are not always compassionate: they must not let us down. We are loath to recognize the pressures created by our expecting herculean feats. Since we are paying their huge salaries through inflated ticket prices, we have the right to expect king-size accomplishments. When some of them stumble, we do not own our part in creating an atmosphere in which they must fulfill our unrealistic dreams. We feel disappointed, disillusioned, and unforgiving, and we are disinclined to consider our contribution to the stress that can lead a hero astray. Thus we are apt to underestimate the burden of stardom—of constantly living up to the performance standard of fans who feed off their success.

In a penetrating article describing the meteoric rise and precipitous fall of Doc Gooden and Darryl Strawberry, Peter Richmond targets the combination of fans' adulation and these stars' self-destructive tendencies as a prescription for their premature demise. Both Gooden and Strawberry had outstanding early success, earmarking them as potential Hall of Famers. Neither one could handle his success and the pressure to surpass enduring records. Richmond suggests that "both became full-blown, always-ready-to-relapse addicts. They were going to be the second coming of Koufax and Williams, until they rejected our mythology and sought solace in the dark safety of their own self-

The Need For Heroes

destruction. Now the question isn't whether they've finally learned their lesson. It's whether we've learned ours."[20] He concludes that "by telling a kid he was a god, we may have given him a false sense of invincibility."[21] Both Gooden and Strawberry were eventually suspended during their downward spiral. Gooden bounced back somewhat, showing that in some cases disciplinary action does serve as a wake-up call and may deter future self-destructive behavior.

In admonishing the fans for their role in the unfulfilled potential of these stars, Richmond concludes, "Gooden is keeping up his end of things. For the time being Darryl is, too. It's the rest of us who show no signs of reforming, who shake our heads at the tragedy of all that wasted talent, at the anti-climatic whimper with which each ended his career, twisting our heads to look for another young man to anoint, someone else to entertain us, to lead us back to the glory days."[22]

Although the public is often in denial regarding the excessive pressure that hero hunger creates, those at the helm of the sports industry are more realistic. The NBA commissioner David Stern has stated, "We must pay the price for failing to meet people's expectations. And we are! . . . We are going through a period where people are questioning our players' conduct. . . . There's a special responsibility that comes from being a professional athlete. . . . The price we pay for being in the fish bowl is that the media plays up the players' frailties. . . . A young man gets into trouble and because of the [media] coverage it gets a lot of publicity. . . . It may not conform to the image of the heroes of yesteryear."[23] Stern is pointing out that our insatiable need for heroes leaves a narrow margin for support when they are tarnished by media attention to their misconduct.

Media attention forces us to deal with the reality that many of our heroes have feet of clay. As novelist R. D. Rosen noted in a letter to the *New York Times*, "Like organized religion (but with beer during the service), major league baseball is a mass mechanism for the experience of hope and the deep contemplation of humility."[24] But when the system fails, when our awareness of our heroes' weaknesses or self-destructive tendencies emerges full blown and our ability to sustain our hopes through our connection to them is significantly compromised, disillusion may set in. Reality is sometimes painful to digest, but as former baseball hero Jim Bouton has pointed out, "athletes are not special people, they are people with special skills."[25]

In truth, herodom is time sensitive. The average professional athlete's career lasts only a handful of years, and time will ultimately erode the most magnificent talent, even if he is relatively immune to illicit temptations or personal demons. Sooner or later our idols must fade, and we must face our disappointment and turn to new heroes as the keepers of our flame of hope. The loss of the blissful and perfect connection we create in our minds is inevitable.

Star athletes face enormous pressure to maintain a positive image in the public eye. Fans eternally seek validation for their devoted worship, so a high-profile athlete is wise to cultivate a positive relationship with the media lest he be depicted as an antihero. The media also play a significant part in creating and sustaining an athlete's image. Hyping an athlete with praise, or even with relentless criticism, brings attention to a sportswriter and builds a following for the writer himself as well as for the player. In 2001 when the Yankees shortstop Derek Jeter hit a home run to win game four of the first World Series ever to extend beyond October, he was quickly heralded on the front page of a New York newspaper as "Mr. November." [26] This story overshadowed the news about the latest anthrax-related death in New York City. Such headlines enhanced Jeter's image as the darling of Yankee fans.

In 2002, during Barry Bonds's magnificent chase of the single-season home run record, fans were less enthusiastic than might have been expected, in part because Bonds had acquired an unappealing image as arrogant and disdainful. Many fans rooted against him, and at times even his teammates seemed unsupportive. In his defense Bonds maintained that his bad-guy image as unresponsive to the fans was an inaccurate invention of the media. If Bonds is correct, it reinforces the common belief that the media have enormous influence over the way fans perceive their sports stars.

This argument can be applied to two superstars of the golden era of baseball. Joe DiMaggio played the media game, gave the press good copy, and was adored as a graceful gazelle. Ted Williams, in contrast, was indifferent to cultivating this aspect of being a famous athlete, so he was often vilified by the press and chronically felt misunderstood and misrepresented.

Joe DiMaggio and Ted Williams may have been the two greatest sports heroes in the middle of the twentieth century, when baseball was the king of sports. The National Basketball Association was not yet in existence, and professional football had only a cluster of teams in one league with a ten-game season that culminated in a playoff between divisional leaders. The age of television, which became the ideal medium for football coverage, had not yet arrived (the Super Bowl, inaugurated in 1967, would ultimately be every year's most-watched television program). So baseball prevailed as America's premier sport.

DiMaggio and Williams were the dominant stars of Major League Baseball in the 1940s, and they played a large role in the dominance of the American League over the National League. The junior circuit, as it was called, won thirteen of the first seventeen All-Star Games played between the two leagues. It wasn't until the late 1940s and 1950s that the National League regained parity, in large measure because of the head start National League teams got in hiring black players. Ironically, the New York Yankees, with Elston Howard, and the Boston Red Sox, with the signing of one Pumpsie Green, were among the last Major League teams to integrate white and black players.

DiMaggio came to the Yankees in 1936, was heralded as the next Babe Ruth (Ruth had left the Yankees in 1934 and retired in 1935), and was an immediate sensation. Williams broke in three years later with the Red Sox; he was less prone to injury than DiMaggio and played for nine years after DiMaggio retired in 1951.

The press fell in love with DiMaggio and pumped him up as a superstar. In fact, he became the first to play on World Series championship teams in his first four years in the majors. Joe DiMaggio—even his name became lyrical. The media enthusiastically dubbed him "Joltin' Joe" and "the Yankee Clipper," and an adoring public made him public hero number one. He could do no wrong on the field; he was considered the best all-around baseball player of his time; and his private life was unsmirched. He was raised in a close-knit family of poor fishermen in San Francisco, the next-to-last of nine children born to Italian immigrants Giuseppe and Rosalie DiMaggio. He grew up without much ambition or direction, did poorly in school, and was expected to follow his father and his older brothers as fishermen. As a young man, Joe recognized he didn't want that life. Instead, he followed his brother Vince, who had pursued baseball and hooked up with the San Francisco Seals of the Pacific Coast League.

As a New York Yankee DiMaggio effortlessly projected an image as a graceful warrior. He carried the Yankees to unprecedented heights—

they won nine World Series championships and ten pennants during the thirteen years of his active playing career. His most remarkable feat was his hitting streak of fifty-six consecutive games in 1941, a record that is unlikely ever to be challenged. The media continued to reinforce and encourage the public's thirst for a hero. He won legendary fame, reflected in three popular songs that embraced his lyrical name. The first was the Les Brown's band recording of "Joltin' Joe DiMaggio," then the Broadway show *South Pacific* made famous the line, "Her skin is tender as DiMaggio's glove." Many years later, during the troubled period of the Vietnam War, Paul Simon's hit song "Mrs. Robinson" included the lyrics, "Where have you gone, Joe DiMaggio? / The nation turns its lonely eyes to you." Thus, in a time of national crisis and angst, DiMaggio represented a hero who could lead us and heal our wounds. These lyrics, written more than fifteen years after his retirement, also reflected the yearning for times perceived as happier.

On only two occasions during his playing days did the fans turn against DiMaggio. His first taste of extended boos and jeers occurred after his prolonged holdout past opening day in 1938. The Yankee management portrayed him as greedy, and many fans felt he had failed as the "pure" hero they needed. Such a hero would not put a salary squabble ahead of his obligation to his adoring public, especially when the country was still reeling from an economic depression. Up to that point he had been viewed primarily as a magnificent player who was unselfish and unblemished.

The second episode occurred in 1942, when he was having a subpar season at the plate. He had not signed up for the armed forces at the beginning of World War II, as other stars like Hank Greenberg and Bob Feller had done. In the patriotic zeal sweeping the country, DiMaggio's image became tainted once again. After that season, in which he did contribute to winning yet another pennant, he enlisted in the army, at age twenty-eight, and he served for three years, until the end of the war.

On his return he led the Yankees to four more World Series championships and resumed his status as the premier baseball hero. As stated by Lefty Gomez, a former teammate quoted in Maury Allen's *Where Have You Gone, Joe DiMaggio?* "He was a guy who knew he was the greatest baseball player in America, and he was proud of it. . . . He was always trying to live up to that image. . . . He knew he was Joe DiMaggio, and he knew what that meant to the country." [27] Between his accomplishments on the field, the media hype, and his uncanny ability to promote his image as the all-American hero, the fans were provided with an ongoing object for worship. As Richard Ben Cramer stated in *Joe DiMaggio: The Hero's Life*, "He was, at every turn, one man we could look at who made us feel good. For it was always about how we felt . . . with Joe. No wonder we strove for 60 years to give him the hero's life. It was always about us. Alas, it was his destiny to know that, as well."[28] After an injury-plagued season, he retired in 1951. According to his older brother, Tom DiMaggio, "He quit because he wasn't Joe DiMaggio anymore."[29]

Throughout his career DiMaggio was admired not only because of his impressive baseball statistics (home runs, batting average, Most Valuable Player Awards, etc.) but also because he was seen as performing day in and day out with a quiet excellence and exuding class and grace. After he left the game he was still venerated for decades. Remarkably, fans continued to more or less unambivalently revere the image of our hero as we needed to see him. It was not until the publication of Cramer's book in 2000 that we posthumously learned more details about his dark side. Cramer depicts DiMaggio as self-centered, emotionally cut off and insensitive to the needs and feelings of others, and obsessed with money. But these personality characteristics were not exposed by a favorable press during his career. According to Cramer, writing about Joe sold newspapers. The public needed him to be larger than life, and he knew instinctively how to perpetuate his image.

The adulation of Ted Williams among Red Sox fans was not nearly as universal as that given to Joe DiMaggio by Yankees followers. DiMaggio fell from grace posthumously, whereas early on Williams struggled with a lack of hero-worship from a significant segment of the hometown fans. At times he was disdainful of the fans as well as the press, which deprived him of the total admiration he felt was his due. Instead, he had a love/hate relationship with the media and the public. When he produced on the field he was a giant and was elevated to the throne. But when he was scornful or indifferent to fans' need for him to cultivate his image as a hero, he was demonized.

Like DiMaggio, Ted Williams came from an impoverished background in California. His mother appears to have neglected her two sons in favor of her devotion to the Salvation Army, a passionate commitment that absorbed her time and energy. According to Williams's biographer, Ed Linn, "Her special mission was ministering to the needs of the drunks, prostitutes, and unwed mothers."[30] His father, a photographer in a small shop in a working-class neighborhood, was also uninvolved at home and gave Ted little time. In his autobiography Williams describes how he and his brother would wait on the porch after dark for one of their parents to come home and let them in. He had little interest in school and was ill prepared for a career after high school. Although he was a scrawny adolescent, he was most comfortable hitting baseballs on the nearby playground. After high school he fulfilled his dream of becoming a ballplayer by signing with the San Diego Padres, the local Pacific Coast League team, and he worked his way up to the major leagues by age twenty. He was an instant success, hitting thirty-one home runs and batting .327 in his rookie season. He became the darling of Boston and soon acquired the nicknames "the splendid splinter" (his tall thin body frame filled out in later years) and "the thumper."

In 1941, his third year in the majors, Ted had an outstanding season, with a batting average of .406. At the time, hitting .400 was not regarded as highly exceptional, since previous stars such as Ty Cobb, George Sisler, and Roger Hornsby had reached that level several times. The Most Valuable Player Award that year went to Joe DiMaggio, who had amassed his sensational fifty-six-game hitting streak. With time Williams's accomplishment in 1941 has taken on greater stature, since no player reached that plateau for the rest of the twentieth century. A few players have flirted with this level, including Williams himself again in 1957, but none have achieved it. With the advent of high-caliber relief pitching and more efficient fielder's gloves, it is questionable whether we will ever see another .400 hitter.

Soon after arriving in Boston, Williams became the new hope of many Red Sox fans. However, he was distressed by the demands for even greater performance being placed on him by a hero-hungry public. At a press conference on Ted Williams Day at Fenway Park in 1991, he complained, "I thought I was doing pretty good in 1940. I ended up hitting .344 and I got booed right out of the park because I wasn't breaking Babe Ruth's record. . . . The press was on me because I wasn't driving in runs. I still drove in 100 runs, but I still wasn't doing enough, and I got a little burned over that. Then they started writing personal things, and that's all water over the dam, and I shouldn't have taken it quite as seriously, but it affected me. It hurt."[31]

Here we see the origin of what became a long-standing feud with the press and the fans. It is likely that the emotional scars of growing up neglected created a deep-seated sensitivity to criticism and a lack of appreciation even when he had made it as a star. He understandably overreacted to rejection and disapproval. When he was criticized or unfairly booed he felt misunderstood and angrily fought back against his disloyal attackers, a thin-skinned and unprofessional response. In 1956 the Red Sox general manager fined him $5,000, a princely sum in 1956 dollars, for spitting in the direction of heckling fans. There had been several similar outbursts earlier in the season. Two years later, after another tirade of spitting at fans, he was fined again, this time by American League president Will Harridge, for "conduct detrimental to the best interests of baseball." Williams later apologized, and though the fine was only $250, he said, "I'm principally sorry about losing the $250." He excelled at the game of baseball, but he didn't care to play the game of dealing with the press and the fans. He often felt beleaguered and was too proud to promote himself as a hero. He came to hate the sportswriters, sometimes treating them accordingly, and they repaid him by overlooking him time and again when voting for the Most Valuable Player Award.

Dave Egan, who wrote a sports column for a Boston newspaper, was often critical of Williams, and Ted came to hate Egan most of all. As Ed Linn noted, "Ted, despite his disclaimers, could not bear to be attacked on any grounds at all. Egan accused Ted of being completely selfish, jealous of the success of various teammates, more interested in fishing than in baseball, and greedy for money. He went so far as to accuse Ted of contributing to juvenile delinquency because he refused to wear a tie or tip his hat, thereby encouraging the youth of the city to rebel against the established rules of society."[32]

Interestingly enough, it was Egan who supported Williams during two major personal crises when other newsmen and fans scorned him. Like DiMaggio, Williams did not rush to enlist in the armed forces at the beginning of World War II, as other Major League stars did. When he appealed to retain his 3A draft listing in 1942, Ted was roundly derided. This was an unpopular decision in a national atmosphere of patriotism, and Williams did join the service from 1943 through 1945, three years of his prime, and again during the Korean War.

The second crisis occurred in 1948 when he was found fishing in the Everglades while his wife prematurely gave birth to their daughter.

When he arrived in Boston five days later, he told reporters he hadn't been able to get a flight out of Miami for five days. When asked if he thought the delay would influence public opinion, he snapped, "To hell with the public. They can't run my life."[33] The press came down hard on him. Paul Gallico, a respected columnist, wrote, "You are not a nice fellow, Brother Williams. I do believe that baseball and sports pages would be better off without you. . . . When, oh, when, will you thick headed athletes catch on that the public is your darling, that you may not disillusion us, that you cannot live as other men but dwell in glass houses and that this is the price you pay for wealth and success?"[34] Of course, as Linn points out, "The public was not Ted's darling. On the contrary, Ted was the public's darling."[35] This incident became magnified because we need our heroes to measure up to our moral, ethical, and personal standards. The fans' resentment and disappointment expressed the attitude, "How dare Ted Williams march to his own drummer and disillusion us by flagrantly indulging his own hobbies instead of being a devoted family man during a time of crisis?"

2. The Psyche of the Athlete

A successful player's ego swells as he progresses and
leaves behind the real world of ordinary people.

Bernie Parrish, *They Call It a Game*

Sports heroes frequently develop unrealistic views of themselves that
are encouraged and reinforced when an adoring world treats them as
elite. For many players a sense of specialness is central to their identity,
strongly influencing their expectations from the world and their treatment of others. Although they may be giants as athletes, many sports
stars have trouble relinquishing this image in daily life. Their personal
interactions are often colored by this inflated view of themselves. It
requires great emotional maturity to maintain relationships based on
equality and reciprocity when you are surrounded by people eager to
anticipate your every need.

Many star athletes have been catered to since childhood and have
come to accept special treatment as their due. Celebrity status can be intoxicating, and as athletes come to believe in their press clippings, they
feed off the constant attention and acclaim bestowed on them. The roar
of the fans becomes necessary to their survival—a form of emotional
oxygen. Pumped up by such affirmation and applause, they feel like
royalty, and they often exist in an unreal sports heaven. When you are
among the high-flying adored, your view of the world becomes blurred.
Off the field, some act as if they are above the rules of society; hubris and
an attitude of entitlement ("I can do whatever I want") become central
to the psyche of many athletes. They may deny that they are vulnerable
to reprisals and feel omnipotent and grandiose as well as entitled.

Our earliest image of ourselves is shaped by our caretakers. When
parents respond lovingly to them, children gradually internalize a picture of themselves as lovable. Thus, how we think about ourselves is a
product of cues we absorb from the world around us.

Many professional athletes are groomed from an early age to view themselves as special. Their athletic talents are recognized early on when their performance overshadows their peers'. While some stars like Joe DiMaggio and Ted Williams developed their exalted status later on, for many the symbolic coronation begins young. Future sports stars usually demonstrate their skills as preteens, and these budding stars begin to receive special treatment from their peers and from adults who live vicariously through their accomplishments.

Tom House, a former Major League player and pitching coach, has coined the expression "terminal adolescence" to describe the emotional state of professional athletes. Because so many have been coddled since childhood, their emotional growth may be stunted. Self-centeredness, insensitivity to the needs of others, and a sense of invincibility, typical of adolescence, are prominent in many of our sports icons. House's phrase might be refined as "interminable adolescence."

Sports stars learn about conditional love early in life. A premium is placed on their physical performance, and their value becomes measured by what they produce rather than by who they are. They learn that in order to receive approval and love, they must constantly live up to their potential. Conditional love, based on someone else's expectations of how you need to be, is different from unconditional love, in which you are loved for yourself.

The downside of being placed on a pedestal is the stress of maintaining outstanding athletic performance. As you breathe the rarefied atmosphere, there is also the constant pressure of living in a fishbowl. The life of the sports hero entails not only basking in the limelight but also dealing with pressures: The pressure of being durable over the long season. The pressure of living up to expectations. The pressure of performing at a consistently high level. The pressure of bouncing back from the inevitable slumps. The strain of dealing with management, the media, and the fans. The strain of having your private life meticulously examined. Expectations are never lowered, and any lapse may be magnified by the press.

Former baseball pitcher Billy Loes, in lamenting the pressures on Major League ballplayers, said he often felt that he would rather have been a truck driver with a modest take-home pay because he would be out of the limelight and would have his nights free.

Thus the young athlete gets special treatment because of what he does and what he represents for us, and this adoration will persist as long as he continues to produce. This conditional love can be intoxicating. Children are generally not yet able to make a conscious distinction between conditional and unconditional love. As Tom House portrays this developmental state, "It starts when they are eight years old, with their peer group, their teachers—the people who have impact on their social environment and allow them to be a what and not a who. . . . Their status as jocks precludes their development as a responsible human being. They have had responsibility all their lives, but they have never been held accountable. When they do something that escalates beyond what their immediate close system can protect, all of a sudden they are saying, 'Why is this happening?' "[1]

A similar portrait is drawn by Jim Bouton, the outspoken former Yankees pitcher, who maintains that "many players are in a dream world and out of touch with reality from the fourth grade on. As soon as they hit the first home run, they start living in a different world."[2]

Of course there are many exceptions to this profile of the athlete's psyche. Nolan Ryan and Pete Sampras stand out as examples of superheroes whose families did not impose the terms of conditional love. In presenting a more humble perspective on the fame-drenched life of sports heroes, Bouton adds, "It's something fun to do with your life for a while."[3] Nonetheless, the description above applies to many sports stars.

As an insider studying how the sense of entitlement evolves among Major League ballplayers, House observes, "It doesn't take him long to get used to people bending over backward to accommodate him, helping him, changing their plans to fit his. . . . It never, ever occurs to him that the special treatment will disappear as soon as his talents begin to wane. He lives by the belief that he is charmed; he doesn't realize that one day the charm is going to tarnish and turn green all over him."[4]

House believes that the typical professional athlete does not evolve into a mature adult: "Put simply he's never really grown up, because he's never had to."[5] He labels this syndrome "the jock's itch," which he defines as "a condition that causes thirty year old men to act the same way they did when they were thirteen. A state of mind that simply refuses to absorb (or even consider) the reality that they'll be 'over the hill' in their jobs before most men their age are even settled into a career."[6]

Bill Bradley, who made the supreme transition from basketball superstar to United States senator, has written about the early indoctrination that causes young athletes to develop a distorted view of themselves, characterized by arrogance and entitlement. Bradley suggests, "The community tells him that he is a basketball star. For the townspeople his future is as clearly outlined as his record-book past. They expect him to become an even greater athlete and to do those things which will bring about the fulfillment of what is wholly their fantasy. The adolescent who receives such attention rarely develops personal doubts. There is a smug cockiness about achievements, or a sincere determination to continue along a course that has brought success and praise. . . . His self assurance is constantly reinforced by public approval."[7]

Bradley agrees that the intoxicating effect of the adoring crowd and the perpetual reinforcement of fame interferes with emotional maturity. He adds, "Self definition again comes from external sources, not from within. While their physical skill lasts, professional athletes are celebrities—fondled and excused, praised and believed. Only toward the end of their careers do the stars realize that their sense of identity is insufficient."[8]

As a result of their inflated definition of themselves, encouraged by public acclaim, many sports heroes come to live in a world of unreality and foster the illusion that they will be treated as special forever and that these glorious days, this heaven on earth, will not be gone anytime soon. They deny the reality that for the vast majority, professional athletes' careers last only a few years. Of course their stars will always shine brightly, their fame will escalate, and nobody will say no to them. Only a few seem to glimpse how they might someday fall from the pedestal. Like the typical adolescent, they are present oriented, navigating their world with an invincible swagger, and they cannot fathom a time of decline and mortality.

Sociologist Steven Ortiz has studied the psyches of professional athletes by talking to their wives. Ortiz conducted in-depth interviews with the wives of football, baseball, basketball, and hockey stars. His findings draw a profile of many athletes as indulged, immature, and self-absorbed—what Ortiz calls "the spoiled athlete syndrome." As one of the wives summed it up, "These guys are babied and spoiled and pampered, totally. In my mind, they lose a sense of reality. They have no responsibilities and, for the most part, they have no cares. The envi-

The Psyche of the Athlete

ronment they are in conditions them to be this way." [9] Many of the other wives echo this view. Ortiz maintains that as soon as they began to show promise in competitive sports, these men were doted on and spoiled by family members and other enablers who surrounded them (coaches, girlfriends, etc.). Such early conditioning interferes with life lessons and truncates the capacity to respect others' rights and to form relationships based on mutuality. When they go into the professional ranks these athletes expect special treatment—and they usually get it. One by-product of this attitude is the promiscuous lifestyle and marital infidelity frequently observed among professional athletes. Ortiz's research examines stresses in the typical athlete's marriage, particularly extramarital sex. The norm may become to function in "a culture of adultery in the high profile world of professional sport—and in a culture of male entitlement." [10] A multitude of factors can lead a married sports star to infidelity. Ortiz observes that "boredom, peer group pressure, team loyalty, opportunity, inflated sense of self, and the availability of women, who seem to be irresistibly attracted to professional athletes, often account for a 'fast-food sex mentality.'" [11]

During the playing season the athlete's central focus is on his performance, his role on the team, and his place among his teammates. It is not surprising, as Ortiz points out, that at certain times the team comes first—he may be married to the team more than to his wife. In many athletes' marriages the balance of power favors the husband because of his fame and money. Many of these wives employ coping mechanisms of denial and avoidance—a sort of a "don't ask, don't tell" approach. Others constantly struggle with fear, insecurity, and resentment. They may use various forms of suspicion management and other coping mechanisms to deal with the ever-present danger of their husbands' infidelities. Ortiz notes one common pattern: "For some wives with a dysfunctional childhood, adultery is a family norm that has become a intergenerational pattern, and they have normalized adultery as a fact of marital and family life." [12]

Because of the power imbalance in their marriages, many sports wives excessively accommodate and defer to their celebrity husbands. Michael Sokolove, in his biography of Pete Rose, writes about the way Rose's first wife capitulated when faced with the open knowledge of her husband's many affairs: "Karolyn Rose even accommodated herself, for a long while, to the most difficult aspect of being married to a ballplayer—the fact that her husband screwed around." [13] Sokolove adds that, according to Rose's teammate Jim O'Toole, soon after marrying Pete Karolyn Rose stated, "I know Pete gets fucked on the road all the time. I say as long as he doesn't do it at home, I don't care." [14] However, according to Ortiz, many athletes do have sexual liaisons and even long-term affairs with women who live close to home.

Another of Ortiz's findings is that many athletes get caught up in the Madonna/whore complex, a polarized view of women as either maternal and nurturing or sexual and enticing. The wife is usually placed in the maternal role, and her sexuality is deemphasized, while the husband seeks other women to fulfill his sexual needs. This dichotomy is poignantly cited by former football hero Dave Meggyesy, who notes in his autobiography that "wives are virginal creatures keeping the home and the kids; other women are meat on the rack." [15]

The typical locker room ambiance of professional teams condones a macho view of women as sexual objects as a common denominator that promotes bonding among teammates. Athletes often accept and tacitly approve of each others' sexual dalliances, and many are not discreet in how they manage them.

Some athletes view "sexcapades" with available women while they are on the road as a perquisite of their celebrity status, and their sense of entitlement prompts them to treat these women as simply convenient objects for their sexual gratification. In some instances their masculine self-image revolves around "scoring" with many women, and like adolescents they show off their records to teammates. It is part of the "adultery culture" described by Ortiz, in which even married players will openly pursue sex partners for the night at the hotel bar in front of their peers. This behavior is another manifestation of the "spoiled athlete syndrome"—"a self-absorbed perception of life [in which players] often conspire to preserve male privileges, which their celebrity status contributes to. Many of the unfaithful husbands are quite indiscreet about their sexual activities with other women on the road." [16]

There have always been numerous groupies who follow sports teams and make themselves available for sex with the players. It is likely that most are trying to enhance their own self-image. The psychological equation, simply put, is: "If this special person wants me, then I must also be worthwhile." After Magic Johnson's 1991 revelation that he had contracted the AIDS virus as a result of numerous one-night stands, the NBA belatedly instituted a mandatory program designed to educate rookies to the dangers of entanglements with groupies.

Many of these women on the prowl are portrayed as exploitative or with no meaningful identity of their own. John Elson, a reporter for *Time* magazine, quotes a groupie: "The only way [these women have] to identify themselves is to say whom they have slept with. A woman who sleeps around is called a whore. But a woman who sleeps with Magic Johnson is a woman who has slept with Magic Johnson. It's almost as if it gives her legitimacy."[17]

In his interview with *Time*, Magic Johnson explained his promiscuous lifestyle: "After I arrived in LA in 1979, I did my best to accommodate as many women as I could—most of them through unprotected sex."[18] The language he uses suggests that he was a good boy who took a somewhat passive, compliant approach to predatory women. To accommodate means to provide, supply, or adapt to the needs of others. His statement overlooks his own motivation in these trysts. Was he simply a poster boy for predatory females to hit on, or did his own strong sexual appetite color his judgment?

While it is easy to cast aspersions on such predatory females, many sports stars evade responsibility for these sexual episodes—which in many instances have led to pregnancies and paternity suits. USC professor Dallas Willard has observed that "a lot of team athletes are ill-equipped to handle pro sports off-field pressures. Many star athletes today are from poor backgrounds—poor not only in a financial sense, but in terms of education, emotional and social preparation for life. They do not have the wherewithal to deal with the availability of sex, the offers to satisfy almost any gratification."[19]

One of the hallmarks of emotional maturity is the capacity for empathy—the ability to understand other people's feelings, experience, and point of view. In essence, empathy involves putting yourself in another person's shoes. Many of our sports heroes are conspicuously deficient in this dimension because they have been conditioned from an early age to be self-absorbed. Their sense of entitlement, the notion that they can do whatever they want without much regard for others (as long as they continue to perform well on the field) has been repeatedly reinforced; and they often do not acquire the emotional skills necessary for reciprocal relationships. Their distorted self-image may prompt them to relate to others based on how well they fulfill their needs. In such cases it is the supplies provided that are paramount and not the other person per se. They may not value others beyond their usefulness. Many athletes become stuck in what psychologists call the stage of need gratification and are impeded from moving on to the higher level called object constancy, in which one can value other people for their own qualities, independent of one's needs.

The prevalence of this profile of the athlete's psyche is confirmed by Tom House, who "sees athletes as part of a system that treats them as objects, thus athletes tend to treat others as objects.[20] As a result they may be prone to transgress the rules of conduct in our society: "Athletes have difficulty identifying society's boundaries because of their programmed insensitivities. . . . The easiest way to say it is that they don't have a thermostat for empathy. . . . They don't have a thermostat for the reality of human interaction. . . . That is a computer chip they don't have."[21]

It can be difficult to sustain empathy when you are being relentlessly pursued by the public and the media. After a while it comes to feel as if you are being hounded, but of course that is part of the landscape a celebrity must learn to negotiate. Nevertheless, it is particularly distressing when famous athletes are insensitive or mocking toward adoring youths. Sportswriter David Remnick reports the following exchange between baseball hero Reggie Jackson and a young admirer: "Once when all of New York wanted to know when Reggie would recover from an injury and return to right field, a young boy said to him in an elevator, 'Hey, when are you gonna play, Reg?' Jackson grabbed himself by the crotch and said 'Play with this.' "[22]

With this lack empathy for others, many stars learn to treat women as objects there to serve their needs. In chronicling his sexual escapades while he was an active player, NBA star Dennis Rodman reflected, "As long as I play ball, I can get any woman I want. . . . If you've got money and the status that comes with playing in the NBA, you can get anybody you want."[23]

Many athletes acquire an attitude of "I can do whatever I want" that leads them to disregard the rules of society off the field. According to a report by the Indiana University School of Law, domestic violence, sexual assault, and drug offenses are the major areas of criminal misconduct among professional athletes, and the author relates these problems to their heightened sense of entitlement.[24]

The Psyche of the Athlete

Several studies indicate that student athletes are accused of more sexual assaults than their peers and that professional football players commit more crimes than their counterparts in the general population. [25] Although these findings have been questioned by NFL commissioner Paul Tagliabue, [26] who attributes them to a misperception about high-profile athletes, they should be looked at further. The *Indiana Law Journal* report suggest that "the most commonly asserted arguments [to explain the possible higher incidence of criminal activity among athletes] are that athletes' disregard for rules, violence against women, and drug related activities result from a combination of factors: (1) athletes are conditioned to believe that they are entitled to behave that way; (2) athletic competition and the subculture of sports perpetuate drug use; and (3) the subculture of men's sports devalues women and encourages violence." [27]

When facing allegations of off-field criminal behavior, professional athletes are sometimes held to a higher standard yet sometimes receive preferential treatment. In the former category, the 1983 criminal case against Kansas City Royals baseball stars Vida Blue, Willie Wilson, Willie Aiken, and Jerry Martin stands out. The four were convicted of trying to buy cocaine, a federal misdemeanor, and sentenced to three months in jail—a penalty far greater than first-time drug offenders normally receive. The magistrate justified his harsh ruling by saying that because these athletes were role models they should be held to a higher standard. Other examples involve the Warren Moon domestic violence case (1996) and the Mark Chmura sexual molestation of a teenager case (2001), which many observers believed were fueled by intense media publicity and pursued by overzealous prosecutors. (Both Moon and Chmura were exonerated, and the consensus among the jurors was that the Moon case never should have gone to trial.)

On the other hand, there is evidence that in general celebrity athletes are convicted of crimes less frequently than others accused of similar offenses. The O. J. Simpson trial stands out as an example of widespread belief that a celebrity's status worked in his favor when the jury found Simpson not guilty. In another high-profile case, Charles Barkley received special treatment in 1997 after he allegedly threw a bar patron through a window. To accommodate Barkley's playing schedule, the presiding judge delayed the jury trial until after the basketball season. Barry Bonds appeared to get preferential treatment in 1994 when he asked the court to reduce his family support payments. The judge, a self-described ardent baseball fan, ruled in favor of Bonds's request, then asked the star for his autograph. It took a public outcry against this favoritism to make the judge reverse his decision toward the multimillionaire player.

When sports stars are arrested, their inflated sense of entitlement frequently leads them to expect preferential treatment. When Michael Irvin was implicated in a 1996 scandal involving strippers and drugs, it is reported that his initial response to the police was the familiar "Do you know who I am?" Only after receiving four years' probation did he remorsefully state, "I'd like to apologize to my father in heaven." Although Irvin is the fifteenth of seventeen children, the seeds of his inflated self-image may have been planted early on. In an interview about her son, Irvin's mother acknowledged, "I knew Michael was special; I knew it before he was born."

Success on the playing field often breeds ever-increasing distortions in athletes' self-image. Intoxicated by the publicity they receive, they come to believe what the media says about them, and ongoing affirmation and applause become necessary to sustain their sense of specialness. The media exalt them as heroes, they wear the mantle of stardom, and they often function as if they are above it all—entitled and invincible.

It is difficult for a star athlete not to become narcissistic. Among the characteristics of the narcissistic personality are self-absorption, an exaggerated sense of self-importance and entitlement, and an insensitivity to the needs and feelings of others. The combination of hero hunger, which creates legions of admiring fans, together with the efforts of sports writers to develop heroes whose feats are noteworthy makes for a situation in which athletes can easily succumb to the adoration that admiring fans bestow on them and come to act as though they are larger than life. Such majestic status is unrealistic and unsustainable, with little tolerance for human flaws. The state of narcissistic entitlement has been poignantly described by former New York Knicks NBA player Dean Meminger, who spiraled into cocaine addiction after his basketball career ended. Meminger credits a mutually nurturing relationship with helping to sustain his recovery. Now a coach at Manhattanville College, Meminger ruefully acknowledged, "My life has been so much egocentric activity. Me, my immediate gratification, my needs, I want what I want when I want it—that whole syndrome."[28]

There is widespread belief in sports circles that athletic success interferes with the development of maturity. Tom House has pointed out that our star athletes don't grow up because they don't have to—that they are accustomed to being catered to from a young age. Bill Bradley has said that the roar of the crowd delays maturity. David Stern has acknowledged that our society programs athletes to become unaccountable, entitled, and insensitive. Impulsive outbursts reflecting such immaturity or insensitivity may occur during competition or off the field. For example, during his march to the U.S. Open tennis championship in 2001, Lleyton Hewitt made remarks to an umpire that were interpreted as a racial slur. Although he was widely criticized by the media for his intemperate statements, Hewitt maintained that they were not meant as a racial slur, and he seemed oblivious to the impact of his remarks. At Wimbledon a few months earlier, the tournament was blemished by sexual slurs aimed at linesmen by Andre Agassi and Goran Ivanisevic when they were upset about calls made against them. When questioned about the remarks, Agassi explained that the intense pressure of such competition can bring out the worst in anyone, and Ivanisevic insisted that his homophobic remark was not intended to be offensive.

Denny McLain, the Detroit Tigers pitcher who rose to the top as a thirty-one-game winner and fell to the bottom as a convicted felon, described the inflated ego of the sports hero: "I learned long ago that when you have a highly sought talent, you can write your own ticket. I was a damned good pitcher, and I knew it. Unless I became intolerable, teams weren't going to discipline me much for breaking a few rules. . . . I blame sports writers in part for giving me the big head. Ever since I was a teenager newspapers have run stories about how great a pitcher I was. That was nice, but the problem was that I started to believe what I read. And the more they wrote, the more I believed it. My ego grew to a proportion that was out of whack with reality."[29]

Former World Series hero Jim Bouton picks up on the theme that the media and the sports industry itself contribute heavily to some heroes' dysfunctional behavior. In a critical appraisal of the factors precipitating Pete Rose's gambling problems, which led to his suspension from baseball and blocked his admission to the Hall of Fame, Bouton accuses Major League Baseball of helping create the conditions for maladaptive behavior to flourish. Bouton maintains that "Pete Rose didn't become a gambler all by himself. Baseball gave him plenty of help he didn't need and no assistance when he could have used it. Just as there was no padding on the outfield walls back then to prevent injuries, there was no guidance to help players cope with life's collisions. No substance abuse programs, no advice on media relations, no psychological counseling . . . and maybe he's in denial about betting on baseball. But Major League Baseball is wrong to deny its role in the development and eventual disgrace of its own true son."[30] In effect, Bouton casts baseball in the role of enabler.

Professional athletes are usually not required to give much back besides sustaining superior athletic performance. On some level they recognize that people's love is conditional, that they are not really valued for themselves—that others define them by their athletic ability. The awareness of conditional love emerges gradually, however, and tends to be pushed aside in favor of enjoying their glory.

Under these conditions, professional athletes are unprepared for the downside of life. When time runs out on athletic ability and they can no longer perform with excellence, they lose their place as darlings of the world, and many face major adjustment problems. It is not easy to make the transition from the spotlight to the background. When football great Jerry Kramer considered retiring from the game, he reflected, "Giving up football is giving up the hero's role. I worry about that. I wonder how much I'll miss being recognized, being congratulated, being idolized. . . . I realized that the odds had to be against me ever being All-Pro again. . . . I made up my mind, finally, definitely, absolutely that I would quit."[31]

Some sports stars make the transition from player into coach, manager, broadcaster, or front office positions, but the vast majority move into the mainstream of the population while they are still young. Some athletes establish productive careers in new directions (e.g., as stockbrokers, congressmen, insurance salesmen, or commercial spokesmen) and are content to be out of the limelight. Former tennis champion Vic Seixas found solace in being a bartender at age seventy-four. But many former athletes flounder and risk slipping into maladaptive and antisocial modes. For example, in a scenario that has become all too familiar, Nate Newton, a former Dallas Cowboys star, was arrested while driving a van containing almost two hundred pounds of marijuana and $10,000 in cash. Newton later pled guilty to drug trafficking and was sentenced to thirty months in prison.

For future professional athletes the commitment to sports is usually established early in life. It is reinforced by parents and coaches, and their identity centers on their performance. This singular focus has been called the "unidimensionality" of the athlete. As Bouton states, "Too many professional athletes are one-dimensional, partially formed people. Think of teenagers in adult bodies."[32] Psychologist Bruce Ogilvie developed the concept of the unidimensional athlete to define the centrality of sports in the identity formation of young athletes. According to Ogilvie,

> The unidimensional athlete has a restricted identity. Based upon social rewards, primarily social recognition, the athlete makes unreasonable ego investments in a single attribute, skill, or ability. In this case, "me the athlete." This identity becomes increasingly narrow until it becomes the only source of reward that has personal meaning. Once threatened by loss, injury, aging, deselection, etc., the athlete fails to find another form of personal meaning. In the extreme situation there occurs a total loss of "athletic identity," They respond as if once they lose this form of self fulfillment there will be nothing to replace it. Many athletes can't find richness or meaning in life beyond their limited identity.[33]

It is understandable that retirement from sports is traumatic for many professional athletes. It implies losing a central aspect of their long-standing identity and giving up all the social rewards that have been bestowed on them since childhood. Most become dependent on and even addicted to public recognition, and they want to hold on to their prestigious self-image for as long as possible. This makes them reluctant to accept that their skills are declining, and they harbor illusions about career longevity when reality suggests it is time to move on.

It is important to distinguish between voluntary and involuntary retirement from a sports career. For every Sandy Koufax, Al Rosen, and Michael Jordan who chooses to retire at the height of his success, there are hundreds of athletes who hang on, stay too long, and postpone their retirement as long as they can. Involuntary retirement occurs when an athlete is released, generally when management fails to renew a contract. At this crossroads many use denial and rationalization to avoid accepting the reality of their declining abilities on the field. The psychic injury of being released can be cushioned by holding on to the belief that it was lack of opportunity to fulfill their role—a premature termination—rather than eroding talent that led to their being cut. In discussing the emotional upheaval that accompanies retirement from professional sports, Reggie Jackson perceptively noted that "you don't retire at your convenience. You don't die when you're ready. . . . It's an inconvenience to die. You don't retire at the top." [34] Jackson's analogy between retirement and psychic death is right on target.

The retirement issues facing the former athlete are profound, and they are often immediate. Jim Bouton described his departure from the team in visceral terms: "As I started throwing stuff into my bag, I could feel the wall, invisible but real, forming around me. I was suddenly an outsider, a different person, someone to be shunned, a leper." [35] The spoiled athlete syndrome and unidimensionality can make it especially difficult for athletes to cope with retirement. The strain on the athlete's marriage is particularly noteworthy. Tom House has researched the divorce rate among former athletes and has come up with the astonishing observation that "some recent statistics indicate that the rate of divorce and separation among newly retired athletes is close to eighty percent." [36] House also notes that when baseball players' marriages do end in divorce, almost 50 percent fall apart within eighteen months after the athlete has left the game! These statistics speak to the magnitude of the stress and adjustment issues they face as they attempt to settle in to life in the real world.

An athlete who makes it beyond the two-year mark in professional sports can expect his career to last five to ten years, depending on the sport. This means that by age thirty-five, when most people are approaching their prime, most athletes are past their peak and must adjust to a more mundane life away from the bright lights. It is shocking to realize that a large majority of professional athletes do not give much thought to their lives after their careers are over, let alone do adequate financial planning. They tend to ride the crest of stardom as young men, yet all but the elite, the best of the best, are out of the game by their thirties. Many of today's heroes do not fare well tomorrow. While some are able to adjust to retirement, many flounder. Their early success and early retirement program them to orient to the past rather than the present or the future. The rate at which former athletes run afoul of the law after their playing days may also reflect their traumatic adjustment to retirement. The extent of problems with drug abuse is especially alarming. The number of former big league baseball heroes who have been convicted of illegal drug possession or sales or who have entered rehabilitation is high. Within baseball alone the list includes such stars as Dave Parker, Keith Hernandez, Doc Gooden, Dennis Eckersly, Vida Blue, Maury Wills, and Hall of Famer Ferguson Jenkins. Denny McLain, convicted and imprisoned for cocaine trafficking, cocaine possession, loan sharking, extortion, and bookmaking, qualifies as one of the all-time corrupt athletes and tragic heroes.

There are indications that antisocial and maladaptive behavior patterns among athletes emerge before they reach the professional level. In a study comparing student athletes with their nonathletic counterparts, psychologist Stephen Weiss found that athletes scored significantly higher on a maladaptive behavior scale than the nonathletes. [37] Such a finding demonstrates the distorted view of the self that many future athletes acquire early on.

For an athlete ensconced as a hero, it is difficult to imagine what life will be like after retirement from the game. For those who permit themselves to envision their inevitable loss of the majestic pedestal, a monumental adjustment looms. They must face both the loss of an inflated sense of specialness and adjustment to a more mundane existence in the real world. Bill Bradley incisively captures this issue:

There is a terror behind the dream of being a professional ballplayer. It comes as a slow realization of finality and of the frightening unknowns which the end brings. When the playing is over, one can sense that one's youth has been spent playing a game and now both the game and youth are gone, along with the innocence that characterizes all games which at root are pure and promote a prolonged adolescence in those who play. Now the athlete must face a world where awkward naivete can no longer be overlooked because of athletic performance. By age thirty-five any potential for developing skills outside of basketball is slim. The "good guy" syndrome ceases. What is left is the other side of the Faustian bargain: To live all one's days never able to recapture the feeling of those few years of intensified youth. [38]

Some stars become disillusioned and dispirited in their retirement transition. The itch to recapture past glory may propel them to attempt a return to professional sports. Most often these attempts are short-lived and highlight the erosion of talent over time. In commenting on Michael Jordan's questionable judgment in planning a comeback in 2001, Bob Cousy, another basketball great, asked, "Why risk tarnishing all that he's accomplished? All of us live in the past, and keep thinking about all the wonderful things we've done. But Old Man Time has a way of rising up and biting you."[39] Against the odds (Jordan being Jordan), he had a very successful comeback with the Washington Wizards at age thirty-nine. Similarly, hockey icon Mario Lemieux regained his former heights when he resumed skating with the Pittsburgh Penguins. Jordan and Lemieux stand out as superheroes who were able to recapture their glory days for another round. But for most sports stars who attempt this perilous route it proves to be an ill-advised adventure ending in failure.

A heightened sense of entitlement and runaway egos can lead to lapses in judgment that set the stage for destructive behavior—generally gambling, drug-related crime, and abuse of women. Gambling and drug-related behavior reflect destructiveness toward the self, while violence and other abuse toward women channel destructiveness toward others.

Until recently, the major sports leagues have assumed a somewhat lenient and forgiving stance toward athletes who self-destruct through drugs or abuse women, in contrast to a long-standing and consistently hard-line approach in dealing with gambling offenses. This puzzling disparity in sanctions can probably be attributed to the belief that gambling improprieties most directly threaten the integrity of the game.

3. Baseball Gambling Scandals

Baseball is something more than a game to an American boy. It is his training field for life work. Destroy his faith in its squareness and honesty and you have destroyed something more. You have planted suspicion of all things in his heart.

Kenesaw Mountain Landis

We create our sports heroes by attributing to them the specialness and greatness that we wish we had ourselves. But this golden image masks the fact that despite their athletic talent they are human beings with flaws that may be exaggerated by a distorted self-image.

There is a downside to stardom. When you sign your contract, you are also signing up for a life in which your off-field activities will be scrutinized and any lapses will be magnified. An ordinary citizen is free to place an affordable bet on a ball game, but an athlete who does so is jeopardizing his whole career.

The Black Sox Scandal

In September 1920 the world of organized baseball was rocked by the news that eight players on the Chicago White Sox had conspired with gamblers to throw the 1919 World Series against the Cincinnati Reds. The White Sox were the stronger team on paper and were heavy favorites to win the series, but before the opening game in Cincinnati the odds had shifted drastically in favor of the Reds. It is likely that word had gotten around to the bookmakers that a fix was in the works.

There are several versions of how the plan came into being, but the view most widely held is that Arnold "Chick" Gandil, the Chicago first baseman, approached a gambler named Sport Sullivan and together they concocted the plot. Gandil then enlisted pitcher Ed Cicotte, who had won twenty-nine games for the Sox that season. As Eliot Asinof reports in *Eight Men Out*, Charles Comiskey, the club's owner, had promised Cicotte a bonus of $10,000 if he won thirty games. He was held out of several late-season starts, and Comiskey denied him the bonus on the grounds that he had not won the required thirty games. Cicotte was being underpaid, with a salary of about $5,000 for the year. His rage and hurt over this unfair treatment led him to justify his lack of judgment, and he agreed to go along with the fix. Next to be solicited were infielders Swede Risberg and George "Buck" Weaver, outfielders Shoeless Joe Jackson and Oscar "Happy" Felsch, pitcher Claude "Lefty" Williams, and utility reserve Fred McMullin. It was well known that the White Sox players were vastly underpaid, but under the prevailing reserve clause that existed at that time, in which players were bound to the team that employed them and could never become free agents, they had little alternative to accepting what Comiskey offered. The players felt very dissatisfied, and the climate was right for a fix. Once things got started it seems it was not too difficult to enlist the eight players. Comiskey's cheapness was readily used to justify taking bribe money.[1]

Sport Sullivan allegedly was connected to the notorious New York gambler Arnold Rothstein, who was supposed to provide $100,000 for the players to throw the Series. The players were led to believe they would each receive at least $10,000, but the plot was bungled badly before it got started. Nobody seemed to know exactly what his role was; it was not clear which games they were to try to win in order to cover up their larger intention; and information about the plan was freely leaked, so that rumors were wildly circulating before the Series. Meanwhile, Rothstein was skeptical about the plan's viability and had some reservations about committing to it. While Rothstein was hesitating, the players were considering a parallel offer. The story goes that in the midst of the floating rumors Cicotte made contact with Bill Burns, a former pitcher, who tried to get a group of Philadelphia gamblers to bankroll the fix. At this point the players seemed ready to accept bribe money from whatever source. Abe Attell, a featherweight boxing champion turned gambler and an associate of Rothstein's, became the liaison with the players for both deals. According to the account given by baseball historian Harold Seymour in *Baseball: The Golden Age*, Rothstein initially turned down the deal, the Philadelphia counteroffer fell through, and Rothstein then changed course and agreed to fund the fix with Attell as the front runner.[2] In a different version presented by sportswriter Leonard Koppett, "Rothstein had, in fact, refused to finance those who first suggested the fix, then used his knowledge that the fix was in to cash in through his own operations."[3] In any case, Rothstein later voluntarily testified before a Chicago grand jury that he did not bet on the

Series and disclaimed any involvement. Curiously, the grand jury believed him; he was never indicted or implicated in the ensuing scandal.

Amid the swirling rumors during the Series, the White Sox manager, Kid Gleason, was suspicious and brought his concerns to the owner. Comiskey in turn reportedly alerted John Heydler, the National League president, who naively chose to believe the White Sox had lost simply because they underestimated the strength of the Reds. He therefore did little to find out what was really going on. Comiskey also turned the matter over to American League president Ban Johnson after the Series; but Johnson's investigation, at least initially, seemed to lead nowhere. Ultimately the matter was left to the grand jury.

On the field the "superior" White Sox played shoddy ball throughout most of the Series games. Supposedly Cicotte, their ace pitcher, was to hit the first batter he faced in game one, as a signal to Rothstein and others that the fix was in. Cicotte did hit the first batter. The Reds knocked Cicotte out of the box in the fourth inning and won the first game 9–1. Lefty Williams started game two and gave up six walks, and the Reds won again, 4–2. Dickie Kerr, who was not one of the tarnished eight, then pitched a shutout, and the Sox won game three. But with Cicotte losing two games (he did win game six) and Williams taking the loss in three games, the Sox lost the Series five games to three. (In that era the format was to win five out of nine for the World Series crown.)

Into 1920, stories continued to flourish about the fix. Comiskey claimed he was pursuing his own investigation, but nothing was done. All the "tainted" players except Gandil returned to play for the White Sox in what turned out to be a close race for the pennant between Chicago and Cleveland, and gradually the rumors subsided. But the whole affair was revived by an alleged fix in a National League game between the Phillies and the Cubs toward the end of the 1920 season. On August 31, 1920, William Veeck Sr., president of the Cubs, received six telegrams and two long-distance calls informing him that that day's game was being fixed for the last-place Phillies to win. Veeck conferred with his manager, Fred Mitchell, and they decided to use their ace pitcher Grover Alexander out of rotation in place of the scheduled pitcher, Claude Hendrix. Veeck intended to send a message that the Cubs were determined to win. But the Cubs were shut out 3–0, intensifying the rumors that the game had been fixed. Veeck launched an investigation and called on the Committee of Chicago Sports Writers to do the same.

Hendrix denied being involved in a fix, and the findings suggested that the calls and telegrams were bogus—attempts by gamblers to get the Cubs to use Alexander and thereby improve their chances of winning the game.

As a consequence of this incident, a special Chicago grand jury was convened to investigate the Cubs-Phillies game as well as to make an overall probe into gambling in baseball. The suspicions surrounding the 1919 World Series were inevitably reawakened. The grand jury probe began on September 22, 1920, and on September 27 a Philadelphia newspaper, which had obtained additional information, broke the story, "Gamblers Promised White Sox $100,000 to Lose Series." The next day the eight players in question were indicted by the grand jury on charges of conspiring to throw the Series, and Comiskey suspended them all indefinitely. He pledged to reinstate them if they were found innocent. All of this occurred while the Sox were in a hot pennant race, and losing the suspended players before the last few games of the season ruined their chances to catch the Cleveland Indians, who finished two games in front of Chicago.

After the Philadelphia news story exposed the conspiracy, Ed Cicotte and Joe Jackson quickly confessed to participating in the fix. Cicotte, plagued with the anxiety and guilt he had been carrying within himself for a year, first went to Comiskey and acknowledged that "I got $10,000 for being a crook." He then made a tearful confession before the grand jury in which he shamefacedly admitted his role in the frame-up. He accused Gandil as "the master of ceremonies," and he described the grandiose mentality among the players: "We talked about throwing the series. Decided we could get away with it. We agreed to do it." In describing his anguish after the fact, Cicotte stated, "I never did anything I regretted as much in my life. I would give anything in the world if I could undo my acts in the last World Series. I've played a crooked game and I have lost, and I am here to tell the whole truth."[4] This White Sox hero, who was a twenty-game winner three times, now at age thirty-six was a pathetic figure in front of the grand jury. His confession epitomized the mind-set of athletes who think they are above it all and can transgress society's standards with impunity. It is likely that Cicotte and the others suffered remorse for many years. After his exposure Cicotte lamented, "I've lived a thousand years in the last year . . . if I had reasoned what that meant to me, the taking of that dirty crooked money—the hours of mental torture, the days and nights of living with an unclean mind; the weeks and months of going along with six of the seven crooked players and holding a guilty secret, and of going along with the boys who had stayed straight and clean and honest—it was hell. I got the $10,000 cash in advance, that's all."[5]

Shoeless Joe Jackson testified before the grand jury in quite a different manner. His admission corroborated Cicotte's version of the fix, but he portrayed himself as the victim of group pressure. He claimed that Gandil and Risberg had pursued him after the others had already committed themselves. Supposedly they told Jackson that since it was already a done deal, he would be a sap to turn down a share of the profits. Persuaded that they were telling the truth and seduced by easy money, Jackson agreed to join in. By all accounts Jackson was a simple, uneducated man who was targeted as easily swayed by group pressure. As the premier hitter, he would be pivotal in throwing the games. Jackson agreed to accept $20,000. He claimed that Lefty Williams gave him $5,000 before the start of the Series but that he never got the rest. In his statement to the grand jury, Jackson maintained that after losing the first two games the eight players had done their best to oblige the gamblers and throw game three, but that things backfired when Dickie Kerr, one of the "clean" Sox, pitched a brilliant shutout. The "fixers," who had bet heavily on Cincinnati and thus lost a bundle, reneged on further payoffs, thereby double-crossing the players for double-crossing them. Jackson led all hitters in the Series with a .375 average, but this statistic was deceptive, since he testified that he deliberately struck out or made easy outs when runners were on base.

Jackson, like Ed Cicotte, felt guilty and remorseful and seemed relieved to testify and get "a big load off my chest." He also claimed he was afraid the other players would retaliate for his exposing the conspiracy. He was particularly afraid of Swede Risberg, and he asked for bailiffs to protect him when he left the grand jury room. Though this may sound paranoid, Jackson feared for his life and wasn't taking any chances. He stated, "Now Risberg threatens to bump me off if I squawk. . . . I'm not going to get far from my protectors until this blows over. Swede is a hard guy."[6] It was when Shoeless Joe Jackson left the courthouse that the legendary incident most closely associated with the scandal supposedly occurred. A young boy, devastated by the allegations against his hero, cried out, "Say it ain't so, Joe!" and Jackson shamefacedly responded,

"It's so." Whether myth or reality, this image of an innocent boy over-whelmed by disillusionment when his hero falls from grace captures the impact the loss of a hero has on his adoring fans.

The eight White Sox players were indicted by the grand jury on September 28, 1920, charged with "conspiracy to commit an illegal act." If convicted, each stood to serve one to five years in prison and receive a fine of up to $10,000.

The trial was delayed until June 1921. In a bizarre twist, the files of their testimonies to the grand jury had been stolen. It was suspected but never proved that Arnold Rothstein, who had allegedly bankrolled the bribes, was behind the theft. Meanwhile the players, as advised by their lawyers, had retracted their confessions. Nevertheless the American League president, Ban Johnson, trying to promote an image of cleaning up the unsavory elements encroaching on baseball, was able to recreate the evidence and secure a new indictment. With all the publicity about the scandal, the public and the press dubbed the eight players the "Black Sox" and were ready to convict them before they went to trial.

The legal case was not strong, and after a five-week trial the jury deliberated briefly and found all the players not guilty on all charges. A wild scene followed in which some of the jurors, perhaps out of admiration and sympathy, carried the players around the courtroom on their shoulders. Later that night the jurors and the players happened to celebrate at the same restaurant and wound up partying together. In the festive atmosphere of exoneration, the players and the jurors left the restaurant together, happily chanting "Hail, hail, the gang's all here."

With the case behind them, the players expected to be reinstated to active status in baseball. It was not to be. On the very next day, August 3, 1921, Kenesaw Mountain Landis, who had recently been appointed as the first commissioner of Major League Baseball with the task of cleaning up the game, declared that all the players would be banished permanently from baseball. Convinced that the evidence incriminated the players, Landis, a former judge, disregarded the jury verdict and ruled as follows: "Regardless of the verdict of juries, no player that throws a ball game; no player that undertakes or promises to throw a ball game; no player that sits in a conference with a bunch of crooked players and gamblers where the ways and means of throwing games are planned and discussed and does not promptly tell his club about it, will ever play professional baseball."[7]

None of the banned players ever played Major League Baseball again. Buck Weaver, one of the accused, tried to clear his name every year until his death; his appeals were repeatedly denied. In addition, Weaver and Jackson, who had long-term contracts with the White Sox, unsuccessfully sued the club for back salary but did reach an out-of-court settlement with Comiskey. Landis's edict against the players stood and ushered in an era of his iron-fisted rule. The players faded into oblivion in occupations ranging from plumber to dairy farmer to liquor store proprietor. Jackson, whose career batting average of .356 placed him third in the all-time list, was never elected to the Hall of Fame.

Finally, in a 1956 article in *Sports Illustrated*, Chick Gandil told his version of the episode. He tried to place some blame for succumbing to temptation on resentment of Comiskey, whom he described as "a sarcastic, belittling man who was the tightest owner in baseball." It is likely that the owner's well-known cheapness sparked widespread discontent and animosity and to some extent set the stage for the events that followed. Nevertheless, Gandil acknowledged that the tainted players needed to take responsibility for their own willingness to be corrupted and admitted that "we had no one to blame except ourselves." Gandil claimed that Sport Sullivan approached him and Ed Cicotte, rather than the other way around, and offered to pay $10,000 to each of the seven or eight players they could influence to go in on the deal. The money was enticing, considering their low salaries, and Gandil and Cicotte carefully selected the other six players who agreed to join in the fix. Meanwhile, according to Gandil, a second proposition emerged through Bill Burns, the former Major League pitcher, who said his group could top any offer they had received. The players now felt they were the prize in a bidding war and, indulging their greed, decided to take any money the Burns group offered. This didn't work out, and Gandil revealed that the players then firmed up the original deal through Arnold Rothstein, who gave them an advance of $10,000, with the promise that the rest would come in installments after each of the first four games. The agreed-on format, proposed by Rothstein, was for the heavily favored team to try their best to win game one behind their twenty-nine-game winner, Cicotte, so that the odds on the Sox would go up, and then to lose the Series "at our convenience."[8]

In his exposé Gandil testified that before the first game too much information had been leaked, rumors of a fix were all around, and the players decided it was too risky to go through with the plot. The fear of getting caught, not a reassessment of the immorality of the plan, supposedly deterred them. Instead, they agreed to double-cross the gamblers by keeping the $10,000 and playing their best to win the Series. Thus, Gandil maintained, although the players' conspiracy was inexcusable, they had reversed their course and attempted to win, and "our actual losing of the Series was pure baseball fortune." For many years Gandil resented Cicotte for caving in and blowing the whistle. Gandil's ultimate lack of contrition is revealed in his statement to *Sports Illustrated*: "I don't believe we would have ever been caught if he hadn't gabbed."[9]

In an eerie postscript, Arnold Rothstein, the gambler who was accused of the conspiracy but cleared in court, was gunned down six years later at New York's Park Central Hotel. Apparently his fellow gamblers had called him to a meeting to force him to settle his debts of more than $300,000 lost in a stud poker game on September 29, 1928. Though he had been unable to cover his losses when the game broke up, they accepted that he was a prompt payer and would soon meet his obligations. Subsequently he maintained that the game had been crooked (a twist from the man who allegedly masterminded the 1919 World Series fix) and refused to pay. It was reported that he was shot by one of the two gangsters his creditors hired as retaliation for welshing on his debt. He lived two days after the gunshot had ruptured his bladder and damaged his intestines, but in a code of silence among criminals, he refused to talk to the police about the shooting. It is estimated that his fortune was worth between $2 million and $10 million. One month later, federal agents seized $2 million worth of narcotics from the biggest drug ring in the United States, and it was disclosed that Rothstein had arranged the financing for this group.

In reassessing the Black Sox episode we might ask, How did this happen? Had similar transgressions happened before? Could they happen again? Among the psychological factors that precipitated the conspiracy were working under an oppressive, belittling, and punitive boss; greed, which the players justified; and group pressure. These factors predisposed them to be susceptible to the fix. And the feelings of specialness and entitlement that characterize many athletes, along with their denial of serious consequences, compounded their poor judgment and their readiness to be corrupted. The group dynamics are particularly interesting. Since Comiskey was probably experienced as a powerful, dominating father figure, it is likely the players wanted to overthrow his tyrannical regime. Resentment at being mistreated and humiliated by Comiskey's "take it or leave it" ultimatums at contract time created a widespread desire to rebel. History and literature are full of oppressed sons who try to overthrow their fathers. The prevailing atmosphere among the White Sox when Gandil and Cicotte assumed leadership in planning the conspiracy bred group contagion. The notion that "we're all in this together" made it easier for the others they approached to collectively act out their rage.

It is generally believed that the image of baseball and its heroes as incorruptible was first tarnished by the Black Sox incident. As the only sport at that time that was organized on a major league level, baseball had been seen as a pure national pastime. But while the magnitude of the conspiracy and the number of players it involved were extensive, it was not the first time cheating had blackened the game. Baseball historians note that the seeds of corruption had been growing for at least twenty years. The climate was very different from what it is today, and it was common for ballplayers and gamblers to have friendly contact and to mix freely. Baseball insiders and players knew there was widespread corruption. Baseball was not well policed, and it was widely acknowledged that individual players had taken bribes to throw games. It is also possible that other incidents, large and small, were never exposed. In the early decades of the twentieth century it was commonplace for players on losing teams to deliberately play poorly toward the end of a season in order to help friends on other teams that were striving to improve their records in the final standings. There had been rumors of fixes in the 1908 National League pennant race, the 1910 American League batting title, and several 1917 games between the White Sox and the Tigers. In the last instance, as Swede Risberg later acknowledged, a pool of $1,100 had been collected from the Chicago players to influence the Detroit pitchers to go easy on them in two doubleheaders during the September pennant race. Thus, although the integrity of the game had been questionable for many years, the Black Sox scandal created headlines because it concerned the World Series, because of the large amount of bribe money involved, and because the widespread suspicions were substantiated.

Could such an event happen again? In hindsight it may seem incomprehensible and perhaps even preposterous to imagine that a scheme could be arranged on such a large scale. But that is judging the event by today's conditions. It is highly unlikely that such a conspiracy could happen again in baseball. With the advent of free agency and multimillion-dollar salaries and the opportunity to earn additional income through commercials, there is little financial incentive to risk such a venture. In addition, the game is policed more rigorously today, and the stigma of the Black Sox scandal and its aftermath continues to be a deterrent if temptations occur. Also, basketball and football games, in which gambling involves point spreads rather than simply winning or losing, may be easier to fix.

Nowadays ballplayers are wary about fraternizing with gamblers. Several years ago I saw Clyde Wright in a hotel lobby, when he was a twenty-game winner with the California Angels, and asked for his autograph. His spontaneous reply was, "You look like a gambler." Only after I had convinced him I was a psychologist did he give me the autograph.

The most notoriously corrupt player of the Black Sox era was Hal Chase. Chase, the premier first baseman of the time, played Major League ball for fifteen years and was known to have been brazenly involved in arranging fixes. It has been reported that in 1919, the year of the World Series scandal, Chase and his teammate Heine Zimmerman, playing for the New York Giants, had unsuccessfully tried to bribe their teammate Rube Benton, a pitcher, to throw a game. Chase and Zimmerman allegedly had also tried to bribe another teammate, Benny Kauff, to help throw a game. This last incident was reported to Giants manager John McGraw, who immediately dismissed them from the team, even though they were in a close pennant race. Neither ever played in the majors again.

In the previous season Chase had played with Cincinnati and had been suspended by his manager late in the season for allegedly betting on games and trying to get a pitcher on the team to throw a game. Earlier in the season Chase and teammate Lee Magee allegedly had conspired with gamblers to throw a game. Reflecting the crookedness that permeated baseball at that time, Magee later denied under oath any involvement in a fix, but he openly admitted intending to bet $500 on his own team (which lost the game). Incredibly, the message Magee conveyed was that it was okay to bet on games as long as you didn't try to fix them. Throughout his baseball career the press accused Chase of throwing games. Seymour portrayed Chase as "the archetype of all crooked ballplayers . . . not only did he throw games himself; he corrupted or tried to corrupt other players . . . he became a full fledged fixer and gambler." [10] Chase arrogantly, blatantly, and repeatedly demonstrated his unparalleled capacity for corruption. His behavior (in the pre-Landis era) epitomized the sense of entitlement and contempt for community values that characterize some athletes. It is significant that after his misdeeds were exposed and he was suspended for the rest of the 1918 season, Hal Chase was permitted to play again the next year. These events showed that corruption in baseball would be tolerated and can be viewed as leading indirectly to the World Series fix; that is, the seeds were planted for the great fix, yet to come. Allowing Chase to avoid punishment and return for the 1919 season reinforced other players' belief that they could play dishonestly without consequences.

It was widely believed that Chase had a part in arranging the World Series fix or, at the very least, knew about it and won $40,000 in bets. He was tried and acquitted along with the Chicago players and other gamblers in 1921. No longer an active player, he was never punished or even chastised by Commissioner Landis.

It took Kenesaw Landis several years after his appointment as commissioner in 1921 to make good on his pledge to clean up organized baseball. Eventually his autocratic regime deterred suspicious behavior, but for a while he was confronted with other attempts to fix games, leading to several more banishments. These included Eugene Paulette, permanently blacklisted in 1921 for offering to throw games; Joe Gideon, in 1921 for "guilty knowledge" of the World Series conspiracy; Phil Douglas, in 1922 for writing to a competing team and offering to abandon his team if it was made worth his while; and Jimmy O'Connell and Cozy Dolan, in 1924 for attempting to bribe another player. In 1926 Landis pursued allegations that Ty Cobb and Tris Speaker, two venerable future Hall of Famers, had conspired to throw a game between their respective teams back in 1919. After an extensive investigation Landis exonerated both players, who were reinstated and resumed playing in the twilight of their careers. During the remaining twenty years of the Landis regime, there were no significant blemishes within baseball.

Since that time there have been three major scandals, involving Leo Durocher (1947), Denny McLain (1970), and Pete Rose (1989).

Leo Durocher

Leo Durocher was known as a brash, fiery competitor, labeled as a good field–no-hit shortstop who made the most of his limited talent and contributed to his team's success with smarts, drive, and other intangibles. He became the ideal manager for the feisty Brooklyn Dodgers of the late 1930s and 1940s, and many of the Brooklyn fans readily identified with his down-to-earth, no-nonsense style. When managing a good club, he seemed able to get the most out of his players and motivate them to achieve. He piloted his 1946 Dodgers, a team much less loaded than the rival Cardinals, to a tie for the pennant and the first playoff series in baseball history. But when managing players with limited talent he was less successful in getting them to maximize their potential, and the team often floundered below their abilities.

Durocher the manager was brazen, arrogant, and defiant and frequently clashed with authority figures. He was nicknamed "the Lip," and his rows with umpires were legendary; he probably was ejected from more games than any other manager before or since. He also was fired for insubordination and subsequently rehired many times by Dodgers owner Larry MacPhail. In 1941, when the Dodgers clinched the pennant, they traveled from Boston back to Brooklyn by train. MacPhail arranged for the train to stop at 125th Street so he could board and lead the victory celebration when they got home. Leo overruled him and ordered the train to streak straight through to Grand Central Station, leaving a gaping owner stranded on the platform. A furious MacPhail fired him for his defiance, but of course he rehired him the next day. How could he fire the man who had led Brooklyn to its first pennant in twenty-one years?

In the following seasons Durocher continued to act as though he could do whatever he wanted. He blatantly associated with gamblers and other shady characters and seemed to enjoy cultivating an image as baseball's bad boy. Like many grandiose individuals who defiantly tempt fate, he was ultimately cut down.

After Kenesaw Mountain Landis died in 1944, A. B. "Happy" Chandler was appointed baseball's second commissioner. After Landis's autocratic rule, it was important for Chandler to set a tone of continued firmness. Durocher's brazen arrogance and his defiant attitude toward authority and moral standards quickly provided that opportunity. It was almost inevitable that Chandler and Durocher would collide.

In April 1947 Chandler took the unprecedented step of suspending Durocher for the entire season for "conduct detrimental to baseball." This stunning edict occurred when Chandler convened a hearing after Durocher accused Larry MacPhail, now co-owner and president of the Yankees, of associating with gamblers at spring training games in Havana—something Chandler had specifically prohibited Durocher from doing. This accusation was the climax of a series of incidents that heightened Durocher's notoriety. As when, many decades later, Bobby Knight, the basketball coach at Indiana University, was fired for grabbing a disrespectful student by the collar, the relatively minor incident in Havana served as a pretext for disciplining Durocher. For the commissioner it was the last straw.

Soon after Chandler took office Durocher was indicted in a Brooklyn court for assaulting a fan who had been heckling him during a Dodgers home game. John Christian, a veteran, wound up in the hospital with a broken jaw. He claimed that Durocher and a security guard had attacked him with brass knuckles. The case was ultimately settled out of court for about $7,000, but it brought Durocher more negative publicity.

One year later, in late 1946, Chandler confronted Durocher about his friendship with well-known mobsters like Bugsy Siegel and Joe Adonis and threatened to suspend him if he continued to associate with them. Baseball was still sensitive about any infiltration by gamblers. At about the same time, Leo's personal life made headlines when he purportedly had an affair with his neighbor's wife, the actress Lorraine Day, whom he later married. This created an uproar within the Catholic Church and led to Durocher's condemnation by the Catholic Youth Organization for "undermining the moral training of Brooklyn's Roman Catholic youth by his conduct both on and off the baseball diamond." Durocher was deemed a bad role model for young fans, and the Catholic Church was hoping to influence a large number of kids who belonged to the Dodger Knothole Club to desert the Brooklyn team.

With the episode in Havana, Chandler had had enough and exercised his unilateral authority to come down hard on Durocher. In the text of his decision to ban Durocher, Chandler, who had been the target of considerable criticism since he became commissioner, took a firm stand:

Durocher has not measured up to the standards expected or required of managers of our baseball teams. This incident in Havana, which brought considerable unfavorable comment to baseball generally, was one of a series of publicity-producing affairs in which Manager Durocher has been involved in the last few months.

Managers of baseball teams are responsible for the conduct of players on the field. Good managers are able to ensure the good conduct of the players on the field and frequently by their example can influence players to be of good conduct off the field. . . . As a result of the accumulation of unpleasant incidents in which he has been involved, which the commissioner construes as detrimental to baseball, Manager Durocher is hereby suspended from participating in professional baseball for the 1947 season.[11]

Thus, with one stroke from the commissioner Durocher became a fallen hero to many of his fans, who admired what he had accomplished as manager of their beloved Dodgers. On learning of Chandler's pronouncement, "the Lip" seemed flabbergasted; his response was to repeatedly shout, "For what?" He had heeded Chandler's previous warnings and had distanced himself from mobsters and gamblers, but his efforts were too little and too late. Durocher's accusations about MacPhail were deemed inflammatory and detrimental to baseball and used as the pretext to suspend him. Chandler stated that the suspension was the "result of the accumulation of unpleasant incidents in which he has been involved." The commissioner's office subsequently revealed that before the Havana incident Chandler had issued an ultimatum to Durocher that "the next offense would be his last." It appears that Durocher did not take this warning seriously enough—that he tested the limits, stepped over the line of acceptable behavior, and was nailed for it. Although Durocher was far from an innocent in terms of his cumulative transgressions, it seems in retrospect that Chandler's edict was excessively harsh. Chandler, in contrast, thought the penalty was lenient, but the Brooklyn fans were outraged at the one-year suspension. In any event, Durocher accepted his punishment (he had no recourse) and returned to baseball in 1948. He probably learned something from the experience, for after his reinstatement he stayed clear of trouble for the next twenty-five years while achieving periodic success as the pilot of the Dodgers, Giants, Cubs, and Astros. The two protagonists in this scandal died within four months of each other in 1992.

Dennis McLain

After the Durocher scandal, baseball's image remained untarnished until 1970, when Denny McLain, the American League's premier pitcher, fell from grace. In the intervening years the national pastime had become revolutionized by the breaking of the color barrier with the acceptance of black players, by franchise relocations and expansion teams, by the introduction of divisional playoffs, by the heightened role of relief pitching, and by the shift from a four-man pitching rotation to a five-man rotation. In 1968 twenty-four-year-old Dennis Dale McLain became the first big leaguer to achieve thirty or more victories in a season since Dizzy Dean in 1934. This remarkable accomplishment may never be duplicated, because McLain was able to start forty-one games, pitching on three days' rest, whereas today's pampered pitchers are traditionally given four days off between starts. He easily won the Most Valuable Player Award and the Cy Young Award that year, and he won the Cy Young Award again in 1969, when he won twenty-four games.

His ruin began before the next season, when he acknowledged to Commissioner Bowie Kuhn that he had been involved in bookmaking back in 1967. Concerned about protecting the integrity of the game, Kuhn followed the lead of Commissioner Chandler in the Durocher episode and suspended McLain indefinitely. In the text of his announcement Kuhn stated that "McLain's association in 1967 with gamblers was contrary to his obligation as a professional baseball player to conform to high standards of personal conduct, and it is my judgement that this conduct was not in the best interests of baseball." [12] On further investigation Kuhn determined that McLain, although admitting he had become financially involved in a bookmaking operation, had been duped by his associates in a confidence scheme. Kuhn ruled that McLain could be reinstated on July 1, 1970. He would miss only half a season. In his defense, McLain claimed he was a victim of his own gullibility. In describing how he often acts before he thinks, he said, "My biggest crime is stupidity." [13]

Robert Lipsyte, a respected sportswriter for the *New York Times*, was suspicious of the naive explanation for McLain's misdeeds and suggested that Kuhn had prematurely "ended the matter with a positive action [the July 1 reinstatement] to avoid further investigation that might reveal widespread gambling, even fixing of games."[14] Fixing games was still the bête noire of baseball. Lipsyte's column also implied that the commissioner did not want a deeper inquiry that might drag a celebrated hero through the mud.

Indeed, an article in *Sports Illustrated* about the time of the suspension reported that during the pennant race in 1967 McLain had been deeply involved with the gambling operation and that a Mafia henchman had intentionally stepped on McLain's toes and dislocated them on the orders of a gambler who had not been paid off on a $46,000 winning bet he had placed with McLain's bookmaking operation.[15] The injury severely impaired McLain's performance on the mound and may have cost Detroit the pennant. In his autobiography *Strikeout: The Story of Denny McLain*, he states that the *Sports Illustrated* story, which defamed him, was based on lies.[16]

In any event, McLain returned on July 1, 1970, but the onetime superhero was ineffective, posting a 3-5 win-loss record. To make matters worse, he was suspended again in August for carrying a loaded gun on road trips. This infraction was a violation of the probationary status of the first suspension. After this disastrous season McLain was traded to the lowly Washington Senators, where he became baseball's losingest pitcher with a 10-22 record. He never recovered his winning form, and after brief stints with the Atlanta Braves and the Oakland A's in 1972, he was out of baseball before his twenty-ninth birthday.

Denny McLain continued to go downhill after his playing days were over. By 1977, after several failed business ventures, he filed for bankruptcy for the second time. He went from one shady scheme to the next, and in 1984 he and several associates were indicted by a federal grand jury for racketeering, conspiracy, extortion, possession of cocaine with the intent to distribute, and conspiracy to import cocaine. McLain claimed he was innocent of all charges except bookmaking. He portrayed himself as victimized by the legal system and by other offenders who were given immunity. Nevertheless, he received a twenty-three-year prison sentence and served two and a half years before his conviction was overturned on appeal based on procedural misdeeds. A higher court determined that the trial had been unfairly rushed and ordered a retrial. But before the retrial McLain pleaded guilty to racketeering and possession of cocaine with intent to distribute. He was given a suspended sentence of twelve years, and he later admitted to extortion, loan sharking, acquiring a plane to smuggle and transport drugs, and shaking down a drug dealer.

In his autobiography McLain describes a long history of having problems with authority and playing by his own rules. He experienced his mother as insensitive and neglectful, and his father, the disciplinarian, died suddenly when he was fifteen, which may have precipitated his subsequent disregard for the rules. Away from the structure of baseball, he acted as if he knew no boundaries. His early celebrity intensified the attitude of "Do you know who I am? I'm Denny McLain!" He frequently externalized his problems, blaming other "scum-bum people" for his legal difficulties. In surveying McLain's many adult transgressions, Fred Goodman wrote in a *Gentleman's Quarterly* article that "the only thing he has proved repeatedly and beyond doubt is that he is a small-time hustler, an unrepentant con artist and an unflinchingly irresponsible man."[17]

After his release from prison Denny was still not persona non grata in Detroit. In spite of the disillusion many fans experience when a sports hero becomes blemished, they often are eager to offer a second chance so they can hold on to the positive image of their hero that they identify with. Thus Denny McLain was welcomed back and became a successful host of radio and television talk shows. Things went well for a while, but his avarice, disregard for the law, and self-destructiveness ultimately prevailed. Although he was making lots of money through legitimate channels such as card shows, endorsements, and nightclub appearances as an organist, he couldn't resist the temptation to try for easy money.

In 1997 he was convicted of conspiracy, theft from a pension plan, money laundering, and mail fraud and sentenced to eight years in prison. There was evidence that McLain and two associates had purchased a Michigan company called Peet Packing in 1993 and had later embezzled $2.5 million of the firm's pension assets. The meatpacking company closed, and about five hundred employees lost their jobs and their pensions.

In 1998, while serving time in a federal correctional center, McLain once again got in trouble with the law. This time he was accused along with Mafia boss John Gotti Jr. and thirty-eight others of selling valueless telephone cards and defrauding phone companies.

Denny McLain stands out as the quintessential baseball hero who spiraled downward as a fallen idol. Can his demise be understood merely as a consequence of a self-destructive core, or did his arrogance propel him to act time and again according to his own rules? Most likely both of these personality attributes contributed significantly to his downfall.

The qualities that link McLain to Leo Durocher before him and Pete Rose after him as the major examples of scandal in baseball after the Black Sox episode are an outrageous sense of self-importance, a defiant attitude toward authority, and a readiness to push their luck to the edge. They underestimated the consequences of their behavior and its impact on their devoted fans while claiming innocence and insisting they were victimized by the system.

Pete Rose

Peter Edward Rose began his Major League Baseball career with the Cincinnati Reds in 1963, the same year Dennis McLain broke in. He was also banned from baseball for gambling, but the scandal that snared him occurred after his playing days were over. Though Rose did not engage in repeated misdeeds, his betting on baseball games was serious enough to bring a lifetime suspension.

In contrast to McLain, whose meteoric career was spectacular and short-lived, Rose had twenty-four seasons of posting Hall of Fame numbers. He is best known for eclipsing Ty Cobb's supposedly unbreakable record of most career base hits. In 1985 Rose surpassed Cobb's long-standing record of 4,191 hits, and he reached a total of 4,256 before he retired. He also holds the records for playing in the most Major League games and for most seasons with 200 or more hits. In 1978 Rose set the modern National League record by hitting safely in forty-four consecutive games.

According to Michael Sokolove's penetrating biography, Pete Rose was not well liked by fellow teammates and was dubbed a "me-me-me" player. Nevertheless he was skillful at cultivating the press, giving reporters his time, insights, and humor, and they helped promote him. The fans loved him and his style of play based on hard work and determination, which personified Cincinnati itself. Thus sportswriters and fans alike were captivated by his charm and his overachieving style, affectionately nicknaming him "Charlie Hustle." As Sokolove noted, "To millions of Americans, he embodied all that was good in the National Pastime, and by extension, so much that was good about America. He was the American ideal of egalitarianism come to life on the field of play; his perpetually dirty uniform, soiled by nothing less than all-out effort, stood as vivid proof that a man who worked hard could triumph over one who was born to greater advantages."[18]

All this changed in 1989 when Rose was investigated for gambling and his arrogance did him in. In the face of mounting evidence that he had bet on sports events, including baseball games, and thereby violated a sanctified code, the sportswriters turned against him. Fans who had previously identified with his accomplishments and hardscrabble work ethic were sadly disillusioned. As Sokolove suggests, "The hero had been too well liked. Too fawned over. The nearly three-decade long diet of adulation, flattery, and praise had bloated him full of his own importance, causing him to feel that he was above the rules that governed the less exalted."[19]

Pete Rose, like his predecessor Ty Cobb, grew up attached to a powerful father who died young, when Pete was twenty-nine. Rose claimed that his father had been the greatest and sometimes the only influence on his life. Both Cobb and Rose attributed their fierce competitive spirit to their fathers, carrying forward the torch of intensity. Sokolove maintains that "for both men, approval from their fathers mattered more than approval from their peers. It was like oxygen, water, food. They couldn't live without it."[20] Both Cobb and Rose may have maintained a connection to their lost fathers by becoming the kind of ballplayers they thought their fathers would have wanted them to be. But they lacked self-discipline and equanimity and developed a grandiose view of themselves that might have been tempered by the presence of a strong and admired father.

The baseball authorities had become aware of Rose's gambling with bookmakers as early as 1977. The commissioner, Bowie Kuhn, started an investigation that went on for years, but there was no conclusive evidence, so nothing was done. This undoubtedly fueled Rose's belief in his specialness. His growing status as an icon seemed to make him untouchable; and though gambling was sufficient grounds for suspension, the baseball authorities did not vigorously pursue the matter.

In 1989, when he was no longer playing but was manager of the Reds, baseball finally launched a full-scale probe of Rose's gambling.

At the same time, a series of articles in *Sports Illustrated* claimed that Rose had regularly placed bets with bookmaker Ron Peters through his associates Paul Janszen and Tom Gioiosa, who had served prison time on drug charges.

Initially Rose denied betting on any sport with bookmakers, but he ultimately admitted to betting on football and basketball games. He steadfastly denied betting on baseball, but Peters, Janszen, Gioiosa, and numerous other sources claimed he had. Rose tried to discredit their statements by pointing out that they were criminals trying to reduce their own penalties.

The commissioner's office appointed attorney John Dowd to investigate Pete Rose; Dowd spent several months gathering information and then submitted a 225-page report condemning him. Rose, the premier player of his era, forlornly acknowledged betting on sports other than baseball and associating with felons, in itself sufficient to ban him from baseball. But Dowd concluded that Rose had also committed the ultimate violation: "The testimony and the documentary evidence gathered in the course of the investigation demonstrates that Pete Rose bet on baseball, and in particular, on games of the Cincinnati Reds Baseball Club during the 1985, 1986, and 1987 seasons."[21]

On August 24, 1989, with the weight of the Dowd report behind him, the newly appointed commissioner, Bart Giamatti, acted. He prevailed on Rose to sign an agreement that he would be suspended from baseball permanently "with the right to apply for reinstatement after one year." As part of the agreement Giamatti added, "Nothing in this agreement shall be deemed either an admission or a denial by Peter Edward Rose of the allegations that he bet on any major league baseball game."[22] Thus Rose was offered an olive branch that let him hope for reinstatement and, more important, future election to the Hall of Fame. At this time Rose has not been reinstated. He remains adamant that he was judged unfairly and that his big mistake, like Denny McLain's, was picking the wrong friends. His detractors note that Rose remains in denial of a serious gambling problem and has never acknowledged the full scope of his misdeeds.

In 1990 Pete Rose was further humiliated by a felony conviction for evading taxes on income derived from baseball card shows; he was sent to prison for five months. The presiding judge, S. Arthur Spiegel, astutely noted, "We must recognize that there are two people here.

Pete Rose the living legend, the all-time hit leader, and the idol of millions; and Pete Rose, the individual, who appears today convicted of two counts of cheating on his taxes."[23]

The Pete Rose saga illustrates how our heroes can be great in some ways and flawed in others. Excellence on the ball field does not correlate with outstanding character. In his insightful biography of Pete Rose, Sokolove observes that "Rose earned his banishment from major-league baseball by flagrantly violating its rules against gambling. And he earned his place in baseball's Hall of Fame. . . . A man can belong both in the Hall of Fame and in Federal prison."[24] It is likely that for Pete Rose betting on sports fulfilled a need for stimulation, action, and another way to feel like a winner. Former Cincinnati Reds pitcher Ted Power said of Rose's gambling propensities, "He has always said that he did everything with average ability and hustle. He beat the system and became the best hitter in baseball history. Maybe he figures if you can beat one system, you can beat another."[25]

Rose is one of many athletes whose character flaws contributed to their ultimate demise—a hero who became a fallen idol. His self-destructive behavior is a classic example of the mentality that says, "I'm above it all. I can do whatever I want and cross the line into shady territory. I won't get caught, and even if I do I won't have to face the consequences."

More than a decade after his suspension, there is still debate over whether Pete Rose deserves to be in the Hall of Fame. In 1989, just before Giamatti's ruling against Rose, I wrote a letter that was published in the *New York Times*, supporting his enshrinement in Cooperstown while pointing out the psychological and sociological trauma Rose's behavior had inflicted on the youth of America.

THE TRAGEDY OF PETE ROSE

To the Sports Editor:

Pete Rose is a national hero whose milestone accomplishments on the field entitle him to a place in baseball's Hall of Fame. A player's personality is not a criterion on which he is evaluated for membership in the hall. His record speaks for itself and his place in baseball history cannot and should not be blighted by his character flaws.

But as a legendary figure his behavior has stirred up considerable distress among sports fans across the country. In the furor, the argument has been raised that Rose's behavior reflects a pattern of compulsive gambling, and, as such it should be treated by a psychotherapist as an emotional problem rather than as a punishment to be imposed by the commissioner of baseball.

While this position has merit, we must not lose sight of the fact that it is the responsibility of professional sports figures to consider the impact of their actions upon those who look up to them and wish to emulate them.

In this era of America when half our youth grow up in broken homes with absentee fathers, they turn more than ever before to their heroes in the world of sports as models to admire, worship, and with whom to identify. Is it fair to inflict the additional pain and disillusionment of a fallen idol upon the lives of these young people? Are we prepared to contend with the hordes of youths, who in their confusion and disappointment will cry out, "Say it ain't so, Pete!"? It is here that Pete Rose has let us down, and this is the ultimate legacy and tragedy of the Pete Rose episode.

Stanley H. Teitelbaum [26]

This sentiment was echoed three years later by Dan Gutman in *Baseball Babylon*: "Leaving Pete Rose out of the Baseball Hall of Fame would make it obviously incomplete. . . . Putting Rose in after what he's done would certainly taint the Hall of Fame's grandeur—if the rest of the members of the Hall were All-American boys like Christy Mathewson. Unfortunately, they are not. . . . Cooperstown is already crammed to the rafters with gamblers, alcoholics, drug users, womanizers, cheaters, drunken drivers, Klansmen, and even ticket scalpers."[27] Clearly, an outstanding career on the playing field does not make one outstanding as a human being.

Through the years an increasing majority of fans are in favor of Rose's election to the Hall, but he will continue to be ineligible unless he is reinstated to the game. Rose maintains that he has been unfairly punished. He argues that "it seems in our society 99 out of 100 guys are given another opportunity. I'm the one out of 100 that's not."[28] His opponents point out that Rose has still not been completely truthful and has shown little contrition through the years. In a scathing article in *Gentleman's Quarterly*, Joe Queenan surmised that "half the sportswriters seem to be working overtime to convince the public that Pete Rose is a green-cathedral Jean Valjean, an errant but contrite scalawag, a man more sinned against then sinning, rather than the lying weasel that he is. . . . Pete Rose is not the victim of a remorseless media witch hunt but a two-faced bounder who dishonored our beloved national pastime by gambling on it and then saying he didn't."[29] And Fay Vincent, who became commissioner after Giamatti's untimely death, has consistently defended baseball's position of not reinstating Rose, based on the overwhelming evidence gathered by the Dowd investigation that Rose had indeed bet on baseball, and on Rose's apparent lack of contrition. Vincent adds, "Any commissioner who reinstates Rose has to accept responsibility for lessening the deterrent to gambling that has been almost totally successful."[30] Thus, by using Rose as a poster boy for the evils of gambling, Major League Baseball attempts to deter future corruption.

In January 2004, after fourteen years of denial, Pete Rose admitted in a new book that he had bet on baseball, including the games of his own team, while he was manager of the Cincinnati Reds. His book became a best seller, but his belated admission was widely criticized as a lame play for reinstatement and election to the Hall of Fame. Watching related television interviews, I had the impression that Rose still didn't get it. He seemed blindly unaware that he is not free from the grip of gambling. Moreover, he misguidedly sought sympathy for all he had endured during the past fourteen years. He is unlikely to get much, because he appears to have made no serious attempt to own up to his addiction and get professional help. And he seems short on genuine contrition.

Other Gambling Episodes

In the past decade there have been several less significant incidents of gambling by prominent baseball figures. The need to compete, something athletes are trained to do well, drives many players toward gambling. It is often not so much about money as about the high associated with winning. Besides betting on sports events, professional athletes often gamble on card games, golf games, and the racetrack.

In March 1993 Lenny Dykstra of the Philadelphia Phillies was put on probation for one year after testifying that he had lost $78,000 in high-stakes poker games. In levying this sanction, Commissioner Fay Vincent mandated that Dykstra regularly report to his office and said that more serious penalties would follow if he continued to gamble. The ballplayer complied, but two months later, after attending a teammate's bachelor party, an inebriated Dykstra crashed his new sports car into two trees, nearly killing himself and teammate Darren Daulton. At this stage of his successful career, Dykstra apparently was committed to life on the fast track, which led him down some perilous pathways.

In 1997 American League slugger Albert Belle acknowledged that he had lost $40,000 betting with friends on college basketball and professional football games. Belle, one of baseball's most controversial figures, had been suspended several times for impulsive violence. He had also received the largest fine in baseball history ($50,000) and had been ordered to undergo anger counseling. Belle's attitude seemed to be that he could dance to his own beat. In defending Belle's gambling admission his agent, Art Tellem, told the press that "Albert's done nothing wrong or illegal. Albert Belle has never bet on a baseball game. . . . It is not uncommon for many athletes, owners or even people in the media to bet on football games."[31] The commissioner took no action against Belle in this matter.

In contrast to the Albert Belle case, it was revealed in 2002 that an investigation some thirteen years earlier, during the era of the Pete Rose scandal, had led to disciplinary action against two umpires as well as Don Zimmer, at that time manager of the Chicago Cubs. The situation was similar to Belle's in that the officials—Frank Pulli and Rich Garcia—and Zimmer had bet on football and basketball but not on baseball games. But the involvement of umpires, who function at the very heart of baseball games, made this a very serious and potentially explosive situation. To make matters worse, it was disclosed that the bookie this trio had been placing their bets with was a known drug dealer—an undesirable associate. Commissioner Vincent determined that those involved had violated Major League rule 21, the "best interests of baseball" rule, and he placed them on two years' probation for "associating and doing business with gamblers and bookmakers." The investigation, conducted by John Dowd, who also handled the Pete Rose probe, was kept secret for thirteen years. When information about these events was eventually leaked, Dowd reported that the umpires and Zimmer were treated more leniently than Rose because they hadn't been accused of betting on baseball and were contrite. Nevertheless, their punishments were greater than that administered eight years later to

Albert Belle for similar offenses. That the investigation and its outcome were kept secret is disconcerting because it makes us wonder whether there have been other such incidents that have not been exposed.

It seems that Major League Baseball is not consistent in applying sanctions to those who violate its rules. The somewhat arbitrary punishments vary case by case. Ultimate disciplinary power is in the hands of the commissioner, who may or may not exercise it to its limit.

Historically, gambling has been a major source of dread within professional sports. When a player associates with figures known to be connected to gambling or gets enmeshed in gambling, it is generally viewed as a threat to the integrity of the sport. In recent times drugs have become a more commonplace problem, and an increasing number of athletes have been suspended for failing drug tests. In most cases these sports stars have been reinstated and subjected to periodic testing. For example, Major League pitcher Steve Howe was suspended and reinstated seven times. It seems that taking drugs is viewed as a health problem that requires understanding and treatment. There has been far less tolerance for gambling offenses, even though they reflect a corresponding behavioral addiction that may also need to be treated as a health problem. The professional sports authorities seem to make a distinction in which an athlete is considered to have a choice about compulsive gambling, whereas drug abuse is seen as a sickness. In truth, such a distinction is blurred by the common ground of addiction. Self-destructive behavior among athletes can be expressed through many pathways.

4. Football Gambling Scandals

> All the conning that I did, I didn't do all this so I could have fancy cars, big houses, mink coats, or eat at expensive restaurants. I did it to feed an addiction. I could have bought 100 Mercedes with the money I've blown.
>
> Art Schlichter in Jeff Benedict and Don Yaeger, *Pros and Cons: The Criminals Who Play in the* NFL

The Early Years of Professional Football

Professional football stands out as being free from gambling for the past two decades, during which football has become the most popular spectator sport in America. In the checkered earlier history of the game, however, several high-profile players were involved in gambling scandals that could have destroyed the appeal of the sport.

Before the television era and the prominence now given this sport, when the National Football League consisted of only ten teams divided into East and West divisions, a major scandal threatened to destroy the league. There were no playoffs then, only an eleven-game regular season culminating in a championship game between the division leaders. The All American Conference, launched in 1946, had not yet attained parity with the NFL, and the Super Bowl between champions of rival conferences did not begin until 1967.

On December 15, 1946, the night before the championship showdown between the New York Giants and the Chicago Bears, two of the Giants' key players—quarterback Frank Filchock and fullback Merle Hapes—were questioned about an allegation that they had been offered a bribe to throw the game. The investigation determined that a small-time gambler named Alvin Paris who socialized with Filchock and Hapes had repeatedly offered each player a payoff of $2,500 and a $1,000 bet on the Bears if they would help throw the championship game. The police had tapped Paris's phone because they suspected his home was a bookmaking establishment. Though they learned that both players had turned down the bribe, neither had reported the attempt to team officials or to the police. This event was the biggest scandal to hit professional sports since the 1919 Black Sox incident, and the mayor of New York City, William O'Dwyer, took part in questioning the players. Filchock denied that he had been asked to fix the game, and O'Dwyer, impressed with his sincerity, believed him. The mayor also thought there was a lack of evidence that he had been offered a bribe. His opinion influenced the commissioner of the NFL, Bert Bell, to ban Hapes from the championship game but allow Filchock to play. Amid the furor Filchock gave a gritty performance; despite a broken nose, he threw two touchdowns in a 24–14 losing cause. He also was intercepted an amazing six times, consistent with his season-long performance of leading the league with twenty-five interceptions. This led some cynical fans to speculate that Filchock may have tried to "lay down" in games during the regular season.

After the game the commissioner suspended both players until the legal proceedings were completed. According to New York law at that time, attempting to bribe a professional athlete was a felony punishable by one to five years' imprisonment and a fine of up to $10,000. It turned out that Paris was the go-between for three higher-placed gamblers: David Krakauer, Jerome Zarowitz, and Harvey Stemmer. Stemmer was serving time in jail for a previous sports fix while arranging this operation. He was under minimal supervision and was somehow able to exploit the penal system to continue his scheme. Harvey Stemmer was a likeable man, friendly, extroverted, and unassuming. He was also my next-door neighbor when I was growing up in Brooklyn. Before he got involved with gambling and rigging games, he was a blue-collar worker who toiled hard for modest wages to support his family. The Stemmers were a sports-oriented family, and his son was amazingly well informed about sports statistics at a very early age. Stemmer played with my father in a weekly low-stakes pinochle game, where he was accepted as a regular guy.

Gradually he became affiliated with gamblers, and his finances improved. The Stemmers were the first family in our apartment building to own a television set. Somehow the neighbors guessed what was going on. Our apartments were next to each other and shared a fire escape. At one point Stemmer was worried that his telephone was being tapped, and he offered to pay our rent if he could hook up an additional line between our apartments. My mother, afraid of getting mixed up in illegal behavior, politely declined.

Everyone knew why Stemmer was imprisoned after his first sports fix. A year later, when the *Daily News* headline screamed something like "Mystery Harvey Sought in Giants Football Fix," we all knew whom they were looking for.

In pursuing "the sure thing" by rigging ball games, Stemmer violated some serious moral and legal standards. The effect his disgrace had on his family is immeasurable. Stemmer and the others were brought to trial on charges of conspiracy and bribery; they were convicted and sent to prison. The judge blasted the three defendants for attempting "to destroy the faith and confidence of the public in American sports," and in meting out the sentence he proclaimed that "anyone who tries to bribe an athlete or fix a sports contest will be dealt with as major criminals." This harsh tone was intended to deter any future attempts to bribe athletes.

Alvin Paris, the gamblers' messenger, received death threats for testifying against the others; he was given a prison sentence of only one year.

While under suspicion from the NFL, Hapes quit playing football and accepted a coaching job at a high school in rural Mississippi. Filchock, who admitted during the investigation that he had lied to Mayor O'Dwyer and had in fact been approached by Paris, was hoping to be reinstated. The day after the trial ended, Commissioner Bell barred both players from football indefinitely. This amounted to a lifetime suspension and was the most severe punishment ever meted out by an NFL commissioner. Bell declared them "guilty of actions detrimental to the welfare of the National League and of professional football." Sportswriter Arthur Daley praised Bell's action in his *New York Times* column and predicted that "their suspensions will have the beneficial effect of serving as object lessons to future generations of players." [1] This turned out to be a very naive prophecy.

After he was banned by the NFL, Filchock signed with the Hamilton Tigers of the Canadian Big Four Rugby Football League and quickly faded into oblivion. His career in the NFL was truncated by his poor judgment in failing to report the bribe offer and then trying to cover it up. He remained bitter about his suspension and maintained that he had been "dealt one off the bottom of the deck," implying that he had been made a scapegoat to convey the message that a professional athlete must be above reproach when it comes to associating with gamblers.

Filchock's suspension was officially rescinded in 1950, and Hapes's was lifted in 1954.

The Scandals of the 1960s and 1970s

Professional football maintained a clean reputation for many years after this incident, and increasing television coverage produced an explosion of interest in football as a spectator sport. The NFL agreed to merge with the All American Conference in 1950 to form an expanded league. In 1960 the American Football League (AFL) was launched, and it too gradually gained equivalence with the NFL. The Super Bowl was organized in 1967 and became the premier annual sports attraction in America.

The integrity of the game and its players remained untarnished until 1963, when new allegations emerged that players were involved in gambling. After an extensive investigation Pete Rozelle, the new commissioner, "indefinitely suspended" Paul Hornung, an offensive star of the Green Bay Packers, and Alex Karras, a defensive star of the Detroit Lions, for betting on football games and associating with gamblers or "known hoodlums." Hornung, known as the golden boy from Notre Dame, was the outstanding player of his era. He had led all NFL scorers in 1959, 1960, and 1961 and was also voted the Most Valuable Player in the NFL in 1961, when he led the Packers to the league championship. His betting on NFL games as well as college football had been a weekly pattern at least since 1959. His bets ranged between $100 and $500 per game, a sizable sum for that time. Neither Hornung nor Karras had ever bet against his own team or been part of any attempt to fix a game, but their gambling was considered a serious violation of their NFL contracts.

When notified of the suspension, Hornung was contrite. He issued a statement in which he acknowledged, "I made a terrible mistake. I realize that now. I am truly sorry . . . I did wrong. I should be penalized. I just have to stay with it." [2] Karras, an All-Pro defensive tackle, was angry about the commissioner's ruling. He maintained that he was being crucified for being acquainted with some shady characters and vowed to appeal the ban. In a television interview Karras claimed he had only wagered for cigarettes, and he indignantly stated: "This is guilt by association and innuendo. I'm not guilty, and I've done nothing to be ashamed of!" [3] He protested that he was the sacrificial lamb in the

investigation after rumors that players were betting on games. In the
NFL legal structure the commissioner's ruling is final, so Karras could
not file a formal appeal. Furthermore, it turned out that his statement
about betting only for cigarettes was false and that he had bet money at
least six times.

The press applauded Rozelle's action, and he received widespread
support for trying to preserve the integrity of the game by intense surveillance and crackdown on any wrongdoing within professional football. An editorial in the *New York Times* declared that "it was reassuring
that there have been no fixed games, but even a suspicion of unethical
conduct cannot be tolerated."[4] Sportswriter Arthur Daley noted in his
column that "the harshness of the Commissioner's punitive action was
governed by his determination to make an example of the guilty. . . .
Uppermost in his thoughts is his conviction that the National Football
League has to be above reproach."[5]

As a result of the suspensions, Hornung and Karras sat out the entire
1963 season. In March 1964, eleven months after the ban was invoked,
the commissioner reviewed the case and decided to rescind the suspensions. The point about preserving the integrity of professional football
had been made, and Rozelle maintained that the penalty was commen-
surate with the offense. He was also convinced that both players now
understood the serious nature of their actions and were repentant. Karras had become more contrite over time as he acquired insight into the
psyche of the athlete. He noted that the suspension "may have been the
best thing that ever happened to me. Pro athletes get lulled into thinking
their sports careers will last the rest of their lives. You don't know how
much you miss something until you have it taken away."[6]

On reinstatement, Hornung rejoined the Packers and played until
1966; Karras resumed his career with the Lions until 1970.

What motivated these All-Pro superstars to jeopardize their careers
by gambling in violation of NFL regulations? Did they fail to take these
infractions seriously? Did they think their elite status exempted them
from the rules—the Denny McLain syndrome? Were they acting on the
principle of "I can do whatever I want"? In any case, given that sports
stars are held to the highest standard and their off-field behavior is
scrutinized, their actions could not be trivialized. They were caught and
punished.

As part of Rozelle's extensive investigation, it came out that five less well known Detroit Lions—Joe Schmidt, Gary Lowe, Wayne Walker, Sam Williams, and John Gordy—had bet on the 1962 league championship game. These players were each fined $2,000 for their onetime infractions. Thus, in the spirit of cracking down on all violations, severe penalties were levied on seven players even though there was "no evidence of criminal wrongdoing designed to influence the outcome of games." In addition, the Detroit Lions franchise was fined $4,000 for not pursuing reports about gambling among its players.

During the course of the investigation, allegations of wrongdoing were also made against Charlie Conerly, a former New York Giants star quarterback, and Carroll Rosenbloom, the owner of the Baltimore Colts. Eventually Conerly was absolved of charges that he had received illegal payments from an indicted gambler, and Rosenbloom was cleared of betting on NFL games while owning a ball club.

During the remaining years of Pete Rozelle's reign as commissioner, several other players were admonished for their alleged ties to gambling figures. In 1969 Joe Namath was in his heyday as a quarterback with the New York Jets and predicted an upset victory for his team against the highly favored Baltimore Colts in Super Bowl III. The Jets won, and Namath was a star of the game. In cultivating his image as a cool, suave man-about-town who flouted conventions, Namath garnered a reputation as an antihero. At the height of his fame Namath became a partner in Bachelors III, a New York bar known for its swinging singles scene. The bar was also frequented by known gamblers, drawing the ire of the NFL commissioner's office. Rozelle threatened to suspend the star quarterback unless Namath gave up his interest in Bachelors III. Having no alternative, Namath was forced to comply with Rozelle's edict.

In 1981 the *New York Times* reported that Ken Stabler, a quarterback who led the Oakland Raiders to victory in the 1977 Super Bowl, had long-term ties to Nicholas Dudich, a convicted bookmaker with connections to the New Jersey–based Simone De Cavalcante organized crime family. Stabler, under surveillance by law enforcement agencies since 1977, denied any wrongdoing. He was never accused of any crime, but any player who associates with known gamblers is considered to be in violation of his NFL contract and can be fined, suspended, or banned for life. The Raiders management, wary of being condemned for complicity, reportedly had notified the league office several times about Stabler's questionable association with gambling.

The concern over the public's perception of damage to the integrity of the game provides the commissioner with the arbitrary authority to act harshly in such cases. The N FL pursued its own yearlong investigation, and although there were widespread reports that Stabler was often seen in Dudich's company, there was not enough evidence to merit strong disciplinary action. Since the long-term independent criminal investigation, as well as the N FL inquiry, yielded inconclusive findings, Rozelle would have seemed excessively dictatorial had he exercised his authority to banish Stabler. Instead he issued a stern reprimand, warning the famous quarterback to avoid "undesirable elements" or risk severe discipline "up to and including suspension," and he extracted a pledge that Stabler would be more circumspect in the future. Stabler was allowed to continue his professional career, and the matter was closed.

After being cleared in the N FL investigation, Stabler promptly sued the New York Times as well as N BC for libel because they had implied that he and Dudich had fixed games while he was playing with the Oakland Raiders. A financial settlement was reached with N BC; the libel suit against the Times was dismissed in 1985.

The Scandals of the 1980s

Shortly after the end of the Stabler affair, an even worse gambling scandal emerged within the N FL. Art Schlichter, drafted by the Baltimore Colts in 1982 and heralded as the next great quarterback in the N FL, was suspended in 1983 for his heavy betting on sports events—the ultimate sin in the eyes of the league administrators. Schlichter is a tragic figure who stands out as a sports hero who had it all and threw it away in the grip of a compulsive gambling disorder. As happens with many addictive personalities, gambling became the central force in his life, and he reportedly lost as much as $1.5 million dollars betting on games. He wagered large sums on exotic parlay bets that required an unrealistic combination of winning outcomes, and despite the long odds against him, he refused to believe he would not win. Like most addicts, Schlichter seemed not to learn from negative experiences, and the illusion that he would beat the odds and win big pushed him out of control.

Schlichter had the typical profile for future sports stars. His outstanding athletic talent was recognized very young. He was a straight arrow boy who didn't drink or smoke and never used drugs, but gambling became his way to rebel against the pressure to be the hero others needed. His gambling began with visits to the racetrack during his high school years and accelerated while he was in college, when he would bet $200 to $300 on college basketball games. He starred as a quarterback at Ohio State University, and as a sophomore he led the team to the Rose Bowl. On signing with the Colts he received a $350,000 bonus as part of a three-year package worth $830,000. At age twenty-two he appeared to be on top of the world, but he quickly gambled away his signing bonus.

In 1982 he lost the starting quarterback job to Mike Pagel, another rookie, and this was psychologically devastating. After this blow the N FL players went on strike, so Schlichter had no opportunity to regain his lost eminence. He sought solace by betting on college football and basketball games and lost up to $30,000 a night. By this time he was so hooked that during the seven-week strike he lost his bonus plus his $140,000 salary. He rationalized that by betting only on college games he was not violating NFL rules, but as his losses mounted he began to try his luck on professional football games as well. For a professional football player this was the kiss of death. He was on a downward course that could only end in disaster. Finally, in April 1983, trying to escape his bookmakers, he participated in an FBI sting. The officers arrested four bookies who had threatened to break Schlichter's passing arm and harm his family unless he paid his remaining debt of $159,000. At this point Commissioner Rozelle investigated and then suspended Schlichter for thirteen months—including all of the 1983 season. Although he was not charged with fixing any games or with betting on any game he had played in or any other Colts game, the league found his gambling on N FL games more than enough to warrant punishment. As he left his lawyer's office one day during the investigation, someone asked if he was Art Schlichter. In wry recognition of the loss of his shining star he replied, "I was at one time." The budding hero on whom others had enthusiastically pinned their hopes was blighted at age twenty-three.

After serving his suspension, Schlichter returned to the Colts in 1984, and for the last five games of the season he regained his spot as starting quarterback. He seemed to have cleaned up his act, and the following season he was again the starting quarterback. Unfortunately he was injured in the season opener, and one month later, amid rumors that he was gambling again, he was suddenly waived by the Colts.

He came back in 1986 for a tryout with the Buffalo Bills but was released during the preseason when the Bills decided to go with Jim Kelly, who ultimately became an NFL Hall of Famer. After losing the job to Kelly, Schlichter sought help from the psychiatrist who had founded the world's first treatment center for pathological gamblers. But he quickly relapsed, and in late 1986 he was arrested for unlawfully betting $232,225. He nevertheless still hoped to catch on with another team. The Cincinnati Bengals tried to sign him for the 1987 season, but with his gambling patterns in full view, the NFL refused to reinstate him.

With his career in shambles, Schlichter financed his gambling by writing bad checks and bilking people. Between 1987 and 1994 he was arrested four times for bank fraud, unlawful gambling, and writing bad checks.

Viewed as a bad apple by the NFL, Schlichter subsequently hooked up with the Arena minor league football league (1990–92), and there too he gambled away his $100,000 yearly salary. After that he hosted a popular sports talk radio show and covered his mounting gambling debts by writing bad checks. Not getting the professional help he desperately needed, Schlichter inexorably got in trouble with the law, and between 1994 and 2000 he was in jail seventeen times.

In 1997, while he was at the Center for Compulsive Gambling in Baltimore, he was found betting again and was remanded to jail. As often happens with severely addicted personalities, Schlichter's pathology outstripped the benefits he gained from psychotherapy. In describing Schlichter's distorted belief system, his former therapist noted that "the high comes in escaping reality and believing that past debts can be repaid quickly and effortlessly."[7]

In 2000 the onetime boy wonder faced federal charges of money laundering, including the illegal use of his father's credit card to obtain $42,000 in cash. He received a five-year prison sentence, and while in prison he was sentenced to six more years for violating probation in a previous conviction. At the sentencing Schlichter's mother made an emotional plea for more rehabilitation rather than prison time for her son. She argued that a gambling addiction is similar to a drug addiction but doesn't inspire the same empathy and social recognition. Her point is well taken. A gambling addiction can be just as lethal to mental health as a drug addiction, but in professional sports gambling has been dealt with more harshly than any other kind of offense.

A part of Art Schlichter is aware of the depth of his pathology, but he has been unable to overcome it. He once told *People* magazine that "when you start stealing from your family and friends, you know it's only a matter of time before you're in jail or you put a gun to your head."[8]

Gambling by College Athletes

The scourge of gambling among football players is by no means limited to professionals. As sports gambling grows widespread in our society, its prevalence on college campuses has mushroomed. This alarming trend has been emphasized by the National Collegiate Athletic Association leadership. Cedric Dempsey, the NCAA executive director, believes that "sports gambling may be the most insidious of all issues facing college sports today . . . [it is] as big an addiction problem on college campuses as alcohol."[9] College athletes are especially at risk, since any sports gambling by an athlete directly violates NCAA rules. These regulations notwithstanding, a University of Michigan poll of 750 collegiate athletes revealed that 45 percent of the male athletes surveyed admitted they had gambled on sports. Even more startling, 5 percent of the male student athletes acknowledged that they had bet on games they played in or had received money to play poorly.[10]

The NCAA has at times taken action against blatant gambling violations among football players. In a high-profile incident in 1995, four players at the University of Maryland were suspended for betting on college games. One of the offenders was the star quarterback Scott Milanovich, who held many of the career passing records at the University of Maryland. At the time these were the harshest penalties directed at Division I athletes for gambling violation of the NCAA code of conduct. The university, worried about the impact of this sanction on the upcoming football season, appealed the NCAA ruling, and Milanovich's suspension was reduced from eight games to four.

One year later a scandal erupted at Boston College. In an effort to police its own football heroes, the school suspended thirteen players for the remaining three games of the season for gambling on sports. Two of the players, Jamall Andersen and Marcus Bembry, were accused not only of gambling on sports, but also of betting that their team would not cover the point spread in a game that Boston College had lost to Syracuse. Although it was determined that no point shaving had occurred, the two were permanently dismissed from the team. Trying to share blame for this episode, Andersen said that the Boston College coaches were aware of the players' gambling and had looked the other way. This incident was particularly damaging to the Boston College athletics program in that a previous basketball point shaving scandal only seven years earlier had had a devastating effect on the school.

A more significant college football scandal emerged in 1998 at Northwestern University, which was already beleaguered by point shaving indictments against its basketball players. The football headlines stemmed from charges that five former players had perjured themselves before federal grand juries that were investigating gambling during the 1994 season. The players, Dennis Lundy, Christopher Gamble, Michael Senters, Gregory Gill, and Dwight Brown, were exposed for allegedly betting against Northwestern with student bookie and former player Brian Ballarini in their games with Ohio State University, the University of Iowa, and the University of Notre Dame. The most serious charge was levied against Lundy, who later went on to play professional football, for denying that he had intentionally fumbled a handoff in a game against Iowa to ensure that Northwestern would lose by more than the point spread. There was no outside bribe involved; Lundy was simply trying to cover his own bet. But it nonetheless was a case of a player's attempting to fix a game. The incident was uncovered when a teammate, who was aware of Lundy's gambling, accused him of deliberately fumbling. An assistant coach picked up on this, and an internal investigation was initiated. Ultimately the findings were given to federal authorities, and the government launched its own extended inquiry into point shaving at Northwestern. When the perjury indictments came out, the NCAA officials acknowledged the serious nature of these infractions and emphasized that this was the first known case of game fixing in college football. Lundy, indicted on one count of perjury, was sentenced to one month in prison and two years' probation. In imposing the sentence the federal judge chastised Lundy and incisively pointed out that "college sports . . . brings adulation. With that adulation comes great responsibility. You didn't handle this well."[11]

5. Basketball Gambling Scandals

It's true that I bet on some of our games, less than a dozen, but I always bet on us to win. I've never done anything dishonest in my life.

Jack Molinas

The integrity of basketball has been repeatedly rocked by scandal—more than that of any other sport. The propensity of college athletes to accept bribes for "only" point shaving has led to many notorious and disgraceful episodes. Young lives have been permanently destroyed by poor judgment and impulsive decisions based on greed and group contagion.

In 2000 Junius Kellogg was nominated posthumously for the Basketball Hall of Fame. He was not elected. He never really had much of a chance, since he never played in the NBA and was not a dominant college player despite being six feet eight inches tall. Kellogg's claim to fame was that as a starting center for Manhattan College, he blew the whistle on a bribe offer that triggered the widespread college basketball scandal of 1951.

At the time, college basketball in New York had attained unprecedented popularity. Five of the local teams were perennial leaders among the nationally ranked teams, and most of their home games were played at Madison Square Garden, the mecca of basketball, rather than at the campus gymnasium. The year-end National Invitation Tournament (NIT) at Madison Square Garden rivaled the National Collegiate Athletic Association (NCAA) tournament for prestige. In 1950 the City College of New York (CCNY) had achieved the remarkable feat of winning both tournaments, and college basketball and New York City were at the center of the postwar sports world. All of that changed dramatically and permanently with the exposés of 1951.

The bribe attempt Kellogg reported ignited a major point shaving scandal that ultimately involved thirty-three players from seven colleges who admitted to fixing forty-nine games dating back to 1947.

The record indicates that in January 1951 Henry "Hank" Poppe, a former basketball star for the Manhattan Jaspers, approached Kellogg about fixing an upcoming game against De Paul University. Kellogg declined the $1,000 offer, but Poppe asked him to think it over. Kellogg did just that and reported the incident to his coach, Ken Norton. At the urging of the college president, they went to the police and told the story to the district attorney's office. The detectives told Kellogg to string Poppe along in order to entrap him. When they met just before the De Paul game, Poppe, working as the go-between for a group of gamblers, told Kellogg he would be paid off if he helped De Paul win by more than the ten-point betting line. Poppe said it would be easy—all Kellogg had to do was to play poor defense, miss some rebounds, and not make it look too obvious. Kellogg was so rattled that he played only a few minutes of the game. He would not have gone along with the fix, but he was not a factor, and Manhattan College won in an upset. After the game Poppe was arrested and made an extensive confession, revealing that in the previous season he and his cocaptain, John Byrnes, had accepted bribes to fix five games. A subsequent investigation found that Byrnes and Poppe had each received $1,000 from gamblers to dump games against Siena College, Santa Clara College, and Bradley College. They also were paid to help their team exceed the point spread in games with St. Francis College of Brooklyn and New York University (NYU).

Poppe and Byrnes (who was not involved in the proposition to Kellogg) pleaded guilty to conspiracy and were given suspended sentences and placed on three years' probation. They were also banned from professional sports by an irate judge, who portrayed them as "traitors who sold out your college. . . . If I find out you are playing professional sports, I will bring you back and send you to jail."[1] Four gamblers, two of whom had previously served time on felony charges, were convicted of conspiracy and given one-year prison terms.

Junius Kellogg, the first black basketball player at Manhattan College, was recognized as a hero in a rally on the school campus. After graduation Kellogg signed on as a second stringer with the acrobatic Harlem Globetrotters, who rarely lost a game. One year into the barnstorming tour, while traveling from one game to another, an auto accident left him a paraplegic. He spent the next forty-four years in a wheelchair until he died in 1998 of respiratory failure. At the time of the scandal Kellogg was canonized by hero-hungry fans and hero-worshiping journalists as a star who took the moral high ground because of his inherent honesty. But there was another factor that motivated him to report the bribe offer to coach Norton—fear. The public and the press always attributed his good deed to his commitment to integrity, but Kellogg acknowledged that apprehension also contributed. He feared that if he failed to report Poppe's bribe attempt and the news leaked out later on, he would lose his scholarship. Kellogg saw himself in a tough spot, with a great deal to lose if he did not come forward.

Though it is widely believed that the point shaving scandals of 1951 were the first to taint the college game, this is not true. There were at least two earlier incidents.

On January 30, 1945, five players on the Brooklyn College varsity admitted they had accepted bribes to throw an upcoming game against the University of Akron. The plot was uncovered somewhat fortuitously when Harry Rosen, one of the perpetrators, was arrested for another reason. The players—Bernard Barnett, Larry Pearlstein, Robert Leder, Jerry Greene, and Stanley Simon—had each received $200 and were promised another $400 after they dumped the game. Rosen was also trafficking in stolen goods, and after he was seized for that, detectives staked out his home. Several hours later Barnett and Pearlstein came to check in with Rosen about the next day's fixed game; and in a comedy of errors, the police, believing these youths were part of the burglary ring, took them into custody. In all the confusion the players panicked and revealed the bribery plan. They confessed that they and the other three players had received money from Rosen and his coconspirator, Harvey Stemmer, to throw the Akron game scheduled to be played in Boston on January 31. Stemmer was the same gambler who one year later brazenly arranged the Giants-Bears football championship game fix, while he was serving time in prison! The Brooklyn College players said that the deal also extended to a forthcoming game against St. Francis; four of the players were being paid to throw that contest as well.

When the plot was uncovered the Akron game was canceled, and Rosen and Stemmer were indicted on charges of bribery and conspiracy. No criminal charges were levied against the players, three of whom were World War II veterans, but they were disciplined by the school, which first barred them from playing intercollegiate athletics and then expelled them. It was discovered that Larry Pearlstein, one of the players involved, was not even registered at the college.

Rosen and Stemmer were quickly brought to trial, convicted, and sentenced to one year in jail. Under the laws of the time their crime was classified only as a misdemeanor, but the New York State legislature amended the law, making it a felony to extend or accept a bribe to throw a game. This measure would apply to amateur as well as professional sports. The bill also upgraded the penalty for such offenses to up to five years' imprisonment and a $10,000 fine. The scandal drew the attention of FBI chief J. Edgar Hoover, who declared that "those guilty should be vigorously prosecuted. Otherwise, the entire American college sports structure will suffer."[2]

That the Brooklyn College plot came to light accidentally raises many questions about other fixes that were never discovered. *New York Times* sportswriter Arthur Daley noted that rumors of other college basketball fixes had been coming to his attention for at least fifteen years. This incident occurred toward the end of World War II, when the issue of good versus evil was foremost in the minds of the American public. In his column Daley underscored the evil of gambling and chastised the players as "five weak-willed boys who didn't have the character or the stability to give two gamblers a couple of punches in the nose."[3]

In defense of the players' moral lapses, these were five impressionable young men, ages seventeen to twenty-two, who were easily influenced. In explaining their readiness to be corrupted, Pearlstein later stated that he and the other players had accepted the deal because they believed other college players were also being bribed.

When an athlete is approached about taking a bribe, he has three basic choices. He can simply say no, dismiss it, and hope the problem will go away. He can report it to his coach, which will set an investigation in motion. Or he can convince himself the offer is worth considering.

In dealing with young college players, especially those from poor backgrounds, it can be easy to induce them to shave points. If they are playing for a good team that is favored to win, the pitch is simple. They are told they don't have to lose a game, merely to win by a smaller margin than the established point spread. They can still contribute to the victory but occasionally be lax on defense or in passing the ball. They could be winners and also make some easy money. They are told they would be foolish to turn down the offer because point shaving is being done throughout college basketball and lots of other players are cashing in.

Brooklyn College's archrival CCNY had its own brush with game fixing in the 1945 season. Its star player, Paul Schmones, was approached by his teammate Leonard Hassman to dump a game. Schmones told his coach, Nat Holman, about the offer, and Holman opted to treat it as private information. He found an indirect way to remove Hassman from the team for subpar academic performance, and he never reported the incident.

Then in January 1949 four arrests were made in New York in conjunction with a four-month investigation into bribes offered to David Shapiro, the cocaptain of the George Washington University team. Joseph Aronowitz, who represented the gamblers' group, initially had solicited Shapiro to throw games in the forthcoming season. Shapiro, who lived in Brooklyn, went to the district attorney's office and was enlisted to set up the gamblers. When the fixers later approached him to throw games against the University of North Carolina and the University of Virginia, Shapiro was told to decline the offers but leave the door open to future contact. Aronowitz persisted, Shapiro agreed to dump the January 4, 1949, game against favored Manhattan College, to be played at Madison Square Garden, by more than eighteen points. He was to be given $1,000 to share with his teammates. Shapiro insisted on a down payment in advance, to be given to his uncle. The "uncle" was a detective, and when the transaction took place Aronowitz was arrested for attempted bribery and conspiracy, along with Jack Levy, Philip Klein, and William Rivlin. Manhattan was an early seven-and-a-half-point favorite to win the game, but heavy betting had pushed the spread up to thirteen points at game time. George Washington University defeated Manhattan 71–63. Shapiro played in the game but fouled out early, and his performance was not a factor in the upset victory.

This was the first legal action invoked under the upgraded New York laws that made offering bribes to amateur athletes a felony. Aronowitz, Levy, and Klein were convicted and sentenced to fifteen months to two and a half years in prison. Rivlin was given a one-year sentence.

In his newspaper column, Arthur Daley lauded Shapiro as "the newest sports hero" for spurning the offer to rig games, and he served notice that other gamblers could face serious retribution if they tampered with the David Shapiros of the world. Hoping this case would stem the tide, Daley asserted that "athletes of his type will force into jail enough would-be fixers to make it an even more hazardous occupation than robbing the United States mails."[4]

Daley was too optimistic. Gamblers were undaunted by the stiffer legal sanctions, and their growing aggressiveness in arranging fixes, coupled with athletes' susceptibility to easy money, led to widespread shadiness. How many fixed games went undiscovered remains unknown. The New York district attorney stated that numerous leads about fixed games came to his attention, but without enough evidence for him to take legal action.

The bribery plots at Brooklyn College and George Washington University were uncovered before the games were played. The same was true for the incident involving Junius Kellogg. But the publicity surrounding the Manhattan College scandal opened up a fuller investigation, and discovery moved from thwarting attempts to fix games to revelations about games that had already been fixed.

Furthermore, the Brooklyn College, George Washington University, and Manhattan College cases all involved attempts to bribe a player to make his team *lose* a game. The gamblers soon realized it would be easier to induce a player on a good team to give less than his best effort. The approach was that they didn't have to throw the game, they merely had to shave points—to see that their team won by a smaller margin than the established betting line. By helping to keep a victory under the point spread, the players could be part of a winning team and still get paid off by the gamblers. The remaining scandals of 1951 demonstrate how appealing this proposition was to many outstanding players on good teams.

The Scandals of 1951

Max Kase, the sports editor at the *New York Journal-American*, had been tracking rumors about fixed games since 1950. Kase had learned that Eddie Gard, a senior at Long Island University (LIU) and a former player, had been the intermediary between gamblers and players in fixing games at CCNY and LIU. After the Manhattan College incident, Kase shared his information with District Attorney Frank Hogan, who immediately tapped Gard's telephone and kept him under police surveillance.

On February 18, 1951, a month after Kellogg told his coach about the bribe offer from Hank Poppe, three stars on the CCNY team were arrested. Cocaptains Ed Roman and Ed Warner and Alvin Roth were charged with accepting bribes to fix three games in the current season. Arrested along with them were Salvatore Sollazzo, the alleged fixer, Eddie Gard, his go-between, and NYU player Connie Schaff, for dumping a recent game as well as offering teammate James Brasco a cut to come in on the deal. Brasco turned the offer down and was exonerated.

Roman, Warner, and Roth agreed to help reduce the margin of victory in games against the University of Missouri (December 9, 1950), Arizona State University (December 28, 1950), and Boston College (January 11, 1951). CCNY was favored by eight to twelve points in three games, and the players were instructed to shave points so that they would win by fewer than seven points. CCNY lost all three games, and the players were paid up to $1,500 a game.

This scandal, which emerged one year after the "Cinderella" CCNY Beavers had managed to win both the NIT and NCAA tournaments, forevermore tarnished big basketball at CCNY. Warner, who was orphaned as a young boy, was widely acclaimed as the number one college player in 1950. For his $3,050 payoff, Warner forfeited his chance to play for big money in professional basketball. Al Roth, when asked why he accepted bribes, lamented, "I know I did a wrong thing. . . . I did it because I wanted to be grown up. . . . I was sick and tired of asking my father for money all the time. Whenever I needed a suit or something I had to go to him. I wanted to be able to do things myself—you know, like a grown-up."[5]

On February 28, 1951, Floyd Lane was added to the list of CCNY players to be prosecuted for accepting money to dump games. Then on March 26 three more CCNY players were arrested: Irwin Dambrot, Norm Mager, and Herb Cohen. This trio was accused of shaving points in three games in the previous season, 1949–50. Mager, who went on to play professional ball with the Baltimore Bullets before the scandal broke, had conspired with Dambrot and Cohen, as well as Roman and Roth, in games against Southern Methodist University (SMU) (December 8, 1949) and the University of California, Los Angeles (UCLA) (December 27, 1949). They were unsuccessful in beating the point spread against the woeful SMU team, and the fixer, a gambler named Eli Kaye (a.k.a. Klukofsky), lost a lot on the game and refused to pay the promised bribe of $4,500. The five players managed to reduce the margin of victory below the point spread in the UCLA game and were given the $4,500. Dambrot and Roman refused to go along with the plan for fixing a game against Niagara University (February 16, 1950), and the other three each collected $1,000 for their role when the favored CCNY lost to Niagara.

A sense of entitlement and a readiness to rationalize behavior underlies the ease with which the seven CCNY stars (Roman, Warner, Roth, Lane, Mager, Dambrot, and Cohen) allowed themselves to be corrupted. Many years later Mager summed it up: "We were just dumb, naive, kids, 19, 20 years old. We didn't know of any law that said you shouldn't shave points—we weren't throwing games, after all. And we thought, hell, the money looked pretty good. Even if it wasn't a lot, it seemed like a lot to us, since we had almost nothing."[6]

Nat Holman, the most famous player among the "Original Celtics" of the 1920s, had been the coach at CCNY for thirty-three years at the time of the scandal. After an internal investigation by the school, Holman and two athletic associates were suspended for failing to report the 1945 bribe offered to player Paul Schmones and for knowing that the academic records of fourteen high school players had been doctored so they could meet the college's admission requirements. The disgraced Holman blamed his tainted players for lacking the moral fiber to turn down the "gangsters" who bribed them to rig games.

With the revelations that players from Manhattan College, CCNY, and NYU had been approached, and in most cases enticed to fix games, the virus that threatened to destroy college basketball was rapidly spreading. The next school to be afflicted was basketball powerhouse Long Island University.

On February 20, 1951, soon after the first round of arrests of the CCNY players, three stars on the LIU varsity were arrested for fixing four games during the current season and three more in the previous year. Eddie Gard, the former LIU player who had been arrested as the intermediary between the CCNY players and the gambler Salvatore Sollazzo, had turned informant to lessen his own penalty. Gard told the authorities he had arranged fixes for Sollazzo with Sherman White, Adolf Bigos, and LeRoy Smith. White was the outstanding player in the country that season and led the LIU Blackbirds to a 20-4 record.

Gard and Sollazzo had courted the players during the previous summer and fall, and when the season opened in December the deal was in place for Sherman and Bigos to receive $1,000 each and Smith to get $500 a fix. In the first two games LIU was a heavy favorite over Kansas

State University (December 2, 1950) and the University of Denver (December 7, 1950), and the players, working the deal to perfection, inched out very narrow victories. The same scenario prevailed on Christmas Day when the Blackbirds, favored by three points, barely defeated the University of Idaho 59–57. The fourth encounter took place on January 4, 1951, when LIU, a seven-point favorite against Bowling Green State University, managed to shave points to emerge with a 69–63 victory. The operation was working according to plan, but many observers were suspicious. Coach Clair Bee received an anonymous letter suggesting that White, Bigos, and Smith were rigging games. When Bee confronted them they denied the allegations, but it scared them into deciding to do no further business with Sollazzo. But it was too late. The damage was done, and it all came to out with Gard's testimony.

The investigation revealed that LIU players had helped fix three games in the previous season, when Eddie Gard was an active player. The first fix occurred on January 17, 1950, when LIU, favored by nine points, lost to North Carolina State University 55–52. Gard and teammate Dick Feurtado shared $2,000 received from Sollazzo. Gard enlisted White and Bigos to shave points in a game against the University of Cincinnati. Although they were favored to win, LIU, with the players underperforming, was trounced 83–65. After cruising to a 19-4 record, the Blackbirds qualified for a berth in the NIT tournament. Once again the players agreed to dump the opening-round game and were beaten by Syracuse University 80–52.

The extensive information Gard provided also paved the way for the arrests of three other former LIU players. Natie Miller, Lou Lipman, and Dick Feurtado were caught for accepting bribes for a game against Duquesne University on January 1, 1949. The fixer of this game was Jack Goldsmith, who had been a former star on the LIU team of 1946–47. Goldsmith had no connection with Sollazzo, and it was reported that Feurtado engineered a double fix by extracting money from both Goldsmith and Sollazzo.

A total of seventeen players from four New York City colleges—Manhattan, CCNY, LIU, and NYU—were involved in fixing games. While they all were enormously disgraced and suffered long-lasting emotional distress, their legal penalties varied. The Manhattan College fixers—Hank Poppe and John Byrnes—were given three years' probation and permanently barred from professional sports. Al Roth, Ed Roman, and

Herb Cohen were given suspended sentences in lieu of jail time and joined the army. Irwin Dambrot received a suspended sentence, and Norm Mager and Floyd Lane were set free. The remaining CCNY player, Ed Warner, was treated more harshly than the others and sentenced to six months in prison. Warner was imprisoned again in the 1960s for attempting to sell heroin. Connie Schaff of NYU received a suspended sentence. The LIU players, Lou Lipman, Adolf Bigos, LeRoy Smith, Natie Miller, and Dick Feurtado, were all let off without penalties, and Eddie Gard was sentenced to prison for up to three years. Sherman White received the severest penalty, a one-year prison term.

Those responsible for bribing the players were not treated leniently. Salvatore Sollazzo, already a convicted felon, was given eight to sixteen years in prison. Jack Goldmsith, a former basketball star at LIU who fixed the LIU game with Duquesne and was a key figure in the bribe of NYU's Connie Schaff, got two and a half to five years. A total of eleven fixers received jail terms varying from six months to seven years. Eli Klukofsky, who had arranged fixes with the CCNY players in the 1949–50 season, beat the system. He had a heart attack and died at age thirty-one, before his trial.

In the first six months of 1951 the scandal was confined to four New York City colleges. Phog Allen, the longtime coach at Kansas University, held a point of view shared by many—that the problem was restricted to the Big Apple. Allen haughtily proclaimed, "Out here in the Midwest these scandalous conditions, of course, do not exist. But in the East, the boys, particularly those who participated in the resort hotel leagues during the summer months, are thrown into an environment which cannot help but breed the evil which more and more is coming to light."[7] And Adolf Rupp, the martinet coach at the University of Kentucky, echoed, "Gamblers couldn't get to my boys with a ten-foot pole."[8] Rupp would later have to eat those words. It was not long before the stain of corruption extended to key players at three more distant high-powered basketball schools.

On July 25, 1951, the ongoing investigation, led by New York district attorney Frank Hogan, indicated that players at Bradley University of Peoria, Illinois, which was runner-up to CCNY earlier in the year in both the NIT and NCAA tournaments, had been rigging games. The fixed games spanned three seasons, from March 1949 to December 1950.

Gene Melchiorre, a clean-cut All-American whose basketball prowess had bolstered the Bradley team to a number one national ranking, was at the center of the storm. During Melchiorre's sophomore season the Bradley Braves reached the NIT postseason tournament but lost to Loyola University of Chicago in the semifinal round. The tournament format called for them to then play a consolation game against Bowling Green. On March 19, 1949, Melchiorre and two teammates, Bill Mann and Mike Chianakas, were approached by gamblers Nick and Anthony Englises to see to it that they lost to the favored Bowling Green squad by more than the established six-point spread. Psychologically, it is a different Faustian bargain to agree to lose a game outright than to try to reduce the margin of victory. The players went with the offer, but Bowling Green won 82–77. A Bradley substitute player scored a last-minute basket, enabling his team to cover the point spread and defeating the plot. The gamblers took a shellacking and declined to pay the bribe money.

The Englises brothers eventually recouped their loss and went back to work on Melchiorre in the next season. They succeeded in bribing him together with Bill Mann and Charlie Grover to shave points to narrow the margin of victory against Washington State University on December 21, 1949. The Braves were favored by ten points and won 67–59. Melchiorre and Mann received $600 apiece, and Grover was given $300. One month later the Bradley players repeated the script in a 64–60 win over St. Joseph's College (Pennsylvania). They were bribed to keep the victory under the established spread of six points. Another player, Aaron Preece, was included in this fix.

The gamblers' "sure thing" approach made it easier for the players to gloss over the issue of dishonesty and seize the opportunity to pocket some quick cash. They rationalized that while the players and fixers made money, no one got hurt and the plot would remain undiscovered. Melchiorre noted, "None of us had any money. We justified our decision to go along with the Englises brothers by saying that the colleges were making plenty out of us. We agreed to go along with them again. We argued to ourselves that what we were doing was wrong, but not too wrong."[9]

When Bradley made it to the NIT finals against CCNY in 1950, Melchiorre was offered $10,000 to throw the game, but he refused. However, he and three other players, Aaron Preece, Jim Kelly, and Fred Schlictman, did succumb to the call to shave points against Oregon

State University on December 7, 1950. The Braves, favored by ten points, managed to narrow the margin of victory to three points in a 77–74 win. Melchiorre was paid $2,000, and the others got smaller amounts. Preece telephoned Eli Klukofsky to confirm that the fix was in. The gambler's line was tapped, and this call turned out to be a key piece of evidence against the players. Ultimately Melchiorre, Mann, and Chianakas were given suspended sentences at the New York trial. No charges had been filed against Preece, Grover, Kelly, and Schlictman. Nick Englises was sentenced to an indeterminate prison term for arranging the fixes, and his brother Anthony received a six-month sentence.

Under Illinois law the players could receive one to five years and a fine of up to $5,000. The indictments against Mann and Chianakas were dropped, and Melchiorre was given a suspended sentence and placed on one year's probation.

The next chapter in the scandal concerned three players at Toledo University who had accepted bribes from Klukofsky to shave points in a game against Niagara University on December 14, 1950. Klukofsky's operation was in high gear at this point; just one week earlier he had succeeded in fixing Bradley versus Oregon State. A year earlier he had bribed players at CCNY to alter the scores in several games.

The Toledo players, William Walker, Robert McDonald, and Carlo Muzi, were induced to keep the winning margin under seven points. They had a tough time accomplishing their task, since Toledo forged to a commanding lead, but at the end they managed to pare it down to a 73–70 victory. The trio of players decided to include Jack Feeman, who was outstanding in the Niagara game, in the deal to shave points against Bowling Green on January 11, 1951, and against Xavier University of Cincinnati on January 30, 1951. In their effort to get under the spread, the players outdid themselves. Toledo was favored by seven points in the Bowling Green encounter and by thirteen versus Xavier, but they handily lost both games.

When the story broke on July 26, 1951, one day after the Bradley exposé, the faithful fans of the Toledo Rockets were protective toward their point shaving athletes. After all, they rationalized, the players didn't deliberately lose any games; they had tried to win by a narrow margin. The distinction between point shaving and outright dumping was emphasized. The Toledo newspapers supported this viewpoint and encouraged the athletes' denial of serious wrongdoing. Resentment toward the investigation prevailed among the loyal fans, who minimized the players' transgressions because they did not want to see their heroes tarnished. There was no Ohio law at the time that covered amateur athletes' offering or receiving bribes, and no indictments were made.

Nevertheless, the investigation by the New York district attorney's office continued and exposed one more long-standing basketball powerhouse, Adolf Rupp's University of Kentucky. The inclusion of Kentucky in the scandal was particularly noteworthy for three reasons. First, some of the players involved were especially talented and among the premier stars of their era. In addition, they were already achieving stardom as professionals in the NBA. Finally, the notion that game fixing was primarily restricted to New York City, promulgated by high-profile coaches such as Rupp and Phog Allen, was permanently debunked.

On October 21, 1951, Ralph Beard, Alex Groza, and Dale Barnstable were arrested for accepting bribes of $1,500 each to throw a game against Loyola University of Chicago in the first round of the NIT tournament on March 14, 1949. Kentucky was ranked number one in the country and was a twelve-point pregame favorite, but with the trio playing ineffectively, Loyola won 67–56. It was a stunning upset in a major tournament, and it marked the first time players had conspired with gamblers to fix a game of this magnitude. The fixers were the Englises brothers, Saul Feinberg, and Nat "Lovey" Brown. Beard had been named Player of the Year in college basketball for the 1947–48 season and again for 1948–49. At the time of the investigation some two and a half years later, Beard and Groza were professional All-Stars for the Indianapolis Olympians in the NBA. With the news of their confessions, they were immediately suspended by the league and were never reinstated.

The three players also admitted that initially they had been paid to help the Kentucky squad exceed the point spread in victories against St. John's University, New York (December 18, 1948), De Paul (January 22, 1949), and Vanderbilt University (January 31, 1949). The arrangement then shifted to point shaving, and in February 1949, as a forerunner to the debacle against Loyola in the NIT, they were paid to go under the spread in a winning effort against Tennessee.

After standing trial, Beard, Groza, and Barnstable were given three years' probation (they could have received prison terms of up to three years) and were barred from sports during this period. In understanding the impact of the scandal on the players, it is useful to distinguish the legal penalties from the emotional penalties incurred. Even though most of the tarnished players did not receive legal sanctions, the emotional toll was substantial. Ralph Beard responded to his sentence by saying, "Yes, I'm guilty. Let me out of here. Let me die." [10] It was a plea for compassion from an athlete racked with torment. Several years later, when sharing the details of the episode with his young son, Beard acknowledged, "I did something wrong. I've paid more than most people because I paid with my life." [11] Yet Beard continued to feel he had been chastised excessively, and with some residual bitterness he proclaimed, "There was absolutely no justice. They didn't catch them all. The only thing I ever wanted was to be a professional basketball player and someday be in the Naismith Hall of Fame. That was my whole life, and it's gone." [12] Dale Barnstable portrayed himself and the others as naive victims of the gamblers and the corrupt atmosphere permeating Madison Square Garden. In his defense he stated, "They [the gamblers] said we didn't have to dump the game. They said that nobody would get hurt except other gamblers. They said everybody was doing it . . . we just didn't think. But if somebody who suspected what was going on at the Garden had warned us that things like that were against the law, we'd never have done it." [13] And Floyd Lane, one of the CCNY players involved in the scandal, who later became basketball coach at the college, later maintained that the press had treated the players too harshly and that the distinction between point shaving and dumping games was not made clear. He rationalized that although he had participated in point shaving, he never would have agreed to deliberately throw a game.

In 1995, when Ralph Beard was sixty-seven, *Sporting News* ran an article campaigning for his admission to the Basketball Hall of Fame. It was pointed out that of the ten players who started in the first NBA All-Star Game in 1951, only Groza and Beard were excluded from the elite Hall. The gist of the writer's argument was that Beard had only taken money from a student who served as a go-between for gamblers, that he had paid dearly for his mistakes, and that based on his talent as a three-time All-American, he deserved to be elected. Bob Cousy, the Boston Celtics legend, echoed this sentiment. Nevertheless, when the Hall of Fame veterans' committee met a month later to consider old-timers, they continued to pass over Beard.

Basketball Gambling Scandals

After Beard and Groza graduated from Kentucky in 1949, Barnstable teamed up with Walter Hirsch and Jim Line for additional point shaving endeavors. This new trio conspired to trim the spread in games against De Paul (December 12, 1949) for $500 each and against the University of Arkansas (January 2, 1950) for $1,000 each. During the overarching investigation Hirsch and Line admitted they had accepted bribes, but they were not indicted.

The next phase of the University of Kentucky exposé occurred in March 1952 and involved Bill Spivey, the team's seven-foot All-American center. The university determined that Spivey had conspired to fix games during the 1950–51 season. In their trial both Hirsch and Line had implicated Spivey, claiming that he had repeatedly approached them to get in on the action and that he had been included in a fixed game against St. Louis University in the Sugar Bowl tournament in December 1950. Spivey appeared before the grand jury exploring the allegations against Hirsch and Line and denied that he was ever involved in any game fixing or had even discussed the prospect. Spivey was subsequently indicted for perjury, and at his trial he admitted he had been offered a $500 bribe to shave points in the St. Louis game and had declined the offer but failed to report it. Eventually, in April 1953 the perjury charge against Spivey was dropped for lack of evidence and because of the questionable credibility of Hirsch and Line, who had been let off when they implicated Spivey.

After Beard, Groza, and Barnstable pleaded guilty to conspiring to shave points, the presiding judge in the overall investigation, Saul S. Streit, lambasted Coach Rupp and the University of Kentucky for an atmosphere contaminated by "the acme of commercialism and over emphasis." Judge Streit proclaimed that both Rupp and the university "must share the responsibility for the plight of the defendants." He stated that the coach had "aided and abetted in the immoral subsidization of the players," and he attacked the university for "the inordinate desire by the school's trustees and alumni for prestige and profits from sports."[14]

In a rather lame rejoinder, Rupp, who all along had vigorously defended his players' lapses, acknowledged that his attitude about point shaving had changed. He stated that previously he "didn't think it was as serious as going out and deliberately throwing a ball game. But now, since it hit into our family, I think it is a bad thing."[15] In November

1952 the NCAA Council determined that Kentucky had violated subsidy and eligibility rules and placed the university on a one-year basketball probation. The council recommended that other NCAA schools remove Kentucky from their schedule, and the university canceled its 1952–53 season.

Finally, after the 1952–53 season District Attorney Hogan officially terminated his investigation of corruption in college basketball. The bribe attempt Junius Kellogg reported in January 1951 turned out to be the tip of the iceberg. The situation ultimately involved thirty-three players (many of them All-Americans) at seven colleges and forty-nine fixed games.

Although it was widely believed that offering or accepting a bribe in a sports event was immoral and should be illegal, most states were lax in drafting laws that applied to such acts. It was as if fixing games belonged to a category of crimes for which the laws to govern such crimes were not yet formulated. As laws gradually were passed, the convicted gamblers were generally sent to prison. Most of the players were given suspended sentences but were left with permanent psychological scars.

In response to the scandals of 1951, the New York State legislature passed a law making it a felony to bribe or attempt to bribe a player in a sporting event, and the bill also doubled the maximum jail sentence to ten years. In signing the bill, New York governor Thomas Dewey took a harsh stance toward the gamblers who promoted corruption and a more compassionate tone toward the young ballplayers: "Bribery or attempted bribery of sporting events is a shameful, evil thing. . . . The young men involved in this scandal have suffered greatly by their exposure and have irreparably injured their entire future lives. The present penal provisions against their acceptance of bribes ranges from one to five years and has not been changed in this bill."[16] California was more even-handed in placing the onus on the players as well as the gamblers, and the State Assembly introduced a bill to make it a felony for a player to accept a bribe to shave points.

A New York Times editorial highlighted the contrast of the CCNY players' attaining their dream one year earlier and then succumbing to sordid enticement. The newspaper chastised those who yielded to temptation, noting that "now some of these young men have, in a melancholy display of weakness, fallen from grace," and depicted the situation as "the cancer of sports."[17]

Blame was cast in many directions for the circumstances that culminated in fixing games. The NCAA issued a report attacking the colleges for illegal recruiting practices, an overemphasis on winning, and greed. FBI chief J. Edgar Hoover even got into the act and blamed "the hypocrisy and sham" of the college system for inspiring these "very atrocious crimes" carried out by the players. The coaches were sometimes accused of laxity. Most of all, blame was assigned to those who seduced the players to step over the line, and even the sordid atmosphere of Madison Square Garden was cited as a reason.

In the aftermath of the scandals of 1951, St. John's coach, Joe Lapchick, like many other coaches, prepared a scrapbook of newspaper clippings about the investigation and showed it to all his players at the beginning of each season. It was designed to deter the next generation of players from temptation. Nevertheless, despite the convictions and the upgrading of laws, corruption in college basketball was not eradicated.

Some players took these warnings seriously and turned in their would-be bribers. In 1959 two members of the University of Pittsburgh varsity, John Fridley and Dick Falenski, notified the school authorities that Dr. Edward Sebastian, a Pittsburgh alumnus, had offered them a bribe to shave points. Dr. Sebastian was convicted and sentenced to eight months to three years in prison. In another incident Lowery Kirk of Memphis State University notified the police that Aaron Wagman, a prolific fixer, had approached him to dump a game. While these players took the high road and set an example of integrity, many others were quietly doing business with the gamblers who preyed on them.

The Scandals of 1961

Only eight years after District Attorney Hogan finished his investigation, the next major point shaving scandal in college basketball erupted on an even larger scale. The probe that began in 1961 covered incidents going back as far as five years and ultimately encompassed as many as fifty players from twenty-five schools and at least forty-four games.

The method of approaching players was significantly different this time. In a highly organized hierarchy, the gamblers established a stable of contact men who had connections with prominent players. In the 1951 cases the gamblers had predetermined which games they would try to fix and approached players accordingly. In the later situation the primary ring of gamblers, which included Aaron Wagman, Joe Hacken, Joe Green, and Dave Budin, responded to calls from their intermediaries, who had lined up players who were eager to dump games for money. The intermediaries, who were often former varsity players, introduced players to the gamblers, and point shaving was arranged. In the organizational structure the gamblers then reported these arrangements to "master fixer" Jack Molinas, a former NBA star who had been barred from the professional league for betting on games, and Molinas in turn "sold" these games to big-time gamblers who made large bets on Molinas's behalf. When the fix was in and went according to plan, everyone along the pipeline was paid off.

The new system dropped the pretense that point shaving wasn't hurting anyone because it only entailed limiting the margin of victory. The bribers took the bolder approach of finding players who were in financial straits and appealing to them with easy money: "Don't be a jerk and pass it up! Everyone's doing it." Group contagion let players justify crossing the line because others were cashing in and they didn't want to be left out. It is a well-known psychological principle that a group norm is a compelling influence leading individuals to depart from their customary behavior. Players who were on the take frequently brought in teammates to participate in additional fixes, sharing the gravy train. For example, Don Gallagher at North Carolina State engaged fellow players Anton Muehlbauer, Stan Niewierowski, and Terry Litchfield, and Gary Kaufman at the University of the Pacific lined up Leroy Wright.

In addition to inducing players to help narrow the point spread, the bolder pattern involved getting them to lose by more than expected. Coach Jack Ramsay of St. Joseph's College in Pennsylvania, who later became a stalwart NBA coach, pointed out that the players' primary method was to play lax defense rather than poor offense. Ramsay noted, "Players would let their man score rather than deliberately miss shots. The reason is obvious. Defensive errors are not reported in the box score of a game, while personal scoring is." [18] Thus in many cases they were being bribed to go substantially out of their way to tank the games. These athletes' readiness to be corrupted was promoted by the special treatment given to prospective players, who are courted with inducements, then wooed with pocket money by the college and alumni alike. Since academic standards are lowered for them, varsity players are conditioned to expect to break the rules and justify wrongdoing.

Basketball Gambling Scandals

District Attorney Hogan had been investigating the situation for two years, and on March 18, 1961, his detectives arrested Aaron Wagman for allegedly bribing University of Connecticut captain Pete Kelly, along with Glenn Cross and Jack Rose, to dump a game against Colgate University. They agreed to lose by eleven or more points, and they succeeded: Colgate won 83–71. Wagman's coconspirators were contact men Jerry Vogel, Dan Quindazzi, and University of Connecticut football captain William Minnerly, who reportedly reached the tainted basketball players. At the time, Wagman was out on bail while appealing his conviction for attempting to bribe Jon MacBeth, a University of Florida football player. MacBeth reported the bribe offer and helped to trap Wagman, who was convicted and given a five-year jail sentence and a $5,000 fine. Hogan's men moved quickly to seize Wagman when they learned he was planning to leave the country. At the same time, they arrested gambler Joe Hacken for bribing Seton Hall University players Art Hicks and Hank Gunter to lose their game against Dayton by more than six points. They were more than proficient in their assignment; Seton Hall lost by the lopsided score of 112–77. Wagman and Hacken worked independently of each other, but they were connected through master fixer Molinas.

Upsets, rumors about fixes, and bookmakers' action to take certain games off the betting board led to an intensification of the probe that had been under way for several years, and the arrests of Wagman and Hacken were the first step in a widespread series of exposures. Hogan's office was most interested in arresting the bribers and treated the corrupted players with leniency. Nevertheless, the athletes were significantly tarnished. In addition to those mentioned above, the college basketball Hall of Shame included Michael Parenti and William Chrystal of St. John's, Ray Paprocky of NYU, Jerry Graves of Mississippi State University, Richard Fisher and Edward Test of the University of Tennessee, Lou Brown of the University of North Carolina, Fred Portnoy of Columbia University, William Reed and Tony Falantano of Bowling Green University, Lenny Kaplan of the University of Alabama, Charles North and John Morgan of the University of Detroit, Richie Hoffman, Larry Dial, Bob Franz, and Mike Callahan of the University of South Carolina, Sal Vergopia and Lenny Whelan of Niagara University, Ed Bowler of La Salle University, and Frank Majewski, Vincent Kempton, and Jack Egan of St. Joseph's University. Among others who had rejected bribe offers but were negligent in not reporting these actions to the authorities were Doug Moe, who later became an established coach in the NBA, and Raymond Stanley, both of the University of North Carolina, and Ron Lawson of UCLA.

The investigation revealed that most of the fixed games took place between December 1959 and March 1960, but some went as far back as the 1956–57 season when St. John's players Parenti and Chrystal agreed to shave points in five games. Jerry Graves of Mississippi State pocketed the most money for agreeing to fix four games in the 1960 season. When he was apprehended, Graves protested that he had never played less than his very best and had hoodwinked the bribers into believing he was shaving points.

Lou Brown, a substitute player at North Carolina, was the player most deeply involved in the scandal. Brown was responsible for setting up contact for Wagman with the four Philadelphia area players—Majewski, Kempton, and Egan of St. Joseph's, and Bowler of La Salle. Frank Majewski brought in Egan and Kempton, the team's two best players, and the trio cooperated with Wagman to fix three contests. Majewski later attributed his readiness to be corrupted to the emotional and financial stress brought on by his father's recent death and his mother's heart attack. Kempton, Egan, and Bowler also claimed that the chief reason for their lapses was their families' dire need for money.

Considering background and finances, Fred Portnoy of Columbia was the player least likely to take part; but probably owing to group contagion, he pocketed $1,000 for agreeing to have Columbia lose to Rutgers University by at least twelve points. With Portnoy dumping, Columbia lost by thirteen points. In his defense Portnoy explained, "You just don't realize the seriousness of what you're doing. It seemed so simple."[19] Ray Paprocky of NYU, who shaved points for Joe Hacken in five games, demonstrated the magnitude of rationalization involved: "I am aware that what I did was wrong, but if I were in the same circumstances, I'd do it again. Not because I'd want to, but because I'd be forced to. It was better than robbing a grocery store. Others wanted the money for cars or girls, I wanted it for my family."[20]

St. John's coach, Joe Lapchick, whose scrapbook about the scandals of 1951 seemed to have little impact on future players, declared, "The thing that frightens me is that this business never stopped after 1951."[21] Lapchick, a straight arrow member of the original Celtics, was stymied in finding an explanation for the prevalence of game fixing. But Joe Hacken, the convicted briber, put his finger on it by identifying the primary motive as greed. Hacken noted, "Everybody did it for a simple reason. Cash money . . . the colleges already spoiled them. The colleges give these kids money and deals. In other words, the kids got into college on a fix. So why shouldn't they fix games too?"[22]

Sportswriter Tim Cohane placed blame for the corruption squarely on the colleges for recruiting players who were academic liabilities. In a scathing attack written for Look magazine, Cohane misguidedly asserted that it was athletes' intellectual limitations that made them easy targets for the gamblers. He maintained that many of them had substandard academic records, were not motivated to learn, and should never have been admitted to college. In maligning the players, he wrote, "Their grades ranged from the eligibility minimum down to the ludicrous or nonexistent. Most of the players lacked the capacity or desire to learn."[23] Cohane's view was that game fixing could be avoided if the schools recruited players with superior intelligence and the integrity to resist temptation. Given the pressure to field winning teams, this proposal seems unrealistic. Furthermore, it is likely that lack of intelligence as measured by academic achievement is not central to a player's readiness to accept a bribe. "Emotional intelligence" is more closely related to the capacity for integrity and the ability to resist temptation.

After his arrest Wagman cut a deal with the authorities in exchange for testimony that further implicated Joe Hacken, Joe Green, and Dave Budin, the other gamblers who worked to set up bribes, and he identified Jack Molinas as the mastermind and head of the bribery ring. The investigators gathered evidence against all of them, and on May 18, 1962, Molinas was arrested on charges of bribery, attempt to suborn a witness, and conspiracy to fix a whopping twenty-five games with twenty-two players at twelve colleges. The law enforcement officials were most eager to snare Molinas as the central figure in the case, and they did so when they induced Billy Reed, one of the players under investigation, to gain lenience by wearing a wire and recording Molinas advising him to lie to the authorities about dumping three games while playing for Bowling Green versus De Paul (December 10, 1959), Bradley (December 12, 1959), and Canisius College (December 3, 1961).

Jack Molinas was an outstanding college basketball player at Columbia and was an NBA star before being banned in his rookie season. Like many star athletes, Molinas was handsome, personable, and popular. He had it all, except for one fatal flaw—he wanted to make big bucks in a hurry, which meant shooting for the big hit by gambling. He was the epitome of the star who disregarded the rules, behaved as if he was above it all, and threw it all away young.

Molinas was a product of an indulgent mother and a harsh father who restricted his son's emerging independence. For example, when everyone in the neighborhood was outside celebrating VE day—the end of World War II in Europe—Louis Molinas forbade his thirteen-year-old son to leave their Bronx apartment.

Jack quickly learned how to work around the system. By defiantly dismissing the rules of society, he was symbolically rebelling against his father's tyranny. As with many athletes, his basketball talent was recognized early in life, and the forthcoming adulation from outsiders reinforced the belief that he could write his own ticket with little accountability.

In his penetrating biography of Molinas, Charley Rosen describes how Jack fell in love at seventeen, but his father vehemently opposed the relationship because the girl was a Gentile and the Molinases were Jewish. His brother maintained that "Peggy was the love of my brother's life, but he didn't have the courage to marry her in the face of our father's opposition. I don't think Jack ever recovered from the whole situation." [24] It appears that since he couldn't defy his tyrannical father directly, other authority figures and the law itself came to represent the oppression he yearned to defeat.

After being banished from the NBA in 1954, Molinas became an attorney, which he used as a sideline to gambling and arranging fixes. Before his trial in 1963, the district attorney's office proposed a deal. They wanted Molinas to admit he was central in several fixes, to accept the revocation of his license to practice law, and to serve a prison sentence of only six months. Always the gambler, Molinas arrogantly turned them down. The case went to trial and Molinas was convicted on all counts; he was given a stiff sentence of ten to fifteen years. In imposing the sentence, Judge Joseph Sarafite said, "In my opinion you are a completely immoral person. You are the prime mover of the conspiracy. . . . You callously used your prestige as a former All-American basketball player to corrupt college basketball players and defraud the public." [25]

Ten conspirators were indicted, and severe sentences were meted out to Joe Hacken (seven and a half to eight years) and Joe Green (six to seven years). Wagman, who had turned state's evidence, was given a three- to five-year sentence, which was suspended because he was already serving five years for attempted bribery in the University of Florida football episode. Jerry Vogel, Dave Budin, Dan Quindazzi, and Lou Brown all received suspended sentences.

Billy Reed and the other players who cooperated with the investigation were granted immunity, but many were expelled from their colleges, and of course their futures were tainted by the stain and scars of the scandal.

One year after Molinas began his prison term, the Appellate Division of the New York Supreme Court ruled that the sentence was excessive, and it was reduced to seven to twelve and a half years. Joe Hacken's term was reduced to six years, and Joe Green's to four to five years. For his cooperation in other criminal investigations, Molinas's sentence eventually was further reduced to six to nine and a half years. He actually served a little more than five years and was paroled from Attica prison in July 1968.

Molinas eventually moved to Los Angeles, where he got involved in pornography productions and other mob-related operations. In 1973 he was arrested for shipping pornographic films interstate. He developed a reputation as a shady character who didn't always make good on his debts, and on August 4, 1975, Jack Molinas was murdered in his home in what the New York Times described as a "gang-style slaying."

Because Molinas was considered to be a sleazy character and a liability to the community, it was reported that the Los Angeles Police Department was not highly motivated to solve his murder. However, three years later the killers were found and tried. Eugene Conner, the hit man, was turned in by his brother, and he received a life sentence. One accomplice was acquitted, and two others got suspended sentences. It was never clarified whether the Mafia was behind the murder.

In his biographical postscript on Molinas, Charley Rosen posed the question, "How could someone who was so smart, so able, and with such a bright future, lead himself down the self-destructive path that he did? . . . In the final analysis, however, it appears that Jack's misdeeds were fueled by that most ancient and universal of sins, hubris. He was too smart. Too smart to think that the rules applied to him. Too smart to even imagine that he could ever get caught."[26]

Of all the players under investigation, Connie Hawkins of the University of Iowa was probably the most talented. Hawkins never dumped a game, but Dave Budin named him as an "intermediary" in finding prospects for the gamblers. After being arrested, Budin admitted to fixing several games, and to lighten his punishment he told the district attorney's office that Hawkins had been given "softening up" money to introduce Molinas and company to potential point shavers. The record shows that Hawkins did receive $200 from Molinas, which they both claimed was a loan, and no player ever acknowledged that Hawkins tried to introduce him to a gambler. Nevertheless, when put under intense interrogation by Hogan's detectives, Hawkins, who was only semiliterate, made self-incriminating statements. He left college, signed on with the American Basketball League, and became an ABL superstar. In recognition of his talent, three NBA teams wanted to acquire Hawkins, but the commissioner, Walter Kennedy, imposed a lifetime ban against him based on the NBA bylaws, which permanently disqualified any player who had associated with known gamblers. Determined to clear his name, Hawkins eventually sued the NBA and won a $1 million settlement as well as admittance to the league.

Later College Basketball Scandals

Since the episodes of 1961, which involved twenty-five schools, there have been no widespread point shaving incidents, but each decade has produced at least one significant scandal.

In the 1978–79 season three Boston College players accepted bribes from Henry Hill, a highly placed Mafia figure. Hill, a government informer who was in the witness protection program and was seeking immunity, told the authorities he had made contact with Rick Kuhn, a reserve forward, who agreed to influence the outcome of games between December 16, 1978, and March 1, 1979. Kuhn was not a good enough player to turn the tide by himself, but he induced teammates Jim Sweeney and Ernie Cobb, the squad's leading scorer, to go in on the deal. Nine games were fixed, and the gamblers bet against Boston College each time—to win by less than the spread when they were favored, and to lose by more than the spread when they were the underdogs. Kuhn and Sweeney accomplished their task in only two of their first four attempts, and the gamblers wanted more of a sure thing. They enlisted

Cobb to fix the last five games and were much more successful. Hill said the trio pocketed about $10,000 each.

In a parallel to the Brooklyn College fix in 1945, the plot was uncovered inadvertently while Hill was being interrogated about a $5.8 million robbery of the Lufthansa freight terminal at John F. Kennedy International Airport in 1978. When questioned about his whereabouts on a certain day, Hill replied, "I was up in Boston that day fixing some Boston College basketball games." This triggered this next round of investigation into corruption in college basketball.

What distinguishes this conspiracy from the previous scandals is that Rick Kuhn was given a ten-year prison sentence for his central role in fixing the games. In the past a double standard had existed in which law enforcement officials treated the players more leniently than the gamblers, who were viewed as preying on naive young students. In this case Paul Mazzei, a convicted drug dealer who was responsible for connecting Henry Hill and Rick Kuhn, received the same ten-year sentence.

Tulane University was the site of the most notable scandal of the 1980s. In March 1985 John "Hot Rod" Williams and four lesser players were indicted for shaving points in games against the University of Southern Mississippi and Memphis State University earlier that year. Two of the players, Clyde Eads and Jon Johnson, were granted immunity and testified against the others. Their testimony indicated that not only were there cash payoffs, but all the players were also supported in their cocaine habits by nonathlete students who arranged the fixes.

At the time Williams was an outstanding senior player and was a shoo-in as an early-round NBA draft pick. Though he reportedly received $5,400 for his role in the two games, his lapse in judgment jeopardized a $1 million NBA contract. Williams's background reveals emotional damage. His mother died when he was nine months old, and his father abandoned the family soon thereafter. He barely learned to read and write, and although he was only semiliterate, he was recruited by Tulane because of his basketball talent. In four years at college he achieved a grade point average of 2.0 while taking a nonchallenging academic program.

Because of a mistrial, the charges were dropped against all the players, and Williams signed on with the Cleveland Cavaliers, where he embarked on an illustrious nine-year career. Throughout the years Williams steadfastly proclaimed his innocence, although other players had testified that he helped dump games.

In the decade of the 1990s two additional point shaving scandals emerged. At Arizona State University (ASU), basketball was emerging as a central attraction, and its team was gaining national recognition. Two varsity players, Stevin "Hedake" Smith, who was the third leading scorer in the school's history, and Isaac Burton helped rig five games during the 1993–94 season.

It appears that Smith was motivated by a $10,000 gambling debt with Benny Silman, a student bookie. Silman arranged the deals for a group of gamblers headed by Vincent Basso, Joseph Gagliano, Joseph Mangiamele, and his father Dominic Mangiamele, who was reputed to be a mob figure. Smith engaged Burton to fix the first two games. The 1994 games were against Oregon State (January 27), the University of Oregon (January 29), USC (February 19), and the University of Washington (March 5). The deal was for ASU, as favorite, to win by less than the betting line. Smith was paid the hefty sum of $20,000 a game, and he gave $4,300 to his teammate Burton for his efforts in two of the games.

This scandal highlights how game fixing can be engineered as readily through defensive lapses as offensive miscues. In a subsequent interview with Sports Illustrated, Smith claimed that his approach was primarily to cheat on defense; that is, he gave his opposing player room to score easy baskets. For example, in the Oregon State game Smith scored a career high of thirty-nine points, but ASU won by only six because of sloppy defense, and they failed to cover the spread.

The point shaving scheme was uncovered when Nevada sports bookies noticed suspicious patterns of betting on ASU games. The casino notified the Pacific-Ten Conference administration, which generated an investigation. The case went to trial, and there were six convictions.

Benny Silman received the stiffest sentence, forty-six months in prison and a $250,000 fine. Stevin Smith received a one-year prison sentence, three years' probation, and an $8,000 fine, and Isaac Burton got two months in jail plus three years' probation and was also fined $8,000. The gamblers, who bet a total of $506,000 on the rigged games, received between three months' probation and a year and a half in prison, depending on their level of involvement. The FBI described this episode as one of the nation's worst sports gambling scandals.

The final college basketball scandal I will document here occurred at Northwestern University during the 1994–95 season. Varsity players Kenneth "Dion" Lee and Dewey Williams were bribed to dump three games by Kevin Pendergast, a former Notre Dame place kicker, and Brian Irving. The games were with the University of Wisconsin (February 15, 1995), Pennsylvania State University (February 22, 1995), and the University of Michigan (March 1, 1995), and the gambler-conspirators bet on Northwestern opponents. A reserve player, Matthew Purdy, was also alleged to have agreed to the deal, but he was not indicted.

Unlike Arizona State, which was a perennial basketball powerhouse, Northwestern was the constant doormat in the Big Ten. In the 1994–95 season it was a poor team and compiled an overall 5-22 record. The team lost each of the three rigged games by at least fourteen points but was not successful in exceeding the point spread as underdog in the Michigan game. In contrast to the large payoffs made to Stevin Smith in the Arizona State scandal, Lee reportedly received $4,000 from Pendergast to fix these games. He also recruited Williams to shave points.

The scandal surfaced during an internal investigation at the university. The four participants were indicted and convicted, and each received a short prison term and two years' probation. The heaviest sentence—two months in prison—was handed out to Pendergast, the former Notre Dame football player. The two players, Lee and Williams, along with Irving, who placed the bets in Las Vegas, were each given a one-month prison term and two years' probation.

In commenting on the Northwestern University exposé, Cedric Dempsey, executive director of the NCAA, cited the prevalence of gambling on college campuses as a cause: "We should not be surprised this is occurring. Gambling is as big an addiction on our campuses as alcohol, and it reflects what is going on in our society."[27] Dempsey estimated that $4.5 billion would be bet on the games of the 1998 Final Four. And Bill Saun, the NCAA representative on the issues of agents and gambling, cited an extensive survey conducted by the University of Cincinnati reporting that more than 25 percent of male athletes in Division I basketball and football programs bet on college games at other schools. Even more significantly, 4 percent admitted to betting on games they had played in.

Such findings raise the question of how many other players at different colleges have been involved in point shaving that we don't know about. It seems likely that there have been fixes beyond those described here that have never been uncovered.

Nonetheless, college basketball has been free from major scandal in recent years. Periodically the opportunity to garner some quick money on a "sure thing" will probably tempt new players into a gambler's den. It is still easy to rationalize point shaving as doing no harm. Most coaches are diligent about alerting their players to the corrupt forces around them. They routinely show clippings of the early scandals or may call in a speaker from the FBI at the beginning of each season. One such speaker has been Michael Franzese, a former captain of the Colombo Mafia family. Franzese described a system the Mafia used to ensnare athletes:. "Many times we would just approach athletes after the game and invite them to have a beer or something like that. That was how we began to get close to them."[28] Franzese revealed how an athlete would then be invited to a party where he would drink a lot and be seduced by a woman. Other men would also participate in sex acts, and the athlete would unwittingly be photographed. Franzese would later confront him with the pictures and insist he cooperate in point shaving or risk being exposed in these compromising circumstances. Franzese claims to have enlisted many athletes through such tactics. A major deterrent is the lure of the millions a star player can make if he reaches the professional ranks. Today's players are generally savvy enough not to risk their future by reaching for some comparatively small payoff in the present.

Corruption in basketball has not been limited to players' doing business with gamblers. On occasion referees reputedly have been on the take as well. The outstanding example was Sol Levy, who was arrested for conspiring with the infamous gambler Salvatore Sollazzo to fix six NBA games in the 1950–51 season. Levy's method was to see to it that certain designated players would foul out early in the specified games, and he was paid $400 to $500 a game.

Professional Basketball Gambling Scandals

In 1948, its third year of existence, when the professional league was still named the Basketball Association of America, Joe Fulks, an outstanding scorer with the Philadelphia Warriors, reported being approached by a local gambler representing big-time racketeers who were attempting to penetrate professional as well as amateur sports. Morris Fleishman was arrested for soliciting Fulks, and the commissioner commended Fulks for rejecting the bribe offer and reporting it. Fleishman was ultimately acquitted because there was no proof he had offered Fulks money. Moreover, Pennsylvania was one of the few states with a professional sports team that had not yet adopted a law governing attempted bribery of athletes. As a result of this incident, the state enacted such a law.

In its infancy the Basketball Association of America survived a number of franchise expansions, contractions, and relocations and emerged as the solidly rooted NBA.

In early 1954, however, the league was rocked by a gambling scandal that involved Jack Molinas. Molinas was in his rookie season with the Fort Wayne Pistons after starring at Columbia University. He had demonstrated outstanding talent in high school and in college, where it was rumored that he had accepted bribes to shave points, but he did not perpetuate this pattern during his brief tenure in the NBA. His transgression was that he was brazenly betting on games he played in, and an investigation launched by NBA commissioner Maurice Podoloff culminated in a lifetime suspension on January 11, 1954. His professional career was doomed after only two months.

Jack Molinas did not take seriously the NBA contractual prohibition against betting on games. Nor did he expect the league authorities to take it seriously. After all, he rationalized, it was widely rumored that other NBA players were accepting payoffs to dump games, whereas he was merely betting on his own team to cover the point spread or to win.

Molinas was having a stellar rookie season with the Pistons when rumors of game fixing prompted Commissioner Podoloff to initiate an investigation that led him to confront Molinas about his betting. When Podoloff asked if he had bet on games, he readily admitted that he had wagered on eight to ten games for the Pistons to win. In his own mind he had done nothing wrong, because he never attempted to lose a game. When Molinas acknowledged that he had bet on the Pistons, Podoloff summarily suspended him. Molinas was astonished. His distorted self-perception prompted him to believe he was beyond reproach.

It appears that Molinas was placing bets independently with a bookie in the Bronx and that there was no connection with gamblers who were trying to bribe him to throw games. In all, he claimed he had won about $400 from his wagering.

Since the wagers had been transacted in New York, a Bronx district attorney investigated, and a grand jury found no evidence that Molinas had committed a crime. Nevertheless, the suspension from professional basketball stood.

After being banned from the NBA, Molinas went on to become a lawyer, and in 1960 he sued the NBA for $3 million for restraint of trade. The lawsuit also sought his reinstatement to the league. Molinas continued to downplay the seriousness of his offense. Although he had not committed a crime, his actions were a breach of contract and a blow to the integrity of the game. He showed little remorse and maintained that he had been treated unfairly: "The punishment given me is more than commensurate with the acts performed." In his defense he pursued the point that when he passed the New York State bar examination the Committee on Character and Fitness of the Second Judicial Department had evaluated his record and decided to admit him to practice law. His lawsuit, presented in federal court, was dismissed, and Molinas was never reinstated. His connection with basketball later took on a different coloration as he went on to become the mastermind of the widespread college fixes uncovered in 1961.

Two other gambling scandals involved unsubstantiated claims about NBA superstars Isiah Thomas and Michael Jordan. In *Money Players: Inside the New NBA*, which explores the seedy side of professional basketball, Armen Keteyian, Harvey Araton, and Martin Dardis assert that Thomas and his teammate James Edwards might have shaved points in two Detroit Pistons games in 1989. The authors suggest the two needed to pay off gambling debts and maintain that Thomas was "said to be in staggering debt to members of a gambling ring involved with organized crime."[29] Their sources include four gamblers who claim to have seen Thomas and Edwards playing in high-stakes craps games at the homes of boxer Tommy Hearns and Emmet Denha, a neighbor of Isiah's. In addition, a former Pistons player acknowledges that he had discussed point fixing possibilities with his teammates in 1989.

The accusation has been discredited in some quarters because it relies on information about Thomas from sources that remain unnamed. Nevertheless, if Thomas and Edwards were suspected of being involved with gambling figures for the purpose of rigging NBA games, the league was remiss in not fully investigating this allegation.

The stain of scandal in professional basketball has also hovered over

Basketball Gambling Scandals

the gambling of Michael Jordan, the premier player in the history of the game. It is purported that huge unpaid losses on wagers with criminals made him vulnerable to pressure to fix a game.

Jordan's accomplishments on the court are legendary, and he led the Chicago Bulls to six championships in eight years. He may have been the most admired and idolized hero of his era. Nevertheless, a series of damaging revelations during the height of his stardom in the early 1990s pointed up Jordan's penchant for high-stakes gambling on golf games and at casinos. Michael Jordan thereby became somewhat tainted as a sports hero.

In December 1991 reports circulated that Jordan had paid $57,000 in lost wagers to James "Slim" Bouler, an amateur golf hustler who was subsequently convicted as a drug dealer. Jordan initially characterized the payment as a loan, but when he had to testify under oath, he admitted its true nature. Shortly after the Bouler incident a North Carolina attorney said he had received checks totaling $108,000 from Jordan on behalf of a deceased client, businessman Eddie Dow, for debts incurred during a spree of gambling on golf. One year later, in June 1993, Richard Esquinas, a golf partner, claimed Jordan owed him $1.25 million accumulated in a ten-day binge of gambling on golf. Esquinas went public with his story and documented his claim in a self-published book. There was additional negative publicity at about the same time, when Jordan was spotted gambling for high stakes at an Atlantic City casino the night before a crucial playoff game against the New York Knicks.

These events suggest that Jordan, sometimes called "His Airness," acted as if he were royalty and could remain an idol in spite of these allegations. Those who defended Jordan took the position that it is common for professional athletes to gamble on the golf course, at the casinos, at the racetrack, and in card games. His supporters held that Jordan was being condemned for doing what many superheroes have done. Although he purportedly wagered $1,000 to $3,000 per golf hole, his gambling was considered to be more about the craving for competition on the golf course than the craving for action of a compulsive gambler. After all, they said, when you earn more than $15 million a year, the money wagered doesn't really matter—it's the thrill of the competition.

Jordan's association with Bouler and Esquinas sent shudders through the NBA hierarchy. The obvious concern was that his playing could be compromised if he was beholden to unscrupulous gamblers.

An investigation was launched in concert with each of the incidents, and in all cases Jordan merely received a mild reprimand. Some critics have postulated that the NBA played things down because it was imperative to protect Jordan's reputation and avoiding tarnishing the NBA's image. Suspending Jordan would have been crippling to the game. We might draw a parallel here with the way Major League Baseball looked the other way in the face of the prevalent gambling of Hal Chase and others in the pre-Landis era. The baseball owners ignored the growing rumors of corruption out of fear that stern action and negative publicity would harm the image of the game. We later came to recognize that such selective inattention indirectly contributed to the Black Sox affair—the epitome of corruption of professional athletes.

In October 1993 Jordan retired from basketball at age thirty, proclaiming that he had nothing further to prove on the court. He had led the Bulls to three consecutive championships. His critics believed his premature retirement was a deal he made with the league in exchange for hushing up the gambling scandal. After a brief and spectacularly unsuccessful effort to make it as a professional baseball player, Jordan returned to the Bulls in the spring of 1995, and beginning with the following season he led the Bulls to win another three consecutive championships. No further gambling episodes emerged. Jordan then retired for a second time, but under the sway of hubris he made an ill-advised comeback, underperforming in an injury-plagued 2001–2 season with the Washington Wizards. The fans came out to see the legendary hero, but Michael Jordan was no longer the Michael Jordan of old.

6. Self-Destructive Athletes

Show me a hero and I will write you a tragedy.

F. Scott Fitzgerald

When an athlete reaches stardom his actions are scrutinized both on and off the playing field. As with any established public figure, his life is no longer his own. Because of intense media scrutiny, the sports hero needs to remember that he will be held to higher standards. Any stumbles off the field will be magnified. If he is prudent, he will be cautious about what he does, where he goes, and whom he hangs out with lest some untoward incident compromise him. Many athletes accept this system and cultivate their hero image, while others dismiss it or defiantly rebel against it. It is debatable whether sports figures get embroiled in drugs, violence, domestic abuse, and other antisocial acts more often than the general population, but when they do their actions make headlines.

A staggering preponderance of sports heroes fall from grace as a result of self-destructive behavior off the field. Drug-related crimes, violence toward women, sexual transgressions, and alcohol abuse have become commonplace in the lives of many of our heroes. And the number of athletes in this category seems to be increasing. Police records regularly inform us of sports stars who have stumbled or been derailed. In some cases the violation involves abuse of others, such as predatory sexual behavior or assault; in others it is a flouting of the laws such as drug trafficking; and sometimes it is simply self-abusive, as with excessive or illegal use of alcohol, drugs, or steroids. What accounts for these celebrity athletes' self-destructive behavior just when they have become so successful and accomplished so much?

Fame is routinely accompanied by the development of an inflated self-image, a sense of invincibility, and in some cases an outrageous sense of being entitled to act beyond the customary boundaries established by our culture. Grandiosity, a sense of entitlement, poor judgment, a denial of vulnerability, and impulsiveness characterize the behavior of many heroes. The triad of grandiosity, entitlement, and arrogance fuels what I refer to as "the toxic athlete profile."

Thus, in spite of their advantages, many star athletes jeopardize their careers. Famous baseball players such as Babe Ruth, Ty Cobb, Billy Martin, Dave Winfield, and dozens more have spent time in jail. The careers of Micheal Ray Richardson and Steve Howe have been truncated by drug problems that led to repeated suspensions and expulsions from their leagues. Impulsive or violent behavior has compromised the careers and lives of Darryl Strawberry, Lawrence Taylor, Anthony Mason, and John Rocker. Their stories and others will be chronicled in this chapter.

In many cases our heroes are boys in men's bodies. When they reach the professional ranks, they have had limited life experiences, their emotional maturity is often stunted, and they are highly susceptible to temptation. Trying to stem the tide of self-destructive misadventures off the field, professional teams conduct emotional seminars to alert their members to the pitfalls they may encounter. Each June the NFL requires its class of rookies to attend a four-day symposium that offers lectures and seminars about paternity suits, domestic abuse allegations, barroom brawls, drug stings, and so on. The NBA and Major League Baseball have similar programs. In their scathing *Pros and Cons: The Criminals Who Play in the* NFL, Jeff Benedict and Don Yaeger indicate that 21 percent of the professional players have been charged with a serious crime during their lives.[1] The league officials contend that this research is flawed and claim that in fact NFL players have a lower rate of arrests than their counterparts in the general population. Nevertheless, mindful of the tarnished image of their sport that such reports convey, the NFL uses these seminars to try to reduce the crimes its players commit. One of the educators, Zachary Minor, offers a symposium titled "Choices, Decisions, Consequences,"[2] designed to get the players to internalize responsibility and ownership of their off-field behavior. The NFL spends $750,000 on the symposium and brands it as successful, though they concede that some players will still misbehave.

Drug and Alcohol Abuse

The most prevalent area of self-destructive behavior among professional athletes has been drug and alcohol abuse. The stress associated with

Self-Destructive Athletes

sustaining a high level of performance has often been cited in explaining athletes' tendency to turn to drugs and alcohol. The sports pages are replete with headlines about athletes arrested on DUI charges. Even players like Denver Broncos quarterback Brian Griese, who recognizes his status as a role model and his straight arrow image, have jeopardized their careers with DUI arrests. After he was arrested in November 2000, Griese remorsefully acknowledged the negative impact of his behavior on his fans. He was determined to accept the responsibility that comes with being a hero, and he pledged, "I'm going to continue to work hard to keep my nose clean . . . because . . . I'm in a situation where I can have a positive influence on kids and people that look up to me. This is a gift."[3]

It is when many athletes begin to recognize their dependence on alcohol or drugs that they publicly acknowledge their problem and sign themselves in to a rehabilitation clinic. Most rehab programs entail about four weeks' stay as an inpatient, followed by return to the previous life circumstances. With luck, the athlete has acquired better tools and strategies for coping with life's stresses and his denial system has been addressed and punctured. Unfortunately, the rate of relapse or recidivism for professional athletes is very high. It is somewhat unrealistic to expect that a short-term rehab program will permanently correct what usually is a long-standing pattern for dealing with stress and distress. When someone returns to the same circumstances that prompted him to use alcohol or drugs in the first place, the temptation to use these familiar escape mechanisms to avoid emotional pain and anxiety often outstrips newly learned coping techniques. What is needed, but often lacking, is long-term outpatient follow-up. When you give up an addiction, it is common for the brain to become rewired so that you feel as if something vital is missing and experience a powerful desire to fill the void. It may require a herculean emotional effort to withstand the pull, especially during the playing season, when athletes feel the constant pressures that accompany fame: the pressures of performing, of maintaining their status as stars, of dealing with the fans, of dealing with the media, and so forth. Not everyone is capable of handling these pressures without taking the path of least resistance—which is to bolster themselves and attempt to reduce their tensions by turning to drugs or alcohol.

We need to understand that the Darryl Strawberrys, Lawrence Taylors, Steve Howes, and other athletes who are repeat offenders are not simply bad people who are determined to destroy themselves and their careers. They are men whose basic emotional frailty underlies their remarkable physical abilities and leads them to undermine themselves. Some deficiency in emotional fiber that interferes with their ability to handle the ongoing pressures they are exposed to may separate these athletes from most of their celebrity teammates.

An athlete who gets involved in heavy drug use is risking disaster, including death from an overdose. On May 11, 1963, Gene "Big Daddy" Lipscomb, an NFL defensive superstar with the Baltimore Colts and Pittsburgh Steelers, died at age thirty-one after being found unconscious at a friend's home. The friend, Timothy Black, acknowledged that they had shared a bag of heroin, which Lipscomb had injected into his own arm. The medical examiner concluded that Lipscomb died of a heroin overdose. The six-foot-six-inch star, a fun-loving and popular player, had surmounted a traumatic background. When he was eleven his mother was stabbed to death; and while he was still in school he had to work in a steel mill from midnight to seven in the morning before attending classes. Big Daddy Lipscomb was one of the few athletes of his era who made it to professional football without having played college football.

Another casualty was Len Bias, the Atlantic Coast Conference basketball player of the year in 1986. Bias was selected by the Boston Celtics in the draft, and less than forty-eight hours later he collapsed in a University of Maryland dorm room. Within two hours he was pronounced dead of cardiac arrest. With a promising NBA career ahead, Bias purportedly was a victim of cocaine intoxication.

Len Bias was a standout high school player, a local hero, and an All-American kid with close family ties and a strong commitment to his community. The experts saw him as an exciting player, and a Celtics scout described him as "maybe the closest thing to Michael Jordan to come out in a long time."[4] His talent and his prospects for stardom in the professional ranks were widely acclaimed. University of Maryland basketball coach Lefty Driesell cited Bias as "the greatest basketball player that ever played in the Atlantic Coast Conference,"[5] and Maryland's athletic director, Dick Dull, described him as "on the threshold of being one of the great, great basketball players ever."[6] Len Bias, the six-foot-eight-inch unanimous first team All-American in 1986, had it made and was apparently riding high when he was suddenly cut down. At the time of death cocaine was found in his urine, and later medical reports attributed his death to a drug overdose.

Postmortem tests determined that Bias had microscopic damage to heart muscle fibers, usually associated with cocaine-induced disease. Len Bias thus had been using drugs repeatedly; his death was not triggered by an isolated drug experience while he was celebrating being chosen by the Boston Celtics. Teammate Terry Long testified that he had been sniffing cocaine with Bias along with David Gregg, another former teammate, and Brian Tribble for over three hours before Bias collapsed. Long also revealed that Bias had introduced him to cocaine and that he had used the drug more than a half dozen times, with Bias present "on most of those occasions." Brian Tribble was accused of supplying the cocaine that killed Bias. He was tried on charges of possession of cocaine, possession with intent to distribute, distribution of cocaine, and conspiracy to distribute, but he was acquitted on all charges for lack of evidence. After his trial Tribble acknowledged in a television interview that he had used drugs with Bias on the morning of his death.

Bias's sudden and tragic death seemed to have little impact on some other professional athletes who were using cocaine. Ten days after the Bias episode, Don Rogers, a star safety with the Cleveland Browns, died of cardiac arrest induced by cocaine. Rogers was twenty-three years old and was to be married the next day. Like Bias, he was an All-American who sabotaged a bright future as a sports hero. And Dwight Gooden, who was already an established hero, was discovered to be using cocaine during spring training several months later. What happened to Len Bias may have served as a warning for many professional athletes, but for some it merely intensified their defense mechanisms of denial and rationalization. When an exaggerated sense of invulnerability and grandiosity is entrenched in an athlete's psyche, it becomes easy for him to avoid the awareness of potential danger. In these circumstances he may develop the attitude that "Bias was a fool. He didn't know how to regulate his use of cocaine. What happened to him isn't going to happen to me!"

The number of former professional athletes who get involved with drug possession or distribution is alarming. I will cite only two examples of a prevalent pattern. Eric Austin, who played briefly with the Tampa Bay Buccaneers in 1996, was arrested in 2000 and charged with three counts of conspiracy to distribute cocaine. He was convicted and given a severe sentence of twenty years in prison for drug smuggling.

Nate Newton was a high-profile offensive lineman who played in the NFL for fourteen seasons, helped the Dallas Cowboys win three Super Bowls in the 1990s, and was a Pro Bowl selection six times. He was convicted in 2002 on charges of conspiracy to distribute marijuana and possession with intent to distribute. He was sentenced to thirty months in prison. Newton had been arrested in Texas with 175 pounds of marijuana. At the time he was facing similar charges in Louisiana, where he had been caught driving a van containing 213 pounds of marijuana. He was later convicted in the Louisiana case and sentenced to an additional five-year prison term and a $50,000 fine. After his retirement from the NFL, Newton had become a popular football broadcaster, but less than two years later this onetime sports hero had self-destructed.

The Bias incident had a profound effect on drug testing in professional sports. Within months of Bias's death, the NCAA, NBA, and NFL adopted drug testing policies or in some cases firmed up loopholes in existing policies. Since the Len Bias tragedy, it has increasingly been recognized that substances such as cocaine and marijuana impair an athlete's coordination. Even the so-called performance enhancing drugs like steroids ultimately break down muscle and tissue, leading to injuries. Therefore it is supremely self-destructive for an athlete to use drugs. Professional teams have come to recognize that some players cannot police themselves, so, to protect their own interests, the leagues have instituted various drug testing policies. Currently in the NBA all players are tested for illicit drugs such as cocaine, marijuana, and anabolic steroids at the beginning of training camp. Rookies are tested randomly four times during the season, and all other players are subject to testing if an arbitrator judges there is reasonable cause to believe they have possessed, used, or distributed an illegal substance. The NFL follows a similar policy in which all players are tested when training camp begins. In addition, there is random testing for steroids during the playing season and random computer testing in the off-season. To its credit, when the NFL learned that many of its players were using ephedra, a dangerous stimulant that can cause death, it barred its use.

Major League Baseball lags behind professional basketball and football in its drug testing policy. The union contract established in 2002 implemented testing for illegal steroid use, but testing for substances such as cocaine and marijuana can be conducted only when there is reasonable cause—for example, when a player has a history as a user. Thus players on a Major League team's forty-man roster cannot be randomly tested, but minor league players are routinely tested. Ironically, this may create an additional incentive for some minor leaguers to reach the majors, where they can use drugs with less chance of being found out. Marijuana, while not generally thought of as lethal, can significantly impair coordination, and according to Dr. Thomas Newton, medical director of the addiction program at the University of California, Los Angeles, the marijuana produced nowadays is substantially more potent than that used twenty years ago. In September 2002 reporters from *Newsday*, a New York tabloid, declared that marijuana use was rampant among the New York Mets team. In addition to citing admitted users—Grant Roberts (as a minor league player in 1999), Tony Tarasco, and Mark Corey (who was hospitalized with seizurelike symptoms after smoking pot earlier in the 2002 season)—the article highlighted ongoing use among four other unnamed players. The Mets management denied the allegations beyond the three. Mets pitcher John Franco was concerned that kids would conclude the Mets were drug addicts and emulate them.

The National Hockey League's policy on drug testing is similar to that of Major League Baseball. The criterion of "reasonable cause" is employed in determining if a player can be tested.

Performance Enhancing Drugs

One of baseball's most troublesome issues has been the increasing use of performance enhancing drugs. Retired home run slugger José Canseco has claimed that 85 percent of big leaguers use steroids, and Ken Caminiti, who died in 2004 from a drug overdose, stated in a highly publicized article in *Sports Illustrated* that the incidence of steroid use has mushroomed to 50 percent of active players. Other players have argued that these figures are significantly exaggerated, but in any case the problem has become widespread within Major League Baseball. Dr. James Andrews, a well-known and highly respected sports orthopedist, asserts that there has been a dramatic rise in muscle and tendon injuries among baseball players related to the increased use of supplements such as creatine, human growth hormone, and steroids. Anabolic steroids are derivatives of testosterone, the body's primary muscle builder. Its use increases muscle mass, which enables a batter to hit a ball farther or a pitcher to throw harder, but it also leads to more frequent breakdown of muscles and tendons. Dr. Andrews explains that "more athletes are carrying more muscles than their frames can support, and therefore the trauma is greater."[7] In addition to more injuries, there are numerous potential side effects from the ongoing use of steroids. According to the *Sports Illustrated* article, "Studies have shown that the side effects from steroids can include heart and liver damage, persistent endocrine system imbalance, elevated cholesterol levels, strokes, aggressive behavior and the dysfunction of genitalia."[8] The best-known case linking steroid use to bodily damage is Lyle Alzado, a celebrated professional football hero. Alzado, who was named NFL defensive player of the year in 1977, died in 1992 from a rare form of brain cancer. Before his death Alzado maintained that his illness was a result of his long-standing abuse of massive doses of steroids, which he had used to make himself bigger and stronger.

Another high-profile case of steroid abuse involves Steve Courson, an NFL offensive lineman with the Pittsburgh Steelers and Tampa Bay Buccaneers from 1977 through 1985. As he recounts in his autobiography, *False Glory*, Courson was a chronic user of anabolic steroids, which substantially increased his size and strength. Three years after retiring from professional football he was diagnosed with cardiomyopathy, a life threatening enlargement and weakening of the heart.[9] Courson later unsuccessfully sought full disability benefits from the NFL on the grounds that his debilitating heart condition was caused by his use of steroids. In 1999 a federal judge upheld the league's decision to reject Courson's claim.

In his book Courson reveals that the use of anabolic- androgenic steroids was widespread throughout the NFL during his playing years.[10] Baseball players' rampant use of stimulants, including amphetamines, has also received much attention. Mark McGwire, during his 1998 endeavor to break the single season home run record, created a firestorm when he revealed that he was taking the supplement androstenedione, a hormone that the liver converts to testosterone. McGwire discontinued the drug the following season. Some physicians have speculated that McGwire's reliance on the stimulant contributed to his premature retirement. It was not until 2004 that the FDA cracked down on androstenedione as a steroid precursor and put a stop to its production. Players are also known to use amphetamine-like stimulants such as ephedra, which is believed to be linked to heart problems, strokes, and seizures. The danger associated with ephedra has long been acknowledged by the NFL, the NCAA, and the International Olympic Committee, and all of them have banned its use. Human growth hormone (HGH), which baseball players often use to strengthen their joints so they can support the muscle mass developed from steroids, can also have damaging side effects, altering facial features, jawbones, cheekbones, and head size and changing the body's entire configuration. In spite of the negative medical information available, it appears that ballplayers continue to ignore the scary reports on the consequences of using anabolic steroids, human growth hormone, and other controversial substances to enhance their performance. Ken Caminiti, who won the National League Most Valuable Player Award in 1996 as a member of the San Diego Padres, attributed his success to the use of steroids. As is typical, with the continued use of steroids Caminiti's body broke down, and he experienced a series of disabling muscle and tendon injuries. He never again approached the level of his outstanding season. There seems little doubt that a significant increase in severe muscle and tendon tears among Major Leaguers has been caused by steroids and similar substances. Furthermore, the time it takes a player to return from the disabled list has increased by 20 percent between 1998 and 2002. In the first year of anonymous drug testing in 2003, under baseball's new collective bargaining agreement, more than 5 percent of the players tested positive for steroids, so more extensive procedures for testing and sanctions were put in place before the 2004 season. Many people question whether these new guidelines go far enough toward curtailing the use of steroids and other performance enhancing drugs. The players' union continues to take the position that if a substance is not illegal, the leagues cannot forbid players to use it. This passes the responsibility to the players to make individual judgment calls and to the lawmakers to ban questionably dangerous substances as they did with ephedra.

In a 2004 Senate Commerce Committee hearing, Chairman John McCain underscored that the use of steroids creates significant anatomical changes such as enlarged heads and shrunken testicles and an increased frequency of heart attacks and strokes. He threatened congressional intervention if the baseball union failed to adopt an even more stringent program of steroid testing.

We must also consider the issue of emulation. Young fans in particular are eager to copy their heroes' behavior. If Mark McGwire is known to use a supplement, it is likely that many young admirers who embrace him as their idol and model themselves after him will do likewise. Sportswriter Buster Olney, in a plea for baseball players to police themselves better, perceptively points out that "it is a reasonable assumption that starry-eyed adolescents are taking supplements because they figure it is the best way to emulate artificially enhanced heroes. . . . If [baseball players] are not going to save themselves, they should at least be concerned about the increasing number of adolescents and young adults who are using supplements, presumably because their heroes are."[11]

In his 2004 State of the Union address, President George W. Bush reminded the country that "to help children make right choices, they need good examples. Athletes play such an important role in our society, but, unfortunately, some in professional sports are not setting much of an example. The use of performance enhancing drugs like steroids in baseball, football, and other sports is dangerous, and it sends the wrong message—that there are shortcuts to accomplishment, and that performance is more important than character."[12]

President Bush's call for the major sports leagues to get tougher in monitoring and restricting performance enhancing drugs is a noble effort, but it may run into resistance because many fans admire the record breaking accomplishments of their heroes in spite of suspicions that their performance might be tainted by steroids and other substances.

Sudden Death

In earlier eras alcohol abuse was a major affliction in the lives of many athletes. Such legendary baseball heroes as Babe Ruth, Mickey Mantle, Don Newcombe, Grover Cleveland Alexander, and scores of others reportedly have had big league problems with drinking. While alcohol abuse continues to be prevalent among sports heroes, in more recent times it is the athletes' attraction to drugs that has garnered most of the negative attention. In fact, headlines about players' involvement with drugs have become so commonplace that when a star athlete dies young we routinely suspect drug abuse.

When St. Louis Cardinals pitcher Darryl Kile suddenly died in a Chicago hotel room in June 2002, many observers immediately wondered

Self-Destructive Athletes

about substance abuse. It turned out that Kile had a congenital heart problem.

Two months later former All-Star catcher Darrell Porter died suddenly in his car. Porter was only fifty years old, and almost two decades earlier he had gone public in a book about his struggle with addiction and recovery. An autopsy determined that he had not died of a drug overdose but that he had a level of cocaine in his system consistent with recreational use. Curiously, the medical examiner declared that the cause of death was "excited delirium," a condition that prompts "behavior that is agitated, bizarre, and potentially violent" and is frequently associated with heavy drug use.

Sudden death among athletes owing to cardiac problems has occurred more often in recent years. Hank Gathers, a basketball star at Loyola Marymount University collapsed on the court and later died from complications of cardiomyopathy.

The most publicized case of sudden death is that of Boston Celtics superstar Reggie Lewis. Lewis was the leading scorer and captain of the Celtics in 1993. In the Celtics' first playoff game on April 29, 1993, Lewis set a torrid pace by scoring ten points in the opening minutes of the game. He then collapsed and was sent for tests at New England Baptist Hospital. A "dream team" of twelve cardiologists arrived at a consensus "clinical impression" that Lewis suffered from cardiomyopathy, a heart condition that can be fatal during strenuous exercise. The tests showed that there were three dead spots on the left ventricle of Lewis's heart, and the doctors agreed that he should no longer play basketball.

The medical findings were also consistent with cocaine-induced damage to the heart, and the lead cardiologist attempted to obtain a urine sample for drug testing. Lewis denied he had ever used cocaine and refused to be tested. Under the NBA drug policy at the time, he could not be compelled to do so unless there was reasonable cause. Those close to him claimed that Lewis refused the procedure because he believed there was a racial issue—that as a black player he was being unfairly suspected of cocaine use by a group of white doctors. Although he had grown up in an inner city section of Baltimore where drugs were abundantly used, Lewis presented himself to the "dream team" as having been free of drugs.

Lewis surreptitiously checked himself out of the hospital and sought a second opinion from Dr. Gilbert Mudge, the chief cardiologist at nearby Brigham and Women's Hospital. Dr. Mudge concluded that the problem was a benign fainting condition (neurocardiogenic syncope). He said he would monitor and test Lewis over the next several months and that it was likely he could resume his professional basketball career. This diagnosis was what Reggie wanted to hear, and he felt confident about playing with the Celtics again. But three months later, on July 27, 1993, while he was taking practice shots at Brandeis University, Lewis collapsed and died. After his death, of course, there were many questions about the cause, about whether his death was avoidable, about whether his heart condition might have been treated more effectively, and about whether cocaine was a factor.

When an athlete who is at his peak and in prime physical condition suddenly collapses or dies, it is only natural to wonder whether drugs have played a part. Is there a self-destructive element contributing to the sudden death of some athletes? Many well-respected cardiologists have noted that "when we hear of an athlete dying suddenly and the autopsy reports that he had a heart attack with multiple dead areas in the heart and dilated cardiomyopathy, think of cocaine."[13]

In response to Reggie Lewis's death, the *Boston Globe* ran articles that raised the specter of cocaine involvement in this tragedy. In a postmortem examination of Lewis's heart, two pathologists said their findings were consistent with a cocaine-damaged heart. However, the medical examiner's autopsy report concluded that the cause of death was a common virus that inflamed Lewis's heart and precipitated his fatal heart attack. The pathologists labeled this official cause of death "absurd," and rumors persisted about Lewis's earlier use of cocaine.

In some quarters it was suggested that the medical examiner was pressured to avoid issuing a controversial death certificate. The mere hint of drugs would have imperiled the payoff on a substantial insurance policy that the Celtics held on Lewis's life. Even more damaging would have been the smearing of the NBA's image by another drug-related death. These smoking guns were retrospectively highlighted by *Wall Street Journal* reporter Ron Suskind, who noted, "Whether Mr. Lewis died from a heart damaged by cocaine—as many doctors suspected then and now—cannot be definitively shown. What is evident: The official cause of death, a heart damaged by a common-cold virus is a medically nonsensical finding by a coroner who was under intense pressure from the Lewis family to exclude any implication of drug use. . . . There was [also] the potential damage to the league and the team if a drug scandal developed."[14]

Derrick Lewis, a former college teammate of Reggie Lewis, maintained that they had used cocaine together back in 1985. And Dr. Mudge, the cardiologist who was caring for Reggie Lewis at the time of his death, claimed at his malpractice trial—in which he was cleared of any wrongdoing—that Lewis admitted to him two weeks before his fatal collapse that he had been a cocaine user. But by then it was too late to save him.

Although the NBA was the first major sport to put a drug testing policy in place, it was the "reasonable cause" clause that deprived Reggie Lewis of the opportunity to be treated successfully. In plain words, if his malady was related to cocaine use, Lewis probably could have been saved; but the NBA regulations and Lewis's denial prevented this. In weighing all the evidence, it remains uncertain whether Reggie Lewis self-destructed by using cocaine that damaged his heart. Was he another Len Bias, who inadvertently crafted his own demise and became another fallen idol?

A more recent incident involved the sudden death of Korey Stringer, the All-Pro offensive tackle for the Minnesota Vikings. Stringer died on July 31, 2001, at age twenty-seven after collapsing during a rigorous practice session. The official cause of death was listed as heatstroke. It was the first fatality of this type in the history of the NFL, although at that time there had been eighteen deaths from heatstroke among college and high school players since 1995.

Stringer had shown signs of succumbing to the ninety-degree heat during the previous day's practice, when he vomited three times and appeared to be gasping for air. After his death it was speculated that the 335-pound player may have been eager to compensate for his lame performance of the day before and that his macho image led him to push himself beyond reasonable limits. If this was the case, the pressure to be a hero and questionable judgment combined to do him in.

Alarm rippled through the NFL, and recommendations were made to avoid such tragedies in the future. Three months later two of Stringer's Vikings teammates reported that Korey had taken a supplement called Ripped Fuel on the morning of his last practice session. This supplement, which has since been banned by the NFL, contains ephedrine, which can increase heart rate, boost blood pressure, and promote dehydration. It is possible that what appeared to be an unexplainable, haphazard tragedy had a self-destructive element.

At the beginning of baseball's spring training in February 2003, Steve Bechler, a twenty-three-year-old pitcher who was trying to make it to the Major Leagues with the Baltimore Orioles, collapsed from heatstroke during a workout and died within twenty-four hours, after his body temperature had spiked to 108 degrees. It was determined that Bechler, who had a history of borderline high blood pressure and liver abnormalities, had reported to camp ten pounds overweight and had been taking the dietary supplement ephedra. It was speculated, as in the Korey Stringer situation, that the stimulant may have been a primary factor in Bechler's heatstroke and death.

Ephedra

Although supplements that contain ephedra are legal and garner more than $3 billion in annual sales in this country, recent research has "concluded that people taking ephedrine [the active stimulant in ephedra], were 200 times more likely to suffer complications as a result of the herb than people consuming other supplements." [15] Several baseball team owners as well as members of Congress have lobbied for the banning of ephedra.

In early 2004 the FDA concluded that products containing ephedra were linked to a higher risk for seizures, strokes, and heart attacks and "pose an unreasonable health risk," and the agency banned the sale and use of ephedra products. Although the ephedra prohibition is heralded as a milestone, athletes who are determined to seek a competitive edge may still find other potentially dangerous performance enhancing substances.

Baseball players as a group continued to have mixed reactions to the dangers of ephedra, even after the Steve Bechler tragedy. David Wells, the Yankees' big winner, acknowledged that a 1996 scare when he was briefly hospitalized with an irregular heartbeat may have been ephedra related. Nevertheless, Wells continued to use the supplement as an energy booster occasionally when he felt sluggish, and he contended that it is helpful and not unsafe when used judiciously.

And Bobby Ojeda, the former Major League pitcher who survived a boating accident that killed teammates Tim Crews and Steve Olin, maintains that players who are trying to reach the big leagues are likely to ignore safety considerations in taking supplements and will do anything they believe will make them stronger or give them with extra energy to help them make the team. Ojeda describes how, after failing to make the Boston Red Sox in his first attempt, he began to use an over-the-counter supplement to build muscle and strength. He credits the supplement with helping him permanently make the grade in 1981. Ojeda, now a pitching coach in the New York Mets farm system, reflects, "Did we cross the line of concern for our long term health? When you are 21 and chasing a dream, there is no line." [16] The temptation to trade long-term health for short-term success may be compelling. Ojeda's argument seems to apply to the suicide in November 2003 of Taylor Hooten, a seventeen-year-old Texas high school pitcher. According to his parents and doctors, Hooten, a cousin of former Major League pitcher Burt Hooten, hanged himself while in the grip of depression and hopelessness during withdrawal from steroids.

I think Ojeda gets it right in recognizing that athletes will seek any advantage to heighten their performance. Even at the risk of death, many are able to disidentify and distance themselves from the tragedies of Len Bias, Korey Stringer, and Steve Bechler.

In the great ephedra debate of 2003, many active players supported the widespread public opinion that the stimulant should be outlawed, since athletes are prone to use poor judgment in their quest for enhanced performance. Others, like David Wells and Chicago Cubs relief pitcher Mark Guthrie, believe athletes need to govern themselves in a responsible manner and should not be prohibited from using legal supplements. Guthrie, who is respected as an intelligent player, defended his use of ephedra: "Xenadrine [which contains ephedrine] helps get me ready to play every night. It helps me focus in games. That's why I keep taking it . . . I don't care what the doctors are saying now. . . . This stuff is not going to kill you if you take it right. I never take more than two a day. . . . I'm not going to stop now." [17]

Although the NFL, NCAA, and International Olympic Committee had banned the use of ephedra, the other professional sports leagues had failed to do so. In the wake of Steve Bechler's death, the use of ephedra was prohibited among minor league baseball players as a precursor to a similar ruling on the Major League level. In addition, the FDA recommended that warning labels be placed on supplements containing ephedra.

In November 2002 the NFL sent a memo warning all teams that they would be fined if they supplied players with banned supplements. White athletes sometimes rationalize that they need supplements to keep up with the dominant black players. In 2001 Bill Romanowski, a Denver Broncos linebacker, was acquitted in his trial for getting prescription diet pills illegally. In a column decrying the self-destructive aspect of athletes who use performance enhancing drugs, sportswriter William Rhoden noted, "A Denver teammate testified that Romanowski, who is white, had said that he took dietary supplements to compete with black players in a mostly black sport."[18] Black dominance in sports is seldom openly discussed.

The dark chapter in American sociocultural history when African American athletes were denied opportunities in professional sports is long gone. Although they were unofficially banned from major sports leagues beginning in the 1880s, African American athletes were recognized for their outstanding talent and were accepted in competitive sports such as running, bicycle racing, boxing, and track and field. Jesse Owens and Joe Louis were early black superstars and heroes to millions. Eventually racial barriers were removed in the professional leagues, and blacks gradually gained equality and then dominance in sports. By 2000, 80 percent of the NBA players and 65 percent of the NFL players were African American. There are contrasting viewpoints about this trend. Some claim heredity accounts for black dominance in sports—that innate physical attributes enable African American athletes to excel. Others maintain that sociocultural factors are primary—that lack of opportunity in other vocational areas because of racism and the paucity of nonsport black role models motivate these players to work hard to succeed in athletics. In the first group is Joe Morgan, the Cincinnati Reds Most Valuable Player, who says, "I think blacks, for physiological reasons, have better speed, quickness, and agility. Baseball, football, and basketball put a premium on these skills."[19] And O. J. Simpson has offered that "we are built a little differently, built for speed—skinny calves, long legs, high asses are all characteristics of blacks."[20] Proponents of the cultural view include Thomas Cureton, who has conducted extensive research on campus athletes. Cureton rejects the heredity position on black superiority in sports and maintains, "Because of years of training, yes. Because of motivation, yes. Because of social goals, yes.

These make a difference, but not race."[21] And according to NBA super rebounder Dennis Rodman, "A black player knows he can go out on a court and kick a white player's ass. . . . The black player is conditioned to think he can take the white guy whenever he needs to."[22] Thus Rodman is highlighting cultural rather than genetic factors as central to this matter. Jon Entine, a journalist who has written a well-documented book on this issue, concludes, "A dispassionate inquirer would have to suspect that there are a host of intertwined cultural and genetic explanations for black athletic success. And the dispassionate observer would be right."[23] This remains a very sensitive and controversial area.

The Leagues' Response to Substance Abuse

At other points along the spectrum of substance abuse are those athletes who fall short of overdosing but find their careers compromised by drugs. One of the saddest cases is Micheal Ray Richardson, a talented NBA superstar whose cocaine use ultimately led to his being banned by the league.

Richardson was drafted by the New York Knicks in 1978 after outstanding varsity years at the University of Montana. He quickly became a high-profile scorer. He was traded to the Golden State Warriors in 1982, and from there he went to the New Jersey Nets in early 1983. His struggle with cocaine first made headlines in May 1983, then again in August 1983, when he voluntarily entered a cocaine abuse rehabilitation program. The dates are important because in September 1983 the NBA and its players reached an agreement in which three-time drug offenders would be automatically banished from the league. Thus Richardson's lapses, because they occurred before the agreement, would not be counted against him. During the 1983 preseason camp Richardson suffered a relapse, disappeared for three days, and refused to enter a rehab program. One week later, in October 1983, he changed his mind and spent two and a half weeks in a treatment facility. After a two-month suspension he was reinstated by the Nets. Although many experts consider addiction to be incurable, it appears that Richardson had a period when he remained clean. He once again became a productive offensive player, and in the spring of 1985 he was named the league's Comeback Player of the Year. The Nets awarded him a four-year contract averaging $725,000 a season.

Unfortunately, in December 1985, after heavy drinking with teammates, he again disappeared. His agent notified the Nets management that Micheal had had a relapse. The team suspended him without pay, and he entered a drug treatment center. At the time he was playing extremely well and was the Nets' leading scorer, with an average of 17.3 points a game. Under the September 1983 drug agreement the NBA ruled him to be a second-time offender, even though this was his fourth stint in rehabilitation. One month later he rejoined the Nets, and Larry Doby, a former Major League Baseball player and current director of community affairs for the Nets, asserted that "Micheal Ray is not a problem child, he's a child with a problem."[24]

The NBA had the most comprehensive substance abuse plan of any sports league. It recognized that a short stay in a rehab clinic usually provided an inadequate solution to a serious problem, and the NBA guidelines called for aftercare for as long as a player was in the league. By this time, however, Micheal Ray Richardson was in a downward plunge that outstripped aftercare efforts, and his off-field behavior was increasingly out of control. During his most recent stay in a rehab clinic Richardson "talked the talk," stating in an interview that "I guess I don't know it all. I know now that there are some things I just can't do."[25] It appears that he was in too deep, however, and as is often the case with addictive personalities, he could not sustain his pledge. Only a few weeks later Richardson was charged with assault for trying to break into his home after his wife had obtained a restraining order, and four days later he again tested positive for cocaine. The next day, February 25, 1986, Micheal Ray Richardson was banned from the NBA. In issuing the suspension, Commissioner David Stern noted with compassion, "This is a tragic day for Micheal Ray Richardson. What we have seen here is nothing less than the destruction by cocaine of a once-flourishing career."[26] It was hoped that Richardson's banishment would be a warning to other players who were using cocaine.

Major League Baseball's equivalent to Micheal Ray Richardson was Steve Howe, who was suspended a record six times for drug or alcohol abuse between 1982 and 1992. Howe had outstanding talent as a relief pitcher, but he is considered one of the most self-destructive ballplayers of all time. He began using cocaine during his sophomore year in college, and it was an established part of his behavior when he reached the majors with the Los Angeles Dodgers in 1980. Despite his addiction, Howe acted as if he were invincible, and for a time he was. Between

1980, when he was the National League Rookie of the Year, and 1983, he was dominant in his sport while becoming more and more involved with cocaine. He entered a rehabilitation clinic for the first time in 1982, and on his release he promptly relapsed. He pitched well in 1983 but had another series of cocaine binging, rehabilitation clinics, and relapses, leading to his suspension from baseball for the whole 1984 season. He returned with the Minnesota Twins in 1985 and pitched ineffectively. It was rumored that his heavy drug use was now affecting his performance. Nevertheless, teams that were short on good pitching continued to hire Howe, hoping his talent would outdistance his addiction. At the end of the 1987 season, while playing for the Texas Rangers, he failed another drug test and was suspended for the sixth time. Ultimately his record of six suspensions and six treatment centers in six years dwarfed even the tragic circumstances of Micheal Ray Richardson.

Eventually Howe found his way to the New York Yankees in 1991, and although he was convicted of cocaine possession in 1992, he generally performed well under close surveillance and the threat of further punishment until the team dropped him in 1996. After his release from the team his self-destructive tendencies found a new outlet, and he was arrested two days later at John F. Kennedy International Airport with a loaded .357 Magnum in his suitcase. He pleaded guilty to gun possession and was sentenced to three years' probation.

Dan Gutman has pointed out that the problem of substance abuse, which mushroomed in the 1980s, has done more than anything else to tarnish the image of our sports heroes. In *Baseball Babylon* Gutman cites baseball great Keith Hernandez as asserting that 40 percent of Major Leaguers were using cocaine. Gutman has compiled a list of baseball's "cocaine All-Stars."[27] Among others, it includes Ferguson Jenkins, Vida Blue, and Joe Pepitone, who were all convicted of possession of cocaine, as well as Dwight Gooden, Maury Wills, and, of course, Steve Howe, cocaine abusers who spent time in rehabilitation centers.

Professional sports teams need to take greater responsibility for helping young athletes, who often come from impoverished backgrounds, make the transition to fame and sudden wealth. Such administrative involvement would also protect the teams' investment. The luster of stardom can quickly vanish when budding heroes find it difficult to handle the intensity of their fame and the ensuing distortions in self-image; they may act out in destructive ways toward others and toward themselves.

Athletes' Disregard for the Standards of Society
The inflated ego shaped by fan adulation, media attention, and in some cases being catered to early in life frequently leads to arrogant and grandiose behavior. Self-destructiveness may follow as athletes underestimate their vulnerability to the temptations and pressures that may lead to alcohol and drug abuse. Or arrogance may emerge as violation of contractual obligations or a more general defiance of rules. Thus, difficulties with internal or external regulation can be a powerful negative force. The self-destructive sports hero typically acts as if the standards of society do not apply to him. He tends to be indifferent or contemptuous toward authority, and he is loath to view himself as having problems or needing help. When he runs into difficulties, he usually resists taking responsibility for his misdeeds. Jim Brown, one of the earliest players to enter the Pro Football Hall of Fame, was convicted in 2000 of vandalizing his wife's car. Brown refused to comply with the court-ordered counseling and community service, and he ultimately served six months in jail.

Some high-profile athletes even attempt to portray their self-destructiveness as a virtue. They take pride in their devil-may-care style and have a fatalistic attitude. It is often not until late in life that they express remorse over their off-field indulgences. Shortly before he died of liver cancer, Mickey Mantle, a flagrant alcohol abuser, quipped, "If I'd known I'd live to be sixty-five, I'd have taken better care of myself."

Lawrence Taylor, the New York Giants football Hall of Famer, is the epitome of the professional athlete bent on flirting with disaster. Taylor recognized his demons—an attraction to cocaine, a powerful antagonism toward authority, and a reckless approach to life—but he proclaimed his determination to do things his own way regardless of the consequences. He was boastful about his wild, arrogant "living on the edge lifestyle."

Taylor's achievements on the playing field were legendary. In his thirteen-year career, from 1981 to 1993, he was named defensive player of the year three times, he played in ten Pro Bowl games, and he led the Giants to two Super Bowl championships. He is credited with changing the role of offensive linebacker from a read and react approach to an attack position. As long as he was a menace to opposing quarterbacks, Taylor could justify his free-spirited, reckless approach to life. He relished his image as a renegade who routinely defied team rules with impunity. Among his infractions were breaking curfew, sleeping during team meetings, refusing to run laps, and repeatedly missing or coming late to practice sessions. He was occasionally fined, but by and large the consequences were minor, which probably reinforced an inflated view of himself and his defiant attitude. Taylor, affectionately referred to by the adoring legion of fans as LT, was a self-described "system breaker." He rejected the responsibility of being a role model and trumpeted his wild side. In his 1987 autobiography he boasted, "I live my life in the fast lane and always have. I drink too much, I party too much, I drive too fast, and I'm hell on quarterbacks. It's always been that way. When somebody calls me crazy, I take it as a compliment!"[28] His disregard for his influence on the young fans who identified with him was apparent in his defense of his reckless driving. He stated, "I don't wear seat belts because if I ever get in a crash at the speed I go, I wouldn't survive anyway."[29] The Giants' general manager, George Young, purchased a $2 million life insurance policy on Taylor out of concern that LT's lifestyle would make him a dead man before he was thirty.

LT's escapades did not lead to an early death, but he did encounter a series of major crises. He started abusing alcohol and cocaine early in his career, and after his sensational 1986 season, he entered a rehab program for about a month. He was not cured, and in the preseason 1988 training camp he failed a drug test and was suspended by the league for four games. Taylor was committed to the world according to LT. In his autobiography he wrote about his need to march to his own drummer. In describing his drug abuse he wrote, "When I started [in 1982] it was just part of a good time. I got high on the stuff, but hell, I drove my car over a hundred miles an hour, closed down more bars than I can remember, went where I wanted, and did what I wanted, and still could go on a football field and knock some dick loose. Cocaine was illegal . . . tell me no and I'll argue and fight you just to be different."[30] Taylor traces his rebellious attitude back to his adolescent conflict with his father. He recalled, "I'd test any rules that were set down. You tell me no, I'll try yes."[31]

At the time of LT's 1988 suspension, *New York Times* sportswriter Ira Berkow expressed the prevalent media view that Taylor was one of the least sympathy-inspiring sports heroes who were contending with substance abuse, because he displayed minimal repentance and insisted he was a free spirit, meaning he "exults in living in the fast lane, which he makes not only unsafe for himself, but for others. That is unconscionable. . . . He is tragic." [32] Berkow also noted that "society might be handed some of the blame for helping mold a guy who feels he can get away with murder, so to speak, as long as he can jump on quarterbacks." [33]

After his retirement Taylor accelerated his self-immolation and repeatedly broke the law. In 1996 he was arrested in South Carolina on charges of buying cocaine from an undercover officer, and two years later he was arrested again on similar charges. He was also arrested in 1997 for failing to pay child support. In 1999 Taylor received five years' probation for filing false tax returns and tax evasion. His drug problems also continued, and in 1998 he was arrested in a New Jersey hotel room for possession of drug paraphernalia, found guilty, and fined $1,100. Although Taylor appears to continue his self-destructive course, he has not spent any time in jail, and he still marches to his own drummer.

In another tell-all book published in 2003, Taylor revealed that during his playing days he had arranged "escort service" for opposing players to make them less effective in upcoming games. Taylor also claimed that Giants players sometimes received a "bounty" for knocking rival players out of a game.

Darryl Strawberry's penchant for self-destructive behavior was a match for Lawrence Taylor's, but he inspired more sympathy. His repeated falling from grace reflects pathos rather than arrogance. When he came to the New York Mets in 1983, Strawberry was heralded as the black Ted Williams because of his smooth and graceful swing. He had a productive career as a slugger, but he never developed as a superstar. It seemed he was not driven to be truly outstanding; instead he displayed a lackadaisical attitude and settled for above-average performance. Nevertheless he was worshiped by the hero-hungry fans (the Mets finished in last place before he arrived), but he did not handle celebrity well.

In his first season he was named Rookie of the Year, and he was an integral part of the Mets 1986 championship team.. Gradually he became immersed in alcohol and drugs, and by 1990 he began the first of many rounds of treatment.

After punching his first wife in the face and threatening her with a

Self-Destructive Athletes

gun, he took refuge in the Smithers Alcoholism and Treatment Center. He then had several below-par seasons in which he was shuffled from the Mets to the Dodgers and then to the Giants, and his self-destructive behavior off the field culminated in an eighteen-month prison sentence in 1998. In addition to charges of spouse abuse, his problems included criminal charges for not paying child support, a tax evasion conviction, and recurrent lapses into substance abuse. In 1994, while playing for the Dodgers, he entered the Betty Ford Clinic for his cocaine addiction. One year later, after being signed by the Giants, he tested positive for cocaine and was suspended from Major League Baseball. As a tribute to his athletic talent, he was picked up by the Yankees in 1996 as a reclamation project, and manager Joe Torre and owner George Steinbrenner became his rescuers and mentors. Strawberry's emotional history included beatings by his drunken father, who left when Darryl was twelve, and he probably yearned for a warm and supportive father figure. The good news was that he contributed to three World Series championships under Torre's paternal tutelage despite a bout with colon cancer in 1998. The bad news was that he continued to periodically relapse into cocaine abuse.

In 1999 Strawberry was convicted of drug possession and solicitation of a prostitute and given eighteen months' probation. He was also suspended from baseball for three months. Less than a year later he again tested positive for cocaine and was suspended by Commissioner Bud Selig for the entire 2000 baseball season. He was never again to play in the big leagues, and his plunge to the bottom gathered speed. In September 2000 he was sentenced to two years' house arrest for violating probation by driving under the influence of a tranquilizer and leaving the scene of an accident. Barely one month later he left the drug treatment center where he was serving his house arrest and went on a binge with crack cocaine and antidepressants. Darryl attributed this blatant violation of probation to stress from the spread of his cancer. He sadly said he had lost his will to live and hoped the drug binge might kill him. He was given a one-week jail sentence and ordered to resume his chemotherapy. Forlornly, Strawberry said, "I can't run from myself anymore. I've got to take responsibility for myself."[34]

Although he made good on his pledge to the extent that he appeared to become free of drugs, he was expelled from his drug treatment center in March 2002 for having numerous sexual encounters with a female resident. Strawberry indignantly protested that he had been singled out for punishment because he was a celebrity. He admitted he knowingly violated the rules by engaging in sex with another patient, but he tried to justify it on the grounds that everyone was doing it and that he had not been sufficiently warned about the consequences. He seemed not to recognize that he was in a precarious position because of his previous offenses, and he expected to be let off because he was being treated unfairly. Instead he was sentenced to eighteen months in prison for violating probation for the sixth time.

Strawberry's personality in many respects is a classic addict's profile. Lack of insight, poor judgment, and low tolerance for frustration led him to try alcohol and drugs as an ineffective way of dealing with stress, including the pressure from the fans and the media to perform even better. What will happen to Darryl Strawberry is anybody's guess. Although there is always hope that a person can change direction, the poor prognosis for his cancer and his addictive personality do not bode well for his future.

Some sports stars do not accept the need to be especially circumspect off the field because they are constantly in the public eye. They seem indifferent to the fact that any hint of transgression, particularly violent incidents, sexual allegations, or drug involvement, will be highlighted by the press and is likely to sully their reputation and their standing with their team. Their adventures create news, and therefore they are targets for negative headlines. Patrick Ewing and Andruw Jones were unceremoniously exposed as patrons of the Gold Club in Atlanta in 2000, where they allegedly were favored with stripper sex. Instead of appreciating that any trace of misbehavior places them in jeopardy, such athletes sometimes gravitate toward trouble zones.

The NBA star Anthony Mason is a player who often seems to be in the wrong place at the wrong time, precipitating multiple criminal charges. Mason's difficulties have revolved around violent episodes off the field. After several arrests Mason protested, "I seem to have a bull's eye on my back," and Paul Silas, his coach with the Charlotte Hornets, said, "He's got to learn sooner or later that people are out there looking for him, and regardless of whether he was at fault or not, it's not a good situation to be in."[35]

In 1989, during his first season as a professional, Mason was arrested for gun possession and given probation and community service. For the next several years he steered clear of trouble as he became a prominent power forward on the New York Knicks. However, since 1996, after he became established as a star, his name appears on the police blotter with alarming frequency. In 1996 he was twice charged with assault at an upscale New York nightclub, and the same year he was charged with assault and resisting arrest while being served with a summons. A sentence of 120 hours of community service was levied. Then in 1998 he and his cousin were charged with statutory rape with girls of fourteen and fifteen. The rape and sexual abuse charges were dropped, and Mason pleaded guilty to two misdemeanor counts of endangering a child. In February 2000 Mason was charged with assault in a barroom brawl in Harlem. In the same year he was arrested in the New Orleans French Quarter for allegedly inciting a riot, assaulting a police officer, and resisting arrest. This case was later dismissed. In all these incidents Mason maintains that he was innocent and was unfairly targeted. Despite a clear pattern of violent episodes, he has suffered minimal consequences. With no significant punishment as a deterrent, it seems reasonable to anticipate that Anthony Mason may continue his self-destructive behavior.

Accidental Deaths of Players

The most extreme self-destructive behavior among athletes culminates in death. The illusion of invincibility fostered by alcohol may have played a part in the death of several sports stars. Just before spring training in 2002, San Diego Padres outfielder Mike Darr was killed at age twenty-five when his sport-utility vehicle went out of control on a Phoenix highway. Darr's blood alcohol level was over the legal limit, and he was not wearing a seat belt, which probably played a significant part in his death.

In January 2000 Bobby Phills, a ten-year NBA veteran, was killed at age thirty when he lost control of his Porsche on a North Carolina highway. Phills was believed to be drag racing with teammate David Wesley, minutes after leaving a practice session with the Charlotte Hornets. He was purportedly driving more than seventy-five miles an hour in a forty-five mile an hour zone when he collided head-on with another car. No drugs or alcohol were involved in this unnecessary death of a sports hero, but recklessness most likely played a part.

Bobby Phills was not the first active NBA star to die in an auto accident in questionable circumstances. That distinction belongs to Terry Furlow of the Utah Jazz, who died in May 1980 at age twenty-five when he crashed his Mercedes head-on into a utility pole in a suburb of Cleveland, Ohio. The police found evidence of marijuana and "a white powdery substance" as well as open bottles of alcohol in Furlow's car. Later reports indicated there were traces of cocaine and Valium in Furlow's bloodstream. Furlow had been struggling with his inner demons for some time, as noted by the Utah coach, Tom Nissalke: "Terry was a very obviously troubled young man and for some reason he was never able to get his life together."[36]

A premature death in an auto accident also felled hockey star Steve Chiasson. Chiasson, a defenseman with the Carolina Hurricanes, was killed in May 1999 at age thirty-two when his pickup truck flipped over in Raleigh, North Carolina, several hours after his team had been eliminated in the Stanley Cup playoffs. Chiasson was not wearing a seat belt, and police speculated that he had been drinking and speeding.

Alcohol may have been a factor in a highly publicized tragedy involving three Cleveland Indians pitchers in March 1993. Tim Crews and Steve Olin were killed instantly one night when their fishing boat, steered by Crews, rammed into a pier on a Florida lake. A third player, Bob Ojeda, survived with severe injuries and later suffered from posttraumatic stress disorder. The crash was sudden and violent, and none of the players saw the pier before the collision in the dark. It was later determined that vodka and beer were on board and that Tim Crews was legally drunk while driving the boat. Whether this tragedy was a freak accident or caused by an alcohol-induced lapse in judgment remains unknown. Gregory Collins, the Cleveland Indians team psychiatrist, ruefully reflected on the effect this incident had on the other Indians players: "Athletes often have beliefs of invincibility that are shattered at times like these. . . . They're young exuberant men. Sometimes they can be a little reckless."[37]

Media Takedowns

In addition to drugs, alcohol, gambling, and sexual abuse, many professional athletes express their self-defeating tendencies in less blatant ways. A prime example is John Rocker, whose big mouth led to his downfall. Rocker, who pitched for the Atlanta Braves, made disparaging remarks about foreigners, minorities, and homosexuals in an interview for *Sports Illustrated*. Rocker said he hated playing in New York and made statements like, "Imagine having to take the [Number 7] train to the ballpark, looking like you're [riding through] Beirut next to some kid with purple hair next to some queer with AIDS right next to some dude who just got out of jail for the fourth time right next to some twenty year old mom with four kids. It's depressing. . . . The biggest thing I don't like about New York are the foreigners."[38]

These inflammatory remarks raised a storm of protest. Baseball commissioner Bud Selig suspended Rocker for the first month of the 2000 season, levied a fine of $20,000, and referred him for a psychological evaluation and sensitivity training. The players' association appealed the punishment, and an arbitrator reduced the suspension and fine to a negligible amount. Rocker's statements were an embarrassment to Major League Baseball and an Atlanta teammate called him "a cancer," yet he was only given a slap on the wrist.

In a subsequent interview with ESPN, Rocker claimed he was not a racist and maintained he had been misrepresented in the magazine article. He later threatened the writer face to face and was fined $5,000 by the commissioner. Rocker protested that he meant his remarks as retaliation against the New York fans, who had abused him on the ball field by dumping beer on him, throwing a battery that hit him in the back, and spitting in his face. Rocker backtracked and made a public apology, but the damage had been done—someone even established a hate-Rocker Web site.

His defenders pointed out that Rocker was being treated harshly by the media: that he was simply expressing what many people feel, that prejudice is widespread, and that he was a scapegoat for all those who share his views. Even John Stossel, a respected reporter on ABC television's 20/20, questioned whether Rocker should be punished for his remarks in a country that espouses freedom of speech. Stossel argued that players who had committed acts of violence, such as José Canseco's hitting his ex-wife or Charles Barkley's throwing a man into the window of a bar, were not suspended or forced to have psychological evaluations, so violent speech should not be viewed as more offensive than violent action.

After this incident John Rocker's career rapidly went downhill. He struggled on the mound, and by June of the next season he was demoted to the minors. Although he returned to the Braves and later pitched for other teams, he has not regained his earlier effectiveness. It seems likely that his damaging remarks and the storm that followed became a long-lasting distraction that interfered with his competence.

In a 1987 interview on ABC television's *Nightline*, Al Campanis, the general manager of the Los Angeles Dodgers, self-destructed when he disparaged the intellectual capacities of black athletes. It was the fortieth anniversary of Jackie Robinson's breaking the color barrier in Major League Baseball, and *Nightline* host Ted Koppel was questioning why there were no blacks on the level of manager and general manager. Campanis, who had been a friend and minor league teammate of Robinson's, explained that while black ballplayers are gifted athletes, "I truly believe that they may not have some of the necessities to be, let's say, a field manager or perhaps a general manager." [39] Campanis seemed unaware that his remarks were offensive and reflected a deep-seated prejudice, but the public uproar culminated in his being fired after serving over forty years with the Dodgers.

We cannot underestimate the media's power to build up an athlete's image or to bring him down. Athletes who extend themselves by providing interviews to the press and making themselves generally available receive positive coverage and are usually shielded from the reaction to their intemperate remarks. For example, when San Francisco Giants star Jeff Kent was about to take off his towel in the locker room after a game toward the end of the 2002 season and provocatively asked whether any of the reporters present were queers or women, his comment was not reported by the media. [40] Had his teammate and rival Barry Bonds made such a discriminatory comment, it more than likely would have been picked up and publicized. In spite of his superstar heroics, Bonds is not media friendly and therefore is often portrayed in a negative light and has his flaws magnified.

The Danger of Hubris

Hubris, in which an inflated ego leads a person to overestimate his standing in the world or to underestimate his vulnerability, has been the downfall of many athletes. In Greek myth, the imprisoned Daedalus makes wings of wax and feathers so he and his son Icarus can fly away to freedom. Icarus becomes intoxicated with his ability to fly. When he ignores his father's warning about flying too close to the sun, his wings melt and he plunges to his death in the sea. The sports world is full of Icaruses whose arrogance leads them to make self-defeating choices.

A relatively obscure but classic example is the career of Charlie Dressen. After retiring as a player, Dressen spent many years as a journeyman manager and coach. After the Brooklyn team underperformed in 1950, Dressen was hired as its manager. In successive years he led the Dodgers to a playoff loss (to the Miracle Giants of 1951) and two pennants. His success was unparalleled in the history of the team. Dressen was flying high, but he misread his worth in terms of how his employers operated. He resented the organization's policy of renewing the manager's contract annually rather than longer term, especially since rival managers Leo Durocher and Eddie Stanky, with less sterling records, were readily being offered two- and three-year contracts. Goaded by his wife to insist on his due, Dressen wrote to the owners demanding an extended contract and was summarily fired. It was 1953, and he had held the second-best manager's job in baseball, in the premier sports city in the world. But he overestimated his value to the organization. Walter Alston was hired to replace Dressen, and he stayed at the helm for the next twenty-three years with annual contact renewals. Charlie Dressen attempted to recover from his disastrous decision, but he moved on to manage other teams with only mediocre results.

Dressen was appropriately assertive in his attempt to get what he wanted, but it backfired because his judgment was questionable. Other celebrity sports figures have suffered a similar fate. In December 2001 George O'Leary, a highly successful head football coach at Georgia Institute of Technology, was hired as head coach by Notre Dame, one of the most sought-after positions in college football. Within five days O'Leary was forced to resign when it was discovered that he had lied about his athletic and academic background. O'Leary's undoing was brought about by a lapse in judgment many years earlier when he untruthfully claimed that he had a master's degree and that he had played varsity football at the University of New Hampshire. These falsifications remained in his biographical sketch and eventually did him in.

Bobby Knight was a basketball icon who played a part in his own termination as coach at Indiana University. Knight had coached the team for twenty-nine years and had led it to three national championships. In his controversial career he was a hero to some and a villain to others. His temper and his old-school discipline made him feared by opposing teams and his own players as well. Knight was fired on September 10, 2000, after he allegedly grabbed and berated a freshman student whom he felt had been disrespectful toward him. Knight had been placed on "zero tolerance" probation by the university four months earlier. An internal investigation into his "persistent and troubling pattern of behavior" had led the school officials to fine him $30,000 and levy a three-game suspension along with the "zero tolerance" edict. It was probably just a matter of time until he crossed the line they had drawn. Bobby Knight had been embroiled in numerous explosive situations along the way. Other supposedly abusive behavior include his allegedly punching a cop in Puerto Rico, stuffing a Louisiana State University fan into a trash can at the 1981 Final Four tournament, flinging a plastic chair across the court to protest a technical foul call, and throwing a vase at an Athletic Department secretary. One of his players, Neil Reed, accused Knight of choking him during a practice session in 1997. Knight denied the charge, and a videotape of the encounter was inconclusive, but this event triggered the investigation of Knight. His history of abusive outbursts leads one to wonder why the university had tolerated such behavior for so long. The answer is Knight's success. Winning basketball teams sell tickets, get alumni support, and bring in millions to enrich the school.

Knight's critics portray him as a poor role model who teaches his players to intimidate others, to ignore authority, to be a law unto themselves, and to blame others for conflict. His defenders admire him as a straight shooter who speaks his mind and is devoted to coaching and getting the best performance from his players.

With his long history of explosiveness, one could say that Knight got himself terminated. He left Indiana with a gracious speech, but two years later he filed a $2 million lawsuit against the university for wrongful dismissal. In 2003 a judge dismissed Knight's breach of contract lawsuit. But in a tribute to his coaching skill, he was hired by Texas Tech University the season after his dismissal from Indiana, and the saga of Bobby Knight continues.

Poor judgment may have blemished the career of NBA superstar Chris Webber. The Sacramento Kings franchise player was indicted in September 2002 for lying to a grand jury about accepting money from a University of Michigan booster more than ten years earlier. Ed Martin reportedly gave Webber $280,000 from 1988 to 1993 while Webber was a high school and college basketball star. If Webber did accept these illegal payments, not only did he use poor judgment, but he further jeopardized his lucrative career with the Kings by denying the charges before a grand jury. If he is convicted, Webber could receive up to ten years in prison and a $500,000 fine. In 2003 Webber avoided jail time by pleading guilty to criminal contempt as his federal perjury trial was about to begin.

Hubris also appears to characterize NBA superstar Latrell Sprewell. In October 2002 Sprewell was suspended by the New York Knicks and fined a whopping $250,000 for violating his contract by failing to report an injury in a timely fashion. He should have known better. Sprewell's career was checkered with violations—the most flagrant was choking his coach in 1997. In the previous season he repeatedly was provocatively late for practice sessions and had been fined for missing a pre-game shoot-around. Now Sprewell claimed he didn't realize that he had broken his hand in a fall on his boat and said he was being scapegoated by management. One newspaper reported that he hurt his hand in a fight on the boat. Despite his history of infractions, Sprewell seemed indifferent to the possibility that failing to report the injury could damage his career.

Randy Moss of the Minnesota Vikings is another superstar who seems to operate with a fearless disregard for consequences. Refusing to be bound by authority figures' rules, he proceeds on a self-destructive course. Moss has performed brilliantly for the Vikings and is the only wide receiver in NFL history to gain more than a thousand yards in each of his first four seasons. Off the field, however, he has been embroiled in a succession of disastrous incidents involving violence, drugs, and verbal abuse.

After an assault charge for beating up a high school classmate in 1995, Moss lost his scholarship at Notre Dame and was sentenced to thirty days in jail. He then transferred to Florida State University, where a marijuana violation led to his banishment from the team and more time in jail. From there he went to Marshall University, where he was charged with domestic battery. His problems continued when he got to the NFL. In 1999 he was fined $25,000 for squirting a water bottle at a referee, and in 2001 the Vikings fined him $15,000 for using profanity toward corporate sponsors on the team bus. In September 2002 his defiance toward authority emerged again when he allegedly pushed a traffic officer half a block with his car because she tried to prevent him from making an illegal left turn. At some point she fell off the hood and onto the pavement, but fortunately she was not seriously injured. Moss was arrested and faced legal charges and, if convicted, disciplinary action by the league. In this serious event it seems that Moss found not being thwarted by an authority figure more important than not injuring others and damaging his career in the NFL. Randy Moss pleaded guilty to two misdemeanor counts and was fined for careless driving and given community service time. He also made an out-of-court settlement with the traffic control agent.

Several weeks later Michigan State University tailback Dawan Moss (no relation to Randy Moss) was arrested for a similar episode. When Moss was told his car was blocking traffic, he drove off, dragging the police officer. The officer had minor injuries, and Moss crashed into a patrol car. He faced a felony charge of fleeing a police officer as well as drunken driving; he was convicted and given twenty days in jail, and he was dropped from the Michigan State team.

These dragging incidents reflect the players' resistance to being stopped from going where they wanted to drive. Preventing an opponent from impeding your forward motion is the mark of a good football player. In contact sports like football and basketball, athletes are trained to be aggressive. This behavior is rewarded and reinforced. But when this approach is seen as a solution to conflict off the field, it can have damaging consequences.

Charles Barkley's aggressive play in the NBA won him All-Star honors, but when a patron in a Milwaukee bar taunted him in 1991, Barkley broke his nose. Charges were filed, but Barkley was acquitted by a jury that accepted his claim that he had been provoked and reacted (overreacted?) in self-defense. Branded as a troublemaker, Barkley was quickly traded away by the Philadelphia Seventy-sixers.

Eleven years later, in 2002, another Seventy-sixers superstar, Allen Iverson, came perilously close to self-destructing through his behavior off the field. Iverson was arguably the most talented and electrifying basketball player to come along since Michael Jordan. He was the NBA Rookie of the Year in 1997, Most Valuable Player in 2001, and scoring leader in 2002. On July 11, 2002, he was charged with three felonies (criminal trespassing, carrying an unlicensed gun, and criminal conspiracy) and six misdemeanors because on July 3 he allegedly forced his way into his cousin's apartment and threatened two men with a gun. This bizarre episode took place after Iverson supposedly had thrown his naked wife out of their house after an argument (a claim she later retracted) and then went searching for her at 3:00 a.m. As a superstar Iverson's actions were scrutinized and then magnified, and the press had a field day with this incident.

The NBA had never had an active player convicted of a felony, and for a while it appeared that Iverson might be the first. He had had previous run-ins with the law. In 1993, as a seventeen-year-old high school senior, he had spent four months in jail after a bowling alley brawl. Since the conviction had racial overtones, Allen was granted clemency, and the conviction was later overturned. In 1997 he was arrested for gun possession and marijuana possession when he was a passenger in a car that was stopped for speeding, and he did community service and served three years' probation. In 2001 the league fined him $5,000 for making derogatory remarks about gays during a game at Indiana.

The charges against Iverson in the July 2002 case carried a maximum penalty of more than fifty years in prison, but he was exonerated when his accusers gave contradictory testimony. In dismissing the charges, the presiding judge sardonically concluded that "it sounds like you had a relative looking for a relative at the house of a relative."[41] Some starstruck court officials crossed appropriate boundaries when they were seen asking Iverson for autographs or handshakes.

Although the charges against Iverson were dropped, it is interesting that his reaction to a volatile family situation was potentially violent. Violence and other antisocial behavior often spring from an impoverished background. Iverson comes from a socioeconomic culture in which the prototype for dealing with conflict is violence. At the time of this incident his father was serving a seven-year prison sentence for stabbing a girlfriend. Allen had seen a friend murdered when he was eight years old, and he claims that the year he was sixteen eight people he knew were murdered. In that milieu, not having a gun might be considered naive and foolish. When a star athlete is charged with gun possession, we tend to think of him as self-destructive because of the risk to his career. But an athlete who grew up in the midst of inner-city violence might consider it self-protection rather than self-destruction.

Five months later, Allen Iverson told reporters that he believed he was being targeted by the Philadelphia police and feared for his life:

"I've heard about police officers toasting to Allen Iverson's next felony conviction. . . . I know if there's a crooked cop out there, they could do anything to me . . . Allen Iverson could wind up dead tomorrow if a crooked cop wants him dead. It's as simple as that."[42]

Female Athletes

As female athletes attain increased presence in sports, we might ask whether they also have self-destructive tendencies. It appears that women may express such tendencies in different ways than men. There are no known gambling scandals or incidents of game fixing involving female athletes, nor do they tend to be violent toward others off the field. Female sports heroes seem less prone to antisocial behavior than their male counterparts and more inclined to act out directly upon themselves. This mirrors a gender distinction prevalent in our culture.

Studies of female athletes show a substantially higher incidence of eating disorders, amenorrhea, and osteoporosis than in the general population. These symptoms, designated the "female athlete triad" by the American College of Sports Medicine, have been on the rise for the past three decades, coinciding with the increased opportunities for women in sports. Dr. Doreen Wiggins, a researcher and clinical professor at Brown University medical school, suggests that "studies show that between 16 and 72 percent of female athletes suffer eating disorders . . . [w]hile that number is 5 to 10 percent in the general population. Being bone thin seems to be considered an inherent part of the aesthetic beauty of such sports as ballet, gymnastics, figure skating, and distance running."[43] Wiggins also points out that the components of the female athletic triad are interrelated. She states that "the three conditions are often linked to female athletes because osteoporosis can result from poor nutrition and inadequate calcium intake typical of eating disorders, and lack of estrogen which is the result of amenorrhea."[44]

Professional female athletes' use of performance enhancing drugs has also received some attention recently. John Mendoza, the chief executive of the Australian Sports Drug Agency, maintains that "the use of performance enhancing substances is rife in pro tennis . . . and the problem is acute on the women's tour, where players must be abnormal in body physique to compete for No. 1."[45] The most widely publicized female sports hero whose involvement with drugs derailed a promising career was Jennifer Capriati. In 1991, at age fifteen, Capriati was her-

Self-Destructive Athletes

alded as the next great women's player when she reached the semifinals in the Wimbledon and U.S. Open tournaments. The following year she won an Olympic gold medal, but in 1993 she hurt her elbow and was eliminated in the first round of the U.S. Open. She then succumbed to the pressure of the expectations placed on her and to the pull of adolescent rebellion. In December 1993 she was arrested for shoplifting a $15 ring at a Florida mall, and the next year she was arrested for possession of marijuana. Two stints in drug rehabilitation programs followed. Capriati's career as a tennis star was all but over at age eighteen. Fortunately, after several years off she became determined to make a comeback, and with the support of her family and coach Harold Solomon she made it all the way back to the top. In 2002 Capriati regained her star status by winning both the Australian and the French Open Grand Slam tournaments.

There have been widespread reports of steroid abuse among female athletes, most notably in track and field and cycling. Although steroids increase strength and boost performance, their numerous side effects include potential damage to the heart and liver as well as general masculinization. It is common for females on anabolic steroids, which increase testosterone levels, to develop husky voices and irregular menstruation. Cindy Olavarri stands out as an example of a female athlete whose career was short-circuited by steroids. Olavarri was an amateur cyclist whose lifelong dream was to make the U.S. Olympic team. She had won three U.S. titles in track as well as a silver medal at the World Championships in 1983. While preparing for the Olympic team in 1984, she tested positive for drugs and was forced to withdraw from the competition. She never again was able to qualify, and she later acknowledged that in her efforts to excel, she had taken performance enhancing drugs for three years before the 1984 Olympic trials.

In 1989 Diane Williams, a prominent U.S. track and field athlete, testified before the Senate Judiciary Committee about her use of performance enhancing drugs and their masculinizing side effects. The Senate hearings revealed that the use of steroids was prevalent among athletes and played a significant role in the outstanding accomplishments attained in sports such as track and field and cycling.

Before these hearings track and field star Florence Griffith-Joyner captured three gold medals at the 1988 Olympics in Seoul. Griffith-Joyner, nicknamed Flo Jo, set world records in the one-hundred- and two-hundred-meter races, and she was acclaimed as one of the greatest female athletes in history. There were frequent rumors that she had used steroids to bolster her performance, but Flo Jo denied ever using drugs, and she never failed a drug test. When she died suddenly in 1998 at age thirty-eight, speculations about chronic steroid use again circulated. Pat Connolly, a former Olympian who also had testified at the 1989 Senate hearings, reflected on Griffith-Joyner's death: "Florence's face changed . . . her muscles bulged as if she had been born with a barbell in her crib. . . . It was difficult not to wonder if she was taking some kind of performance enhancing drugs." [46] The official coroner's report after an autopsy showed that Flo Jo had died of asphyxiation as the result of an epileptic seizure. Since it was not the job of the coroner's office to assess previous drug use, Joyner's critics continued to voice suspicion about the influence of steroids in her career and in her death.

Acting out by female sports figures has been rare indeed. The most bizarre scandal involved the ice skating star Tonya Harding. While Harding was preparing for the Olympic trials in 1994, her rival Nancy Kerrigan was attacked after a practice session. On January 6, 1994, Kerrigan was clubbed above her right knee by a man wielding a retractable metal baton. The injured Kerrigan was forced to withdraw from the figure skating trials but was later voted onto the team. The investigators determined that the attack was part of a plot to disable Kerrigan, who was one of the favorites to win a gold medal at the upcoming Winter Olympics, and thereby enhance Harding's chances for a place on the U.S. Olympic team. Within a week, arrests were made in the case. Harding's ex-husband, Jeff Gillooly, had masterminded the plot and conscripted her bodyguard, Shawn Eckhardt, to arrange the assault on Kerrigan. Eckhardt hired two acquaintances, Shane Stant, who hit Kerrigan, and Derrick Smith, who drove the getaway car.

Harding had maintained she was innocent, but after Gillooly's arrest she admitted she had learned about the plot after the attack took place. Gillooly first tried to protect Harding, but when he learned she had testified against him to the FBI, he told investigators she knew all about the plot and had approved it in advance.

While the legal proceedings were unfolding, the Winter Olympics took place in February 1994, in Lillehammer, Norway. Both Kerrigan and Harding competed; Kerrigan performed brilliantly and won a silver medal, and Harding underperformed and came away empty. One month later Harding pleaded guilty to conspiracy to hinder the investigation. This was a felony conviction, but it spared her a prison sentence. Instead, she was fined $100,000 and given three years' supervised probation and five hundred hours of community service. In a separate inquiry, the U.S. Figure Skating Association concluded that Harding "had prior knowledge and was involved prior to the incident." The organization banned her for life and stripped her of her 1994 National Championship title.

Jeff Gillooly was treated more harshly for his role in the plot. Convicted of racketeering, he was sentenced to two years in prison and fined $100,000. His accomplices, Eckhardt, Stant, and Smith, each got eighteen months.

Sometimes in the world of sports even unsubstantiated rumors can have devastating consequences. Speculations about a sexual liaison between Nancy Lieberman, coach and general manager of the Detroit Shock professional women's basketball team (WNBA), and Anna DeForge, one of her players, rocked the team shortly before the end of the 2000 season. Some of the players complained to the team president that the pair had exchanged hotel room keys and were spending late-night time together, implying that they were having an affair. The additional implication was that DeForge was receiving preferential treatment by being assigned to a starting position because of their romantic liaison. Both Lieberman and DeForge denied the accusations. According to a *Sports Illustrated* article about sexual relationships between coaches and athletes, Lieberman, who was married at the time, protested that "such talk was born of players' petty jealousies. . . . I would never jeopardize my profession or my character to be with one of my players."[47] Nevertheless, the scandal was a distracting influence, and the team floundered to a losing season. Lieberman, a Hall of Famer, was abruptly terminated, and the president of the Detroit Shock acknowledged that the "tense locker room was a factor in the firing."[48]

7. Athletes and Violence toward Women

It's not right to slap your wife and see the fear and the anger inside of her.
It's not right to make her afraid that you are going to kill her.

Vance Johnson

It is generally believed that we are becoming a more violent society. In addition, the media coverage of violence is more extensive now—the television news is typically replete with reports of violent acts. We have been made aware of the prevalence of domestic violence in our culture; the FBI claims that every fifteen seconds a woman is being beaten by a husband or boyfriend![1] Correspondingly, rapes and other assaults on women by professional and college athletes are almost everyday events, and they receive widespread coverage.

In earlier eras athletes' abuse of women may or may not have been less common, but it was certainly given much less publicity. In 1952 Jim Rivera (nicknamed Jungle Jim), an outfielder with the Chicago White Sox, made headlines when he was accused of rape. When confronted with the scandal Ford Frick, the baseball commissioner, said, "To the best of my knowledge, this is the first time a commissioner ever had to make a decision on a morals charge."[2] Fortunately for Rivera, the charges were dismissed and he had a productive ten-year Major League career. In 1958 Edward Bouchee, while playing with the Philadelphia Phillies, was arrested for exposing himself to a six-year-old girl and was placed on probation. In 1970 Lance Rentzel, a Dallas Cowboys football hero, was arrested on similar charges. But such headline-making incidents involving prominent sports figures were rare. By contrast, in more recent times such legendary heroes as Jason Kidd, Scottie Pippen, Barry Bonds, Darryl Strawberry, and Warren Moon have all been accused of domestic violence. And that is just the start of a long list of sports stars whose names appear on the police blotter, including José Canseco, Mark Chmura, Corey Dillon, Riddick Bowe, Dave Meggett, Moses Malone, Al Unser, and Robert Parish.

There is an ongoing debate over whether athletes are violent toward women more often than are nonathletes. Sports researchers Todd Crosset, Jeff Benedict, and Mark A. McDonald published a controversial study indicating that male college athletes commit more sexual assaults than other students. Moreover, their study shows that when college and professional athletes are charged with rape they tend to be treated leniently. The authors collected information from ten Division I colleges about male athletes and sexual assaults. They compiled their data from both campus police reports and the schools' judicial affairs offices. Their findings showed that in the campus police reports recorded from 1991 through 1993, the college athletes did not commit more sexual assaults. But when they examined the data from the judicial affairs offices, which they considered a more reliable indicator, they found that 19 percent of the sexual assault complaints involved student athletes, who made up only 3 percent of the male students.[3] Although the sample size was too small to yield definitive conclusions, the authors did find a statistically significant relation between male college athletes and complaints of sexual assault.

Jeff Benedict was the director of research at the Center for the Study of Sports in Society, and he had been assigned to gather information about the growing belief that athletes' violence toward women had reached excessive proportions. According to Benedict, the center, which receives financial and political support from professional sports leagues as well as college athletic programs, had hoped his research would refute the public perception that athletes tend to abuse women. But when the findings were published and publicized, indicating a significant relation between college athletes and sexual assault, Benedict claims that the center's director pressured him to resign from his position. The research was criticized as flawed, primarily because it was based on a relatively small sample size of sixty-nine cases and did not take into account other factors in violent behavior, such as alcohol use.

Benedict continued to pursue his interest in athletes' crimes against women, and in Public Heroes, Private Felons (1997) he developed the thesis that celebrity status predisposes sports stars to violate "behavioral boundaries," which may result in violence toward women. It seems likely that the distorted self-image and sense of entitlement that many athletes acquire as a by-product of being heroes places them at greater risk in this area. Benedict further asserts that athletes' crimes against women are rising dramatically and that their rate of conviction is disproportionately low compared with the general population: "Between 1986 and 1996 over 425 professional and college athletes were publicly reported for violent crimes against women. Few were successfully prosecuted, much less incarcerated. The fact that popular athletes, society's most recognized male role models, routinely escape accountability for domestic violence, rape, gang rape, and other crimes has dulled public consciousness of their increasing levels of deviance."[4] In support of his position Benedict reports that of 172 professional and college athletes arrested for alleged sex felonies between 1986 and 1995, only 31 percent were convicted, compared with Department of Justice statistics showing that in the general population more than 50 percent of such cases ended in conviction. Benedict's research also revealed that the vast majority of domestic violence complaints made against professional and college athletes are not prosecuted. Between 1990 and 1996 there were only 28 convictions among 150 such complaints. In many cases the victims may have backed away from the allegations because they anticipated that the accused athletes might receive preferential treatment.

The Crosset, Benedict, and McDonald research corroborated an earlier study by the *Philadelphia Daily News* that found college athletes were disproportionately involved in sexual assaults. Among the sixty incidents tracked between 1983 and 1987, the Philadelphia study found football and basketball players 38 percent more likely to be involved than their nonathlete peers.[5]

A comprehensive study by the Indiana University School of Law has pointed out the inequities within the criminal justice system in dealing with charges against athletes. They maintain that there is a tremendous range in the way high-profile sports figures are treated by the law.[6] While some are afforded excessive leniency, others are prosecuted more vigorously than may be warranted. For example, in his highly publicized attempt to reduce his family support payments, Barry Bonds seemed to receive special treatment from a judge who described himself as an "ardent baseball fan" (the ruling was later reversed). Colorado Rockies pitcher Marcus Moore was acquitted of raping his girlfriend. One of the jurors later acknowledged that although everyone thought he was guilty, they didn't want to convict him because of his "status as a ballplayer."[7]

At the other end of the spectrum are cases in which sports figures

Athletes and Violence toward Women

were prosecuted more aggressively for their alleged assaults on women. Many people believe that the sexual assault case against Green Bay Packers star Mark Chmura and the domestic violence case against the famous NFL quarterback Warren Moon fall into this category. Both players were acquitted after stormy trials, and in the Moon case some jurors contended that the case should never have been brought to trial. In another example, Miami Dolphins star Lamar Thomas was arrested and held without bail on charges of possible violation of probation from a prior domestic violence incident when the media publicized a subsequent instance of domestic violence in which no charges were pressed against Thomas.

The Indiana Law School Study concluded that "some professional athletes are targeted for prosecution, while others are able to escape major punishment; in either case, such discriminatory treatment is the result of who professional athletes are. Overall athletes are both held to a higher standard and above the law."[8]

It appears that athletes' abuse of women has become an epidemic. In addition to the studies by Benedict and his coauthors and the *Philadelphia Daily News*, studies conducted by the *Washington Post* and the *Los Angeles Times* reported a disproportionate number of sexual assaults committed by athletes. Furthermore, a survey conducted by the National Institute of Mental Health found that between 1988 and 1991 athletes were involved in approximately one-third of the 862 sexual assaults on college campuses.[9] And a 1985 study by the Association of American Colleges indicated that next to male fraternities, athletes were the group on campus most likely to engage in gang rape.[10]

However, some claim that the perception of the problem is skewed by excessive media attention. An editorial in the *American Journal of Sports Medicine* notes that "the apologists for professional athletes (club owners, general mangers, agents) say that all this violence is nothing more than a mirror on society in general. They say that the high profile of the athlete brings media attention and that athletes are involved in this situation no more than others."[11] In other words, this group takes the position that domestic violence among athletes merely reflects what is happening in our increasingly violent society. After Minnesota Vikings defensive end James Harris allegedly slapped his wife and broke her nose and collarbone, the Vikings' vice president of administration and team operations, while acknowledging the seriousness of the incident, suggested there might even be less violence by athletes than two or three decades ago, since such incidents were underreported by the media and police in earlier eras. [12]

This point of view was attacked by Calvin Griffith, the longtime former owner of the Minnesota Twins. Griffith bluntly stated, "That's a crock. I spent the first seventy years of my life in major league baseball, and I could tell you lots of stories of players cheating on their wives, but never beating them up like I'm reading today." [13]

But Greg Aiello, an NFL spokesman, maintains that the prevalence of domestic abuse among NFL players is no greater than in the general population, and he points to the league's educational and counseling programs designed to limit the problem. [14] In early 2001, after the high-profile trials of NFL stars Rae Carruth, Ray Lewis, and Mark Chmura, Commissioner Paul Tagliabue sought to refurbish the tarnished image of NFL heroes. Tagliabue said he was distressed over the misconduct of players who victimize others and stressed that "the overwhelming number of NFL players are good people and good citizens. We are extremely proud of NFL players as a group. As a league, we need to have, and do have, a wide array of strong programs and policies not just to support our players, but also to hold them accountable to higher standards. . . . If the rest of society can do as well as we do in the NFL, America's crime problem will be well addressed." [15]

Additional research is needed to determine whether athletes perpetrate more violence toward women than do men in the general population. To be sure, the overwhelming majority of athletes do not abuse women, but there is anecdotal evidence that, to the extent that such abuse exists in our culture (and indeed its existence is a harsh reality), it occurs more often among college and professional athletes. In addition, the apparently disproportionate incidence is magnified by the intense media coverage given to allegations against athletes.

There are several theories about this pattern. When athletes are unsuccessful or ineffective in competition, they may take out their frustration on those they see as less formidable foes, often the women in their lives. This is the mechanism of displacement. The well-known psychological principle of frustration-aggression says that the threshold for aggressive behavior is lower under conditions of marked frustration. Thus women often become targets when athletes have a particularly bad day on the job.

Athletes and Violence toward Women

Insensitivity toward women, and seeing women as objects to be used and abused has a long-standing history in the jock culture. Mistreatment of women has also been the theme of much locker room humor. For example, the legendary Penn State football coach Joe Paterno, after a frustrating loss to Texas in 1990, quipped, "I'm going to go home and beat my wife." [16] Paterno was not serious, but his remark reflects an insensitive and disrespectful attitude shared by many in sports.

The second theory about athletes' abuse of women centers on the generalization of aggression training. Its proponents contend that athletes are trained to be aggressive and perhaps even violent on the field. In the NFL, for example, players are conditioned, starting every Tuesday, to build up maximum physical aggression, to be released against the next Sunday's opponents. The object of the game is to destroy their rivals, and each week they prepare to do so. This heightened aggression, they say, makes athletes more likely to behave abusively in their relationships off the field. When you are trained to be highly aggressive in competition, it is difficult to turn off that side of your personality outside the playing arena. Hence it can be difficult for an athlete to leave his violent emotions on the field; instead, he transfers them to his home. Professor Merrill Melnick, who has researched the relation between athletes and sexual assaults, speculates that "aggression on the playing field, sexist language, and attitudes used in the locker room and an inordinate need to prove one's maleness can combine in complex ways to predispose some male athletes towards off-the-field hostility." [17] Many athletes maintain that this position is an excuse that a minority of players use to justify their proclivities toward domestic violence. Michael Strahan, the New York Giants defensive end, bluntly emphasizes this point: "Can't turn off the aggression? That's a cop-out. I don't like that at all." [18] And Jonathan Ogden of the Baltimore Ravens football team declares that "the vast majority of us can control our tempers off the field. We view it as a job, have fun with it. But then we go home and try to relax." [19]

This sentiment is echoed by Harry Carson, a New York Giants linebacker during the team's glorious Super Bowl championship years. He maintains, "You're trained to be aggressive [but] when the whistle blows you need to leave that on the football field and go home and do whatever else you need to do." [20] Carson believes that athletes generally can compartmentalize their aggression so that they use it in their game effort and are not programmed to extend it beyond that. He mused, "You work yourself into a frenzy prior to the game. You go into a game and you see bodies flying all over the place, but then the whistle blows after a play [and] you get up and walk back to your huddle. And you do that for an entire game. Once the game is over you see players walking off the field talking, chatting, and smiling, and so forth."[21]

Carson acknowledges the prevalence of athletes' violence toward women and suggests that such incidents are often a by-product of a "toxic relationship." He takes exception to the one-sided presentation in which the athlete is pictured as a violent abuser and the woman as an innocent victim. He sees these violent episodes as an interaction between men who overreact and abuse their power and women who may be provocative. His point is not to condone athletes' violent behavior but rather to plead for women to share some responsibility for triggering these reactions. "Everyone has to understand that you have a boiling point. . . . Anyone who is involved with an athlete has to understand that there are certain buttons. Don't push those buttons."[22] He describes his own relationship with a woman who intentionally started a fight with him; as things heated up she urged him to hit her. Carson recalls, "I was under a lot of stress and could have very easily hauled off and hit her. But something inside of me—like God touched me and said—don't touch this woman, because if you touch this woman, you're going to be on the front page of every paper in the free world tomorrow morning. I could just see myself being led out of my house in handcuffs. I knew that if I lashed out, I would have to pay a price."[23]

Carson's ability to anticipate the consequences of his actions enabled him to restrain himself. Had he given in to his violent impulse, he would indeed have paid a high price in media attention and possibly legal trouble. Unfortunately, many athletes have not acquired the "personal infrastructure" (a term coined by Judge Norm Early) that helps them not to overreact when provoked.[24]

The third theory, and the one I most fervently espouse, concerns the background influences that may predispose some athletes to abuse women. Two contrasting backgrounds come into play. On the one hand, many athletes grow up in an atmosphere of derogatory attitudes toward women as well as violent behavior. Their histories are checkered with scenes of domestic abuse. Troy Vincent, a premier player with the Miami Dolphins and the Philadelphia Eagles, captured the essence: "Do-

Athletes and Violence toward Women

mestic violence was the way of life in my home. . . . To see my mother get beat was just part of my life. . . . It was just part of the community to beat your wife or your girlfriend."[25] Vance Johnson, a Denver Broncos wide receiver who admitted violence toward his first two wives, reports similar exposure. In his autobiography Johnson wrote about his early life in Trenton, New Jersey, where "everywhere I looked men abused women. There was absolutely no respect given to women in Trenton. All of the women were really battered and abused emotionally and physically. It was just a way of life, and no one ever did anything about it."[26] This is a typical scenario in the early lives of many of our sports heroes. When boys are exposed to this value system daily, they breathe it in emotionally. This way of relating to women becomes implanted in their psyches. Without positive role models, athletes from this background identify with and emulate the abusive behavior they have witnessed.

At the other end of the spectrum are those athletes who have always been catered to and overindulged. Many athletes get special treatment from an early age, and they come to believe the rules are different for them. In an interview with Geraldo Rivera, Judge Norm Early observed that "elite athletes know that the rules do not apply to them from a very early age, whether it's going to class, whether it's getting grades, whether it's DUI, whether it's rushing them out the back when a cop comes into a barroom brawl."[27] Dr. Joseph Pursch, who has studied the personality characteristics of college athletes, suggests that "because athletes receive preferential treatment from early ages, their social consciences are often underdeveloped. . . . At home he gets away with talking back; in school he gets good grades even when he cuts classes, and his third drunk driving charge is covered up. . . . And when he gets rough with a cheerleader at two o'clock in the morning, the coach smooths things out with her father."[28] Elsewhere I have noted, in accord with this view, that "male athletes are conditioned to think they're special and feel they can function on a different plane. . . . Athletes are prone to think their needs have to be responded to fast, and if they're not, it can trigger violent responses."[29] Many athletes are accustomed to getting whatever they want, and when their desires are frustrated their highly developed sense of entitlement overpowers their underdeveloped social conscience. Many cases of sexual assault and domestic violence involving athletes probably are based on this scenario. In the words of researcher Jeff Benedict, "When surrounded by women, these players' unfamiliarity with behavioral boundaries can easily lead to sexual assault."[30] Benedict concludes that "stardom by nature dulls adherence to social norms, luring athletes to overindulgence in illicit temptations."[31] The Indiana University Law School Study pointed out that "when one has a sense of entitlement, one feels that the rules and laws that apply to the rest of society, do not apply to him. Receiving special treatment tends to perpetuate athletes' sense of entitlement."[32] On a similar note, Jackson Katz of the Center for the Study of Sports in Society adds, "Elite athletes learn entitlement. . . . They believe they are entitled to have women serve their needs. It's part of being a man. It's the cultural construction of masculinity."[33]

The sports culture that reinforces athletes' profound sense of entitlement also contributes to the prevalence of sexual assaults and violation of boundaries when they relate to women. In many cases the sexual acting-out not only is aimed at sexual gratification but also makes a statement about masculinity within the jock culture. According to the Indiana University Law School Study, "Experts contend that the male sports culture encourages athletes to engage in these activities [sexual acting-out], not for sexual pleasure, but to prove their virility or sense of worth to other men. Ultimately, the culture instills the idea that women are sexual objects."[34] The view of women as compliant sexual objects is graphically depicted in coach Bobby Knight's infamous interview with Connie Chung in which he stated, "If a female knows that rape is inevitable, she should just sit back and enjoy it."[35]

Respected sportswriter Robert Lipsyte has stated that easy access to women has blurred the distinction between consent and force in high-profile cases of alleged rape by professional athletes. Lipsyte cites the research of Jeff Benedict, whose master's thesis describes how these athletes, because of their celebrity status, are socialized to expect a lack of accountability for sexual abuse of women, whom they perceive as sexually compliant. The constant pursuit by sports groupies—women who readily make themselves available for sexual encounters with athletes—further complicates this problem. Benedict defines three categories of groupies: "the one-night stand 'collector,' the 'would be wife,' who is hoping an affair will lead to a long term emotional relationship, and the 'sniffer,' whose aim is to bask in the reflective glow of the sports hero."[36]

Athletes and Violence toward Women

Athletes and Domestic Violence

Athletes who come from impoverished backgrounds frequently have had few opportunities to develop effective coping skills. This is a primary factor in many cases where conflict between spouses is dealt with through violent behavior. In a typical history the player identifies with the aggressor—he has been abused himself or has identified with the abusive behavior of the men he knows and has learned to respond violently to a perceived provocation. Spouse abuse as a solution to conflict, though never justifiable, is often an impulsive overreaction based on the need to exert dominance and control.

The sports culture is also cited as a major factor underlying spouse abuse. Marriah Burton Nelson, the author of *The Stronger Women Get, the More Men Like Football*, has argued that "sports create an aggression found in men who beat their wives. It is not the sports themselves, but the culture of the sports in which male athletes and coaches talk about women with contempt. The culture of sports is a breeding ground. It begins with the little league coach saying 'you throw like a girl.' This teaches boys to feel superior. Masculinity is defined as aggression and dominance. In order to be a man, you have to be on top, to control, to dominate."[37]

High-Profile Cases of Assaults on Women

Kobe Bryant, the Los Angeles Lakers' twenty-four-year-old superstar, was arrested on July 4, 2003, and charged with assaulting a nineteen-year-old employee at the Colorado spa where Bryant was staying before having arthroscopic knee surgery. It was the major sex scandal of the year. Bryant, who was the youngest player ever to join the NBA when he was drafted directly out of high school at age seventeen, had become a poster boy for the league.

Unlike many world-class basketball stars, Kobe, whose father had been an NBA player, did not come from the inner city. In contrast to other icons' blemished images, Bryant was packaged by the media as a clean-cut, likeable boy next door with solid values, worthy of emulation. His carefully crafted squeaky-clean persona helped him land multimillion-dollar endorsements with McDonald's, Sprite, and Nike.

In a tearful press conference after his arrest, Bryant denied forcing himself on the woman, but he did admit to having consensual sex with her. He berated himself for having committed adultery and professed his deep love for his wife. One of the things that makes this case so compelling is the apparent dissonance between Bryant's flawless image and his human frailties. While his hero-worshiping public was fed a spotless picture of Kobe, those closer to him were more realistic in their assessment. After the scandal broke, *Sports Illustrated* reported that a source within the Lakers organization described Bryant as "an extremely cold and calculating man," and a *Newsweek* article reported that his teammates viewed him as aloof and selfish and not a team player. He was a valuable player who helped the Lakers win three championship titles, but he was not popular with his teammates.

Bryant's legal defense team was certain to emphasize the distinction between consent and force in the hope that Kobe would then not be convicted as a sexual predator. The outcome of this trial will send a message to athletes regarding their sexual conduct. If Kobe is convicted, they may "get it" that a high-profile sports star must be circumspect. But if Kobe is acquitted, there is danger that athletes will be encouraged to indulge their sexual appetites indiscriminately and expect to get a free pass by alleging consent if they are accused of rape.

It is also important to consider this episode within a cultural context. It occurred at a time when our society is litigious and in no mood to be deceived by our leaders or our icons. The nation was divided over the government's misleading statements about the reasons for waging war against Iraq. And there was a parallel split in the public's reaction to the Bryant case. Many people felt deceived by Kobe's self-destructive actions, which forced them grudgingly to view their hero in a more realistic light. Others felt he was being persecuted by the legal system and rallied behind him. Had this incident taken place in the era of Babe Ruth or Wilt Chamberlain, it might not have led to criminal charges or received the same media attention, and Kobe Bryant's one-dimensional image would have remained unsullied in the eyes of a blissfully ignorant public. The prevailing cultural attitudes play a large part in how our heroes are perceived and judged.

Vance Johnson, the Denver Broncos wide receiver, was a classic product of an impoverished background and the sports culture. These factors contributed substantially to a pattern in which he sexually exploited and abused women once he made it to the NFL. In his tell-all autobiography he describes a compulsively promiscuous and irresponsible lifestyle fueled by a grandiose self-image and a sense of invincibility. He captures the mentality of many high-profile athletes in reflecting, "I believed that I could do anything I wanted to do, and people all over the city were helping me cover my mistakes." [38] Such introspection was anathema to him during his early years in professional football, however, as he pursued an unlimited number of sexual conquests and fathered four illegitimate children. He married the first of three wives impulsively, only to soon learn that she had been a groupie. The police were repeatedly summoned to their home in response to domestic disputes. Angela Johnson later claimed that Vance had held a gun to her head and threatened her. She also alleged in an interview with the *Rocky Mountain News* that he had pushed her downstairs when she was pregnant and that he gave her a black eye. [39] Nevertheless, in spite of multiple acts of domestic violence, she did not press charges because she feared the repercussions. Johnson also physically abused his second wife, Chri, and in 1991 he spent seven days in jail after he rammed her car.

To his credit, Vance Johnson belatedly came to recognize how distorted his perceptions of himself and others had been. He had even empathized with O. J. Simpson's "pain" when he was accused of murdering his wife, Nicole. Eventually, after several years of professional counseling, Johnson purports to have gained insight into his behavior and cleaned up his act. He summarizes his tumultuous life during his playing years as follows: "After being a second round draft pick for the Broncos in 1985, I quickly became intoxicated by the trappings of fame and fortune. I had a God complex. I thought I could do whatever I wanted to do, so I did. I was 22 years old . . . but my attitudes and actions were more like those of a two year old. . . . I had thousands of affairs with women. . . . I was abusive to my wives and girlfriends. . . . I served time in jail for ramming my second wife's car. . . . I eventually got counseling for my abuse problems and I finally regained control of my chaotic life." [40]

Many athletes like Vance Johnson have repeatedly behaved violently toward women. Darryl Strawberry punched his wife, Lisa, in the face and broke her nose in 1987. Three years later he was arrested for again beating her up and threatening her with a gun. And in 1993 his soon to be second wife, Charisse, alleged that Strawberry had physically abused her, but she declined to press charges.

The most highly publicized case of domestic violence by an athlete involves O. J. Simpson. Simpson had repeatedly abused his wife, Nicole, who frequently called the police. After many such incidents Simpson was charged with assault in January 1989; he pleaded no contest, portraying the incident as just a quarrel despite pictures showing that Nicole was bruised and battered. The whole world knows that five years later O. J. Simpson was charged with the brutal murder of Nicole Simpson and Ron Goldman. He was exonerated in "the trial of the century" and was set free, though he was later held liable in a wrongful death civil lawsuit and was ordered to pay $8.5 million in compensatory damages and $25 million in punitive damages to the families of Nicole Brown and Ron Goldman.

In the 1990s the University of Nebraska football team spawned several athletes who were repeatedly abusive toward women. The most infamous were future NFL players Christian Peter and Lawrence Phillips.

While he was at Nebraska, Christian Peter, a three-hundred-pound defensive linesman, was arrested eight times and convicted four times for offenses including assaults on women. He was convicted of raping Natalie Kuijvenhoven, a former Miss Nebraska, in 1993 and received eighteen months' probation. In 1996 he was again convicted of assaulting a woman and disturbing the peace and served ten days in jail. In between these events Kathy Redmond, a student athlete at the university, filed a civil suit alleging that Peter had raped her twice. The case was settled out of court, and Redmond later became director of the National Coalition against Violent Athletes. Peter left the University of Nebraska before graduating, and in 1996 he was drafted by the New England Patriots. Three days later, after widespread public protest, Robert Kraft, the owner of the Patriots, released him. Kraft was applauded by many for placing integrity above the need to win at all costs. Meanwhile Peter was picked up by the New York Giants and played for them the next four seasons. He was taken on by the Giants as a reclamation project, and he was not involved in any additional misbehavior off the field while with the team. Peter attributes his abusiveness at Nebraska to his alcoholism and attention deficit disorder, which can trigger impulsive behavior. Since turning pro, he has been in ongoing counseling and has regularly attended Alcoholics Anonymous meetings. He acknowledges that "the person I was is not a person I'm proud to have been, or to have known."[41]

Lawrence Phillips came from a troubled background. His father left when he was very young, and there was a stable period while his mother raised him alone. But things changed abruptly after another man moved in with the family when Lawrence was twelve. According to sports researcher Jeff Benedict, his mother kicked Lawrence out of her house after a violent incident, and he lived in a halfway house from the age of thirteen. [42] He reportedly felt rejected and abandoned by his mother, who seemingly chose to live with another man instead of him. [43]

He was recruited by the University of Nebraska, which recognized his exceptional athletic talent. Once at Nebraska, he soon ran into trouble. In September 1995, after a previous assault charge, he was arrested for the brutal assault of Kate McEwen, a former girlfriend. According to a later lawsuit filed by McEwen, "Phillips beat and kicked her while she was at a friend's house. She contends he then grabbed her hair 'caveman style,' pulled her down three flights of steps and slammed her head into a wall." [44] Apparently there had been a long history of violence in his two-year relationship with McEwen, who played on the university women's basketball team. McEwen recounted an earlier episode in which "Phillips shoved her head into a wall so hard it broke through the wall, then choked her and would not allow her to leave her apartment," [45] and in other incidents she reports that he raped her and threatened to kill her.

Phillips pleaded no contest to the 1995 attack and was given one year's probation. Coach Tom Osborne dismissed him from the team, but Phillips was an outstanding running back, and after missing six games he was reinstated in time to play in the National Championship game. Osborne purportedly knew about Phillips's violent relationship with McEwen and had warned him that he would be dismissed from the team if there was further abuse. [46] Osborne initially made good on his pledge, but perhaps because of intense pressure from alumni and the university administration to produce football victories, he later reneged. In view of the serious charges against Phillips, what message was Osborne sending? His decision seems to reinforce the public perception that sports stars often receive special treatment. Osborne was widely criticized, particularly by national women's groups, for reinstating Phillips, and people asked whether he was motivated by a genuine wish to defend an accused player or by the team's need to have Phillips on the field. Osborne seemed to underplay the seriousness of Phillips's violent pattern: "It's not as though Lawrence is an angry young man all the time and a threat to society. But there are occasions every four to five months where he becomes a little explosive."[47]

In his book chronicling the turbulent events of the 1995 Nebraska season, Coach Osborne describes how his decision to reinstate Phillips was influenced by a report from the Menninger Clinic. Lawrence had been sent to Menninger, one of the finest mental health facilities in the country, for an evaluation. According to Osborne, the extensive psychological assessment showed that "there was no psychotic or neurological disorder that rendered him dangerous to himself or others. . . . His previous experiences made close relationships difficult, yet Lawrence didn't appear to be a serious threat to the victim and didn't appear to be one who had a significant problem with control. . . . It was recommended that Lawrence enter into therapy. . . . It was not recommended that Lawrence be put on medication . . . [and] it was stated that football could be an important part of his recovery."[48]

The psychological report further suggested that the brutal attack on McEwen was triggered by the breakup of their romantic liaison, which Phillips experienced as a repetition of losing a significant figure. As Osborne interpreted it, "Obviously, Lawrence's family history and his sense of abandonment was intensified by the loss of his girlfriend."[49]

In spite of his violent record, in 1996 Phillips was selected as a first-round draft pick by the St. Louis Rams. He had a stormy relationship with the Rams, and after playing in twenty-five games he was dropped for repeatedly breaking team rules. During nineteen months in St. Louis, he was arrested three times and spent twenty-three days in prison for violating his probation when he was charged with drunk driving. The police reported that he was driving his Mercedes up to eighty miles an hour with a flat tire. He was later signed by the Miami Dolphins, but again encountered difficulties off the field when he was convicted on a battery charge of hitting a woman in a bar. He then went to play in NFL Europe, and after a productive period he was signed by the San Francisco Forty-niners in 1999 but was soon dropped for missing practice.

On May 27, 2000, Lawrence Phillips was again arrested for allegedly beating a girlfriend. *Sports Illustrated* reported that "Phillips is charged with felony counts of false imprisonment, corporal injury to a cohabitant, making a terrorist threat, and conspiring to dissuade a witness."[50]

At this point it seems that Christian Peter and Lawrence Phillips went in opposite directions after their violence toward women at the Univer-

Athletes and Violence toward Women

sity of Nebraska. They both made it to the pros, but whereas Peter appears to have benefited from professional help and has not committed more abuse, Phillips has continued to lose control.

Mark Gastineau was a football hero in the 1980s as a member of the New York Jets. Known for his ferocious pursuit of opposing quarterbacks, in 1984 he established the record for most sacks in a season as part of the infamous "Sack Exchange." (The record was not eclipsed until Michael Strahan surpassed it in 2001.) Gastineau coasted on his celebrity status and seemed to disregard the traditional norms. His propensity for violence off the field first made headlines in 1984, when he and another Jets player became embroiled in a nightclub brawl. After a three-week trial, which his supporters believed was based on overzealous prosecution because of his celebrity, he was convicted but was sentenced only to ninety days of community service. The presiding judge, Alan Marcus, perhaps somewhat in awe of Gastineau's hero status, stated, "I accept the fact that you are not a criminal in the true sense of the word . . . the only people who should be afraid of you are the opposing players in the National Football League." [51] This prediction turned out to be too optimistic. In 1988 his wife, Lisa, accused him of domestic violence, and one year later his girlfriend, actress Brigitte Nielson, made the same allegation.

After he retired from the game, he broke the law on several occasions, and in 1998 he was arrested for assaulting his second wife, Patricia. Court documents reveal that he had repeatedly abused her, and in one altercation he slapped and choked her and threatened to kill her. He pleaded guilty to the charges and was ordered to attend an anger management program. Then in September 2000 Gastineau was sentenced to eighteen months in prison for failing to complete the program.

Sometimes a dethroned hero can belatedly own up to his flawed personality. After serving eleven months of his sentence at Riker's Island, Gastineau appeared repentant and conceded that "the adulterous life I lived, the way I lived my life, not respecting my wife or my marriage, it took its toll." [52] Showing some insight into his powerful need to control and dominate women through physical intimidation, he acknowledged that his abuse of women was triggered by his "wanting my wife, girlfriend, to be submissive to me in the world." [53]

Jeff Benedict has presented a detailed account of the assault record of Marcus Webb, the Boston Celtics basketball rookie phenomenon. [54]

Webb was arrested on March 15, 1993, after a physical assault claim by Quientina Brown, the mother of his young son. This followed a rape complaint filed against him only a week earlier by another woman, Erika Gomes, after Webb terminated their three-month relationship. An investigation by a *Boston Globe* reporter uncovered a long-standing pattern of "irresponsible behavior that a career in professional sports had only exacerbated." [55] The case with Gomes was resolved with a plea bargain in which Webb admitted a lesser crime of indecent assault and battery. It was classified as a felony and he was sentenced to thirty days in jail, but a rape conviction could have led to a twenty-year sentence. Judge Robert Barton underscored the arrogant and entitled attitude common to many elite athletes in describing Marcus Webb as "a very cocky individual through this whole legal proceeding. He couldn't believe it was happening, and it was all a little bit ridiculous to him. . . . Athletes are spoiled as men because they have women throwing themselves all over them. . . . After a while they begin to believe that they personally are something special. They can't believe that anybody would ever say no to them." [56]

In the midst of the combined assault allegations, Webb was dismissed from the Celtics. Like Lawrence Phillips a few years later, Webb pursued his basketball career in France, where he became a star player. It seems that American athletic pariahs are welcomed in Europe.

In considering the background of athletes who abuse women, the themes of either overindulgence or neglect often emerge. As I noted in chapter 2, many athletically gifted players have been pampered since childhood, when their talents were first recognized. They are not accustomed to having anyone say no. On the other end of the spectrum are athletes who were abused or neglected as children. They have learned to interact in violent ways because that is what they have seen and experienced.

The common denominator linking these two backgrounds is that once players are recognized as outstanding athletes and are treated as special by an adoring public, they often acquire an inflated self-image. Under these conditions an athlete may be conditioned to expect that his needs will be met in accordance with his own self-centered viewpoint. Instant gratification and limited tolerance for frustration may become the rule.

An emotionally compromised background in which early loss or

Athletes and Violence toward Women

abandonment is central, especially the loss of maternal figures, can establish a template in which future loss, abandonment, and rejection may precipitate violent behavior. The psychological wounds left by early neglect or abandonment can be deep and may make a person hypersensitive to rejection, abandonment, and loss in future relationships. For example, Lawrence Phillips's violent assault on Kate McEwen might partially be understood from this perspective. It is common for individuals who have been damaged to develop emotional scars and to remain unaware that under adverse conditions they are at risk of becoming abusive toward their partners. These wounds may be easily reactivated in future situations when their personal needs are not being fulfilled. Thus certain athletes cannot tolerate disappointment, either because they are accustomed to being gratified or, conversely, because early neglect has left them vulnerable to being hurt again.

The need to control another person has often been cited as the root of domestic violence. The question is why an athlete needs to dominate women. I believe we should view the need to control as an effort to ward off the repetition of psychological trauma. Dominance can be a way to force others to meet your needs in the way you feel you require. But it can also be an impulsive response to perceived rejection or abandonment. The athlete who feels entitled to have his whims met may overreact if he feels he is not being given his due. It seems likely that much domestic violence by sports heroes is based on this scenario.

Scottie Pippen, the basketball star who played alongside Michael Jordan with the Chicago Bulls championship teams, was charged with domestic battery in May 1995 after a fight with his fiancée, Yvette Deleone. Deleone later dropped the case, but it emerged that Pippen had previously been accused of violence toward women. Two years earlier Deleone told the police her hand and wrist had been fractured when Pippen threw her six feet in the air and out the front door for accidentally breaking his pager. That case was also dismissed when Deleone refused to sign a formal complaint. Accusations against Pippen extended back to 1989 when his former wife, Karen, told the police he had hit and choked her after she asked the court for protection. The combination of athletes with violent tendencies and women who are reluctant to let their complaints play out in the judicial system spawns recurrent violence.

Although we are repeatedly being exposed to stories about athletes and abuse of women, sometimes these incidents, like Scottie Pippen's earlier episodes, are underreported by the media. For example, in 1991 divorce court documents revealed that former heavyweight champion Sugar Ray Leonard had admitted to physically abusing his wife as well as to using cocaine and abusing alcohol over a three-year period. In an astute analysis, Michael Messner and Donald Sabo pointed out how the story was framed in terms of drug abuse rather than domestic violence by the Los Angeles Times, New York Times, and National Sports Daily.[57] Leonard was a poster boy for the "just say no to drugs" campaign. Juanita Leonard, in her divorce proceedings, asserted that Leonard had frequently been violent with her over a two-year period. She claimed that he "[would] throw me around and harass me physically and mentally in front of the children. . . . I was holding my six month old child and [Leonard] spit in my face. He pushed me. He shoved me. . . . I was on my way out the door. He wouldn't let me out. He took a can of kerosene and poured it on the front foyer in our house. He told me he was going to burn the house down . . . that he wasn't going to let me leave the house or anything."[58] According to Messner and Sabo, "Sugar Ray Leonard in his testimony, did not deny any of this. He agreed that he sometimes threatened her and struck her with his fists."[59]

The ensuing newspaper stories played down the piercing information on domestic violence and instead highlighted the alcohol and drug abuse aspect. Contrition and redemption became the focus of follow-up pieces in the newspapers.

Women who claim to have been physically abused by their athlete husbands or boyfriends frequently decide not to press charges. The partners of Darryl Strawberry (Charisse), Scottie Pippen (Yvette), and of course O. J. Simpson (Nicole) represent only a few of the women who turn to the police with claims of domestic violence and then refuse to pursue their cases through the legal system. We can speculate that among the reasons they fail to follow through are the fear of publicity, disruption of their families, economic reversals, and further violence from their abusers.

Vance Johnson has written about his abuse of his first two wives, usually triggered by his philandering. He also revealed how in the years before his recovering as a chronic abuser, his wives often bought into even his blatantly transparent lies because they were eager to believe him. He capitalized on their loving feelings, smooth talked them, and repeatedly got them to overlook his transgressions. He describes how when he was courting his future third wife, he perpetually lied to her about being married. He once went so far as to tell her, "If you ever call my house and a woman answers, don't get pissed, it's just my house-keeper."[60]

In August 1995 Irving Spikes, a Miami Dolphins fullback, was accused by his wife, Stacey, of grabbing her neck, choking her, and throwing her on the floor in the course of an argument. Stacey revealed that she had endured four years of violence that began when she was seven months pregnant and Spikes bloodied her nose after she struck him. She blamed herself for his attack because she had started it. Subsequently, she claimed, there was an ongoing pattern of violence and her football hero husband once put her in the hospital with upper body injuries. She left him for six months but came back when Spikes pledged to treat her better. In a typical battered wife scenario, Stacey rationalized: "Basically I just loved him, so I felt it was worth the chance. So I left my house, I packed all my stuff up and my kids up and moved down here just on the whim of 'I'm going to do better.'"[61] In spite of the renewed violence, Stacey Spikes declined to press charges against her husband, but she did resolve to get a divorce.

An even more chilling history of domestic violence involves Tito Wooten, a star defensive back with the New York Giants. In December 1997 Wooten was accused by his girlfriend, Akina Wilson, of punching her in the face, choking her, and kicking her to the floor. Wilson was two months pregnant, and though she filed a police report, when the case went to court she dropped the charges. Wooten had been arrested five times in the previous six years, including two assault charges. In 1994 he was charged with battery of his wife, Brenda, after police saw him punching her in the face, but she declined to press charges. Two years later he was arrested again for assaulting a girlfriend, but she also refused to testify against him. Tito's mother abandoned him at a very young age, and we might speculate that this predisposed him to aggression toward women.

One month after Wooten's egregious abuse of her, Akina Wilson committed suicide by carbon monoxide poisoning in Wooten's garage. She was twenty-two years old. Friends and family blamed her death on her volatile relationship with Wooten. Joyce Wilson, Akina's mother, bitterly resented the negative impact the relationship was having on her daughter. She said that her efforts to get Akina to break up with

Tito were to no avail: she "was in awe of him because he was a football player."[62] This case further exemplifies how some star athletes can repeatedly engage in domestic violence and avoid the legal consequences when their victims decline to press charges.

One of the most widely publicized cases of sports heroes' domestic violence involved the perennial All-Star quarterback Warren Moon. On July 18, 1995, the Moons' son Jeffrey, a frightened eight-year-old, called 911 with the help of the Spanish-speaking maid and reported that his father was choking his mother. For an eight-year-old to witness possibly life-threatening violence between his parents is always traumatic. Felicia Moon told the police that "Warren has struck her on the head with an open hand and 'choked her to the point of nearly passing out.' "[63] After the episode Warren Moon privately and publicly apologized and pledged to get professional help to save his marriage and family. Moon acknowledged that he had lost control in the heat of a "domestic dispute" and stated, "It scared me. I made a tremendous mistake. I take full responsibility for what happened. . . . I want to make sure this doesn't happen again."[64] At this point Felicia's mission appeared to shift from protecting herself from a violent spouse to protecting her husband's upstanding image. Moon was a former NFL Man of the Year (1989) and had a sterling reputation as a community leader.

Reluctant to disrupt the family life of their four children, Felicia Moon insisted she would not press criminal charges. If the wife doesn't press charges of spouse abuse, the prosecutor's office generally drops the case, because without her cooperation they don't have a strong enough case. Nevertheless, under a new Texas law by which spouses can be compelled to testify, Moon was arrested and the prosecutors elected to pursue misdemeanor charges against him. It is possible that they decided to prosecute Moon because this incident occurred soon after the O. J. Simpson trial, which heightened awareness of domestic violence in this country. The prosecutors appeared to have a strong case against Moon. They presented a tape of the 911 call in which a terrified Jeffrey cried, "My daddy gonna hit my mommy" and a sworn statement from Felicia that Warren had struck her and had choked her nearly into unconsciousness. But when she was forced to testify against her will, Felicia asserted that she had been to blame for the violent episode and that Warren "was merely trying to calm her down when he grabbed her by the throat, causing her to cough."[65]

　　　　　　　　　　　　　　　Athletes and Violence toward Women

The jury quickly acquitted Moon, and several jurors later said they thought the case never should have come to trial and that Moon was vigorously prosecuted because he was a celebrity. Although it was not entered as evidence, there was a record of three earlier reports of Moon's assaulting his wife and a 1987 restraining order against him for allegedly threatening her. Moon denied the prior abuse and protested that the highly publicized 1995 episode "was a misdemeanor case. The way the media covered it was as if I had chopped somebody's head off."[66]

The incident did receive excessive media attention, perhaps because Moon, as a future Hall of Famer, was the most famous active professional football player at that time to be tried for spouse abuse. It is reasonable to say that he was treated unfairly by the media; but Moon's statements about what happened appeared to minimize the incidents. The case also led to an extensive scrutiny of Moon's personal life, which revealed a pattern of extramarital affairs and frequent attraction to strip bars. According to Jeff Benedict, Moon's "time away from the field was increasingly filled with sexual activity."[67] Such a profile is characteristic of some sports heroes, whose inflated egos prompt them to feel they can do as they like.

The year 1995 was difficult for Warren Moon. Just two months before the reported assault on his wife, Michelle Eaves, who had been fired as a Vikings cheerleader, sued the club and Moon for sexual harassment and sexual assault. Moon denied the charges, but Eaves received $150,000 in an out-of-court settlement.

A more well rounded view holds that domestic violence is not simply a matter of a violent perpetrator and an innocent victim—that often both people participate, though not necessarily in equal amounts. In an Oprah Winfrey television program addressing family violence, Oprah concluded that "you teach people how to treat you!" An exchange between a young couple on the show illustrated their understanding that their pattern of family violence was a two-way street. Through extensive counseling sessions this couple acquired insight. The husband recognized that "I used my size to try to intimidate her. That was my way of getting back at her, when she was telling me I was a bad person." This is a plausible description of what may trigger a man to abuse women. What generally receives less attention in these situations, however, is the "dance" between the two participants that can culminate in violence. This view was expressed by the wife, who came to realize that "I provoke the men in my relationships to treat me this way. . . . There was a part of me that felt I deserved to be treated this way. . . . That's how unlovable I really believed I was. . . . Somebody saying to me you're so unlovable, I can hit you. . . . The familiar pattern was a dance that I was doing and what I realized was that I could choose a different dance."[68] A similar point of view is offered by *New York Times Magazine* writer Deborah Sontag, who observes that "domestic violence is construed as one-sided aggression, when often there is a warped dynamic of intimacy in which both the man and the woman are players."[69] This perspective is not meant to imply that spouse abuse is ever justifiable or acceptable; it is simply considering it from an additional angle.

We seldom address this side of the equation when examining domestic violence involving athletes. Because of his vastly greater size and strength, it is generally more compelling to characterize the athlete as a bully who loses it when he cannot tolerate being challenged or not being catered to and who attempts to control his woman through force. In addition, the power imbalance related to his fame and fortune gives the woman less say in the relationship, and she frequently feels she has to endure whatever abuse he dishes out. What is sometimes obscured is her role as a coparticipant; she may provoke an argument that escalates into violence. Her own background may prompt her to feel that she deserves to be mistreated, or in some cases, she may even be repeating familiar patterns in which men are violent toward women. This formulation may also help explain why many women who are abused by celebrity athletes do not press charges.

When Warren and Felicia Moon appeared on *Larry King Live* after Moon's acquittal, King asked whether Warren viewed domestic violence as a two-way street. Moon replied, "There is a statistic out there that 35% of domestic violence out there is caused by the woman or provoked by the woman. Only 2% of those are ever talked about by men."[70]

A high-profile case exemplifying a wife's belief that abuse is central to a marriage is that of Boston Celtics basketball star Robert Parish and his wife, Nancy Saad. Just before a playoff game in 1987, Saad, who was estranged from Parish at the time, went to his hotel room to confront him about neglecting his parental and financial obligations. In an interview later given to *Sports Illustrated*, Saad maintained that Parish, who was entertaining a naked woman in his room, "grabbed her by the throat and threw her out the door and into the hallway, and she remembers being punched and thrown into a wall and spinning and thumping off the door of an adjacent room."[71] Saad was hospitalized for seven days with severe head, neck, and eye injuries, and afterward she suffered periodic headaches and convulsions. This incident occurred one year after the couple had separated because, according to Saad, the seven-foot-one, 230-pound player "threw her down the stairs of their house and kicked her as she stumbled out the front door."[72]

Saad described a pattern of violence in their ten-year relationship and cited other instances, such as when her husband " 'pushed me down a flight of stairs' because she kept badgering him to tell her why he wasn't coming home at night"[73] while she was eight months pregnant and when he literally kicked her out of the car with her infant son in her arms because she criticized the way he was driving.

Nancy Saad belatedly recognized that their backgrounds played a large part in their violent interactions. She noted that Robert had been exposed to many violent exchanges among his relatives while he was growing up, and that she had grown up with a battered mother and a violent father. Accordingly, "because of her upbringing, she thought that being battered was the natural order of things. . . . If a man wasn't aggressive and abusive, he didn't love me."[74] Thus in Parish she found a partner who would repeat the patterns they both knew best. As in many relationships, this repetition of personal history is not a coincidence. The psychological formulation is that couples like Robert Parish and Nancy Saad have an "overdetermined" liaison in which they both repeat relational patterns familiar to them from their childhoods.

After their divorce, Saad came to view Parish as also a victim. She stated that "this [abusive behavior] was something he learned from somebody before him. He never got help."[75] Saad claims that she eventually was able to forgive Parish.

Abuse of Pregnant Women

In one of the most heinous forms of violence toward women, some athletes abuse their pregnant wives or girlfriends. Many such incidents have made headlines in recent years. When a woman is pregnant it is typical for her to become more self-absorbed and to direct her energies inward. During this interlude she is generally less responsive to her partner. When the woman has served as a satellite to her sports-hero husband, this shift in availability can strain the relationship. As she becomes less accommodating to her spouse, heightened conflict may escalate into violence.

In addition to the reports cited above of assaults on pregnant wives or girlfriends by such sports stars as Vance Johnson, Irving Spikes, Tito Wooten, and Robert Parish, a number of other incidents exemplify this problem. In July 1994 Mark Fitzpatrick, the Florida Panthers goalie, was charged with aggravated domestic battery against his eight-months pregnant wife, Susan. She alleged that Mark, then twenty-five, "pushed my head back, kicked me in the back, and just kept yelling for me to get out."[76] She also said she had repeatedly been the target of physical violence, and she filed for divorce shortly after this latest attack. After his arrest Fitzpatrick denied the charge, which was a felony, and accepted placement in a pretrial diversion program.

In September 1995 Dan Wilkinson, a Cincinnati Bengals defensive lineman, was arrested and charged with punching Shawnda Lamarr, his four-months-pregnant girlfriend, in the stomach during an argument. Wilkinson, who was six-feet-four and weighed 315 pounds, pleaded innocent, and in a statement to the media he proclaimed, "I have known Shawnda for a few years, we have spent much time together, and she is very important to me. Our life together is very important to me. I hope and I pray with all my heart we will be able, over time and through hard work, to find the solution to our problems."[77] Wilkinson was eventually convicted on a misdemeanor count, and neither the NFL nor the Bengals meted out any punishment.

Back in 1999 Mustafah (Steve) Muhammad, an Indianapolis Colts rookie defensive back, was charged with domestic battery for allegedly beating his pregnant wife. Nichole Muhammad tragically died one week later after an auto accident that resulted in excessive bleeding from premature labor. Muhammad was later convicted of the misdemeanor battery charge and received a one-year jail sentence. The sentence was suspended, and he was placed on probation along with counseling and community service. Under the newly established NFL personal conduct policy, Muhammad was suspended for two games.

Sexual Assaults on Minors

Sports figures have also occasionally been accused of sexual assaults on minors. Rafael Septien was a star place kicker with the Dallas Cow-

Athletes and Violence toward Women

boys when he was charged with sexually assaulting a ten-year-old girl in 1987. Septien portrayed the incident as a misunderstanding, and the child, who was a friend of his roommate's daughter, offered to drop the charges; but the Texas district attorney pursued the case nonetheless. If convicted, the thirty-three-year-old Septien faced a sentence of up to life imprisonment. Septien eventually pleaded guilty to a reduced charge of indecency with a child, and he was given ten years' deferred probation and fined $2,000. He was released by the Cowboys shortly thereafter, marking the end of his career in the NFL.

In a widely publicized case, Tim Barnett, a wide receiver with the Kansas City Chiefs, was charged with felonious sexual assault of a four-teen-year-old housekeeper in a Milwaukee hotel in June 1994. Barnett had a history of domestic violence, and at the time of these allegations he was free on appeal of a thirty-day jail sentence. He had first been arrested in 1992 after allegedly battering his wife. He pleaded guilty to a reduced charge of disorderly conduct and received a suspended sentence with probation. One year later, before completing his probation, he allegedly beat his wife and threatened her with a gun. Once more he pleaded guilty to a lesser charge; his earlier suspended sentence was revoked, and his jail time was reinstituted. Through legal maneuverings Barnett was able to remain free on appeal, and he played a big part in two playoff victories for the Chiefs.

In the midst of a storm of publicity surrounding the Milwaukee sexual assault on a minor, the Chiefs suddenly released Barnett, ending his career in football. He was later convicted and given a three-year sentence. After serving one year in prison, Barnett was paroled.

Gang Rape

According to the Web site of the American Civil Liberties Union's Sports Hall of Shame Hate Crimes against Women, in August 1995 five football players at Idaho State University were charged with statutory rape of a minor. The fourteen-year-old girl declined to testify, and the players pleaded guilty to a lesser charge of misdemeanor battery. They each got off with a $350 fine. There have been several other allegations of gang rape by athletes. At about the same time as the Idaho State incident, four players on the New Orleans Saints football team were accused of raping a thirty-year-old woman in their preseason training dormitory. The players were not indicted because the prosecutors believed that the woman, who was an exotic dancer, would not be able to present a credible case that the sex was not consensual.

Athletes at several colleges have been accused of gang rapes. In 1989 three football players at the University of Oklahoma—Nigel Clay, Glen Bell, and Bernard Hall—were charged with raping a twenty-year-old woman in a dormitory. More recently four former members of the Notre Dame football team—Donald Dykes, Justin Smith, Lorenzo Crawford, and Abram Elam—were accused of the gang rape of a twenty-year-old student.

In April 1992 the New York Mets baseball franchise was hit with a scandal when three star players—Dwight Gooden, Vince Coleman, and Daryl Boston—were accused of raping a woman in Gooden's apartment in Port St. Lucie, Florida, one year earlier. That the woman waited almost a year to file a complaint and the prospect that the players would claim any sexual relations had been consensual led the prosecutors to decide against pursuing criminal charges.

Gang rape by athletes is sometimes rationalized as group sex. A quasi-sexual situation may get out of hand when athletes respond to peer pressure to demonstrate their sexual prowess. Performing sexually in front of peers may reinforce an athlete's virile image. Promoting macho status with peers may drive gang rape, which in essence is masquerading as group sex, more than a pressing need for sexual satisfaction. The male sports culture perpetuates the notion that women can be sexually exploited. Former University of Oklahoma quarterback Charles Thompson illustrates this point in describing how a teammate paraded naked through a dormitory brandishing condoms and inviting teammates to participate in sex with a girl staying in his room. Thompson reports that fifteen players responded to the offer.[78]

In April 1992 nineteen players on the Cincinnati Bengals were accused of having gang-raped a woman eighteen months earlier in a Seattle hotel suite. Victoria Alexander allegedly had had consensual sex with one of the Bengals players, Lynn James, and subsequently was sexually assaulted by his teammates while they cheered each other on. The woman threatened to go public with allegations of gang rape, and several of the players, wanting to avoid a scandal, contributed $30,000 as a settlement. She later decided to sue the nineteen players she claimed had engaged in the multiple rape, but because she had signed off on the settlement release, her case was denied in court. No criminal charges were brought against the athletes, and several players characterized the incident as group sex with a willing participant who was known to be a sports groupie.

In his autobiography, Vance Johnson describes numerous situations in which athletes have sex in front of their teammates in an atmosphere of camaraderie, nonchalantly and apparently unselfconsciously. According to Robert Lipsyte, some experts have questioned whether this activity may also reflect homosexual leanings and represent an indirect homosexual connection among athletes.[79]

Abuse of Women by Other Sports Heroes

Assaults on women extend beyond the major sports leagues. The spectrum includes athletes from noncontact sports such as golf and motor racing to boxers at the other end.

Professional golf star John Daly was arrested in January 1993 on charges of assault. His wife, Bettye, claimed the twenty-six-year-old Daly had "just lost it" at a party at their home when she asked a guest to restrain his girlfriend, who was "hitting on John." Daly allegedly responded by pulling his wife's hair and throwing her against a wall. He also trashed the house, smashing a television set and punching holes in a basement wall. Bettye Daly did not press charges, and Daly acknowledged that the incident was triggered by alcohol. The 1991 PGA champion, who had already had two alcohol-related hospitalizations, then entered an alcohol rehabilitation program, where he stayed for one month before returning to the next PGA Tour.

Motor racing hero Al Unser Jr., a two-time winner of the Indianapolis 500, was arrested in July 2002 for allegedly assaulting his girlfriend after the couple had spent several hours at a strip club. The misdemeanor charges were dropped by the Indianapolis prosecutor after the forty-year-old Unser agreed to enter an alcoholism treatment center. In a previous incident Unser's ex-wife sought a restraining order after claiming he had physically abused her while drinking.

Both Daly and Unser blame their violent tendencies on alcohol. Some researchers maintain that this excuse is too easy—a way of disclaiming responsibility for one's actions. Authors Mike Messner and Donald Sabo point out that "the drunken bum theory of wife abuse is largely a myth: only about one out of four instances of wife abuse involves alcohol."[80]

Coaches and Managers as Abusers

Sometimes a team's coach or manager is violent toward women. Since coaches are authority figures who set a path for players to follow, such episodes potentially have a widespread impact on the players' moral values. Two such cases are the assault complaint filed in 1994 by the estranged wife of Dan McCarney, then an assistant football coach at the University of Wisconsin, and the battery charge against Bobby Cox, the manager of the Atlanta Braves. According to the ACLU Sports Hall of Shame Hate Crimes against Women, McCarney's wife alleged that she had been physically abused by her husband twenty to thirty times during their eight-year marriage. Yet in spite of these allegations McCarney was named Iowa State's head coach in November 1994.

Bobby Cox's wife, Pamela, called the police in May 1995 to report that her husband had hit her. After thinking things over, and possibly to protect her husband's career and avoid disrupting a long marriage, Pamela retracted her complaint the following day. Under Georgia law, however, as in many states, the police are now authorized to make an arrest when they feel it is warranted without the cooperation of the spouse. After the couple went for counseling the battery charge was dismissed provided that Pamela enroll in a battered women's program and that Bobby continue violence counseling and undergo an alcohol evaluation. As in many similar cases, including that of Warren and Felicia Moon, the Coxes played down the violence and preferred to call the episode simply a "domestic dispute." No legal sanctions were rendered, and Cox continued as manager of the Braves with tremendous success.

Boxers as Abusers of Women

Boxing, the most violent of sports, has had its share of champions who have been charged with abusing woman.

In 1992 Trevor Berbick, a former world heavyweight champion who lost his title to Mike Tyson, was convicted of rape. The victim was the family's twenty-six-year-old baby-sitter. Berbick, whom the court ordered to be assessed by psychiatrists to determine his mental competence, accused his wife and attorney of conspiring against him. He was ultimately sentenced to four years in prison. Berbick was paroled after fifteen months, but in 1997, after violating parole, he was deported to Canada, where he had previously lived. He later was found to have reentered the United States illegally, and this time he was deported to his native Jamaica.

Mike Tyson, who succeeded Berbick as the kingpin in the world of boxing, is in a league of his own when it comes to accusations of abusing women. In describing his sadistic approach, Tyson confessed, "I like to hurt women when I make love. I like to hear them scream with pain, to see them bleed. It gives me pleasure."[81] In this attitude women are seen as receptacles for aggression and then discarded.

As a child Tyson saw his mother repeatedly abused by boyfriends. As a twelve-year-old he was arrested for purse snatching and sent to the Tryon School for Boys. Boxing trainer Cus D'Amato rescued him from an environment of violent street crime and groomed him for competition in the ring. In dethroning Berbick in 1986 at age nineteen, he became the youngest heavyweight champion in history. As a famous athlete, Tyson undoubtedly found many women who felt honored to be sexually exploited by him. In February 1988 he married actress Robin Givens, and eight months later she filed for divorce. In a nationally televised interview with Tyson at her side, Givens claimed that he was manic-depressive and that their marriage was "a living hell." Givens also claimed Tyson had battered her during their brief marriage.

Among numerous accusations of sexual assault by Tyson were a 1986 incident in which he allegedly asked a salesclerk for sex and turned violent when she rejected his overtures and two lawsuits in 1988 in which women alleged that he had grabbed them at a New York nightclub. While Tyson seemed to be growing more and more out of control in his behavior toward women, his aggression was also productively channeled within boxing. Between 1986 and 1990 he successfully defended his heavyweight crown seven times, mostly by knockout, until Buster Douglas defeated him in February 1990.

In February 1992 Tyson was forced to deal with the consequences of his sexually predatory behavior when he was convicted of rape and criminal deviate conduct in an assault on Desiree Washington in an Indianapolis hotel room.

Washington was an eighteen-year-old Miss Black America contestant when Tyson pursued her in July 1991. She somewhat naively went with him to his hotel room to pick up some things he needed before taking her to a nightclub. Once she was in his room, Washington claims that Tyson brutally raped her, and she pressed charges. It was reported that shortly before the trial began Tyson's representatives offered her $1 million to drop her charges. Washington declined, and a sympathetic jury convicted Tyson. He was sentenced to six years in an Indiana prison and served three years before being released on probation.

After the highly publicized trial, Tyson engaged Alan Dershowitz, of O. J. Simpson's team of attorneys, to conduct his appeal. In an attempt to persuade the court that Desiree Washington shared the responsibility for what happened in Tyson's hotel room, Dershowitz portrayed her as behaving like a sports groupie: "In some respects, she should have known that when you go to the room of an athlete at three o'clock in the morning, who is used to groupies, you better make it very, very clear that you are not a groupie. And she didn't make that clear."[82] In spite of Dershowitz's skillful efforts to discredit Washington, the Indiana Court of Appeals upheld the rape conviction.

Washington also pursued a civil suit against Tyson, which was ultimately settled out of court.

Bizarre Cases

Riddick Bowe is another former heavyweight boxing champion who has assaulted his wife. Bowe became champion in November 1992 by defeating Evander Holyfield. By the time he retired in 1997, he had compiled an amazing record of forty victories, one loss, and one draw. His problems with domestic violence were publicized in 1997 when his wife, Judy, filed for divorce. She claimed that Bowe punched her in the face and back: "He knocked me out in front of my three year old. . . . I was out cold for several minutes. It never fazed Riddick. He thought nothing of it."[83] Determined to free herself from her husband's abuse, Judy Bowe mustered her courage and took their five children to a small town in North Carolina.

Several months later Bowe kidnapped Judy Bowe and their children and drove with them two hundred miles into Virginia, at which point she was able to call for help. Judy Bowe recalls how traumatized she was during the episode, in which he threatened her with a knife: "I was in fear for my life the whole time."[84] Bowe was charged with interstate domestic violence, and after a brief stay in a psychiatric facility, he pleaded guilty. Riddick Bowe's defense lawyers and doctors argued that he had acted misguidedly as a result of brain damage from boxing, and Judge Graham Mullen compassionately sentenced him to thirty days in jail and four years' probation. The prosecutors appealed such a lenient sentence, and in July 2001 a federal appeals court upheld their appeal and ruled that Judge Mullen must resentence Bowe. Mullen complied by imposing a prison sentence of eighteen to twenty-four months, but he reduced the time by the eighteen months that Bowe had spent on probation, thus avoiding time in jail. The prosecution mounted a second appeal, and this time the court ordered Judge Mullen to resentence Bowe to serve eighteen to twenty-four months behind bars in a federal prison. In January 2003 Mullen implemented the court order.

On February 8, 2001, while the case was still under appeal, Bowe was again accused of domestic violence after allegedly dragging his wife across the floor, cutting her knees and elbows. He was arrested and charged with third-degree assault and a violation of his probation. Two years later, on March 10, 2003, just a few days before he was to begin the prison sentence imposed by Judge Mullen, Bowe was arrested again on charges of domestic violence toward his second wife.

Bowe's story is especially sad because he was dedicated to his family, using his $80 million in purses to support many relatives and even to buy them fancy homes. Riddick Bowe, who was twelfth out of thirteen children in an impoverished Brooklyn family, maintained a close attachment with his mother, who was a single parent. He claims to have had contact with his father only a handful of times during his childhood. Bowe had also experienced the tragic losses of a sister who was murdered and a brother who died of AIDS.

The story of Lewis Billups has more sinister overtones. Billups was a star defensive player in the NFL. His career, which ended in 1992, spanned seven seasons, mostly with the Cincinnati Bengals. Billups had been accused of sexual assault several times while he was an active player, including initiating the 1990 gang rape of Victoria Alexander in a Seattle hotel suite, but he had never been prosecuted. After he retired, his propensity for violence toward women accelerated dramatically. As chronicled by Benedict and Yaeger in their exposé about the criminal activities of NFL players, "In the eighteen month period following his retirement and leading up to his death, Billups was reported to authorities thirteen times for assaulting women, convicted once for raping a woman in Florida, and imprisoned by Federal authorities in Georgia for stalking another woman."[85]

Billups's assaults cannot be considered merely impulsive acts by a sexually addicted athlete. The malevolence of his predatory behavior toward women is best exemplified by his calculated plan in the Florida rape case. In this episode Billups, along with a friend, allegedly drugged and then raped a woman, videotaped the sexual encounter, and later demanded $20,000 from the victim to keep them from showing the videotape to her prominent husband. Apparently this had been an on-going method for Billups. When the charges were made public, six other Florida women reported similar experiences with Billups. A plea bargain was reached in this case when the victim declined to testify.

In an unrelated case, Billups was imprisoned for one year for making threatening calls to another woman across state lines. On April 9, 1994, six days after his release from jail, Lewis Billups was killed when his car crashed into a metal barrier on a Florida highway. The police estimated he could have been driving as fast as 140 miles an hour.

On February 27, 1998, Dave Meggett, the NFL's leading career punt returner, was involved in a strange sexual imbroglio in a Toronto hotel room. Meggett, who was employed by the New England Patriots at the time, and Steven Brannon, another former Patriots football player, had arranged a sexual liaison with a prostitute who was an acquaintance of Brannon's. The athletes allegedly joined in having group sex, but according to the woman's complaint, things went wrong when their condoms broke and she demanded they discontinue sexual intercourse with her. She maintained that Meggett beat her and forced her to return the money she had been paid. Meggett and Brannon were charged with sexual assault and robbery, but the charges were dismissed when a jury failed to reach a unanimous verdict. The Patriots dropped Meggett after this incident. He was then signed by the New York Jets in December 1998, after claiming he had been set up in the Toronto affair.

Three years later Meggett was again arrested and charged with criminal sexual conduct in Charleston, South Carolina. According to the police, he forced a woman he had met in a bar into his Porsche and compelled her to have sex. Under state law he could not be charged with rape because the woman was drunk.

A different kind of bizarre incident involved San Diego Padres outfielder Al Martin. On March, 20, 2000, during spring training, Martin and Shawn Haggerty-Martin, who claimed to be his second wife, engaged in a prolonged confrontation that ultimately became violent. The couple exchanged punches, resulting in minor injuries, and the

Athletes and Violence toward Women

police interceded and arrested them both on domestic assault charges. According to Haggerty-Martin, in the midst of their fight her husband threatened her: "If you cheat on me, lie to me, betray me, I will O. J. your ass so quick. I will torture you. I will tie you up and cut you and pour alcohol on you."[86]

What began as a routine domestic altercation turned into a case of bigamy when Shawn charged that Al Martin was already married to another woman, Cathy Martin. Martin emphatically denied the charges. He acknowledged that although he had participated in a Las Vegas wedding ceremony with Shawn in 1998, "he did not think it was real"—he thought it was not legally binding.[87]

Women's Violence toward Male Athletes

When domestic violence involving athletes is reciprocal, the star player is sometimes the victim. In 2002 two athletes were stabbed by a wife or girlfriend. Former Major League outfielder Jeff Stone suffered multiple stab wounds to his upper body, allegedly in a fight with his wife at their home. Stone was hospitalized, and Linda Stone was charged with first-degree assault.

Several months later twenty-year-old Anthony Davis, the University of Wisconsin's star running back, who led the Big Ten in rushing yardage in the 2001 season, was stabbed in the left thigh during a fight with his girlfriend. The knife came perilously close to a major artery. His girlfriend was charged with second-degree recklessly endangering safety.

A lethal encounter occurred on August 28, 2000, when Fred Lane, a running back with the Indianapolis Colts, was shot and killed, allegedly by his estranged wife Deidra. The police report said the twenty-four-year-old Lane was shot in the head and chest as he entered the couple's home. According to the prosecutors, Deidra Lane committed the premeditated shotgun murder in order to collect a $5 million insurance policy on her husband.

Earlier stars who reportedly were wounded during domestic disputes include professional football great Irving Fryar and baseball hero Jim Wynn.

On January 8, 1986, before a Conference Championship Game, Irving Fryar, a New England Patriots wide receiver, claimed to have severed a tendon in his right pinky in a "kitchen accident." The press later reported that the injury was the result of a violent encounter with his wife Jacqueline, who was four months pregnant. The *Boston Globe* said the couple had argued in a local restaurant and its parking lot, and that when Fryar pushed his pregnant wife down she attacked him with a knife. The twenty-three-year-old player, who was the league's leading punt returner in the regular season, adamantly denied the report.

Fryar recovered in time to play in the Patriots' Super Bowl game, and he scored their only touchdown in a crushing 46–10 loss to the Chicago Bears. His troubles mounted later in the year when he was investigated for allegedly betting on one or more NFL games. Fryar later acknowledged his destructive behavior and may have sought professional help. His best NFL years followed his turnaround, and he even became an ordained minister.

In December 1970 Jim Wynn, a Houston Astros outfielder, was reportedly stabbed by his wife during a domestic imbroglio and needed abdominal surgery to repair his wound. The twenty-eight-year-old Wynn, who had pointed an unloaded shotgun during their argument, declined to press charges against his wife and blamed himself for the incident.

Recent Allegations of Violence toward Women

Educational efforts and the beginning trend toward policies to deter assaults on women have had a meaningful effect on sports. There appears to be a significant drop in incidents compared with the barrage in the middle to late 1990s. Nevertheless, some athletes still have a long way to go toward facing this problem.

Mark Chmura, a Green Bay Packers All-Pro tight end, was acquitted on February 6, 2001, of third-degree sexual assault and enticement of a minor. The charges stemmed from the previous spring, when he was accused of raping a seventeen-year-old at a high school after-prom party. The alleged victim, who had previously been a baby-sitter for the Chmuras, claimed the attack occurred after a romp in a hot tub. At the very least, the thirty-one-year-old football star, whose public persona was that of a straight arrow and who had declined to visit the White House with his teammates after their Super Bowl victory in 1997 because of President Bill Clinton's "immoral behavior," may have used poor judgment in attending a high school party.

A different kind of case involving a professional football player took place in July 2002 when Derrick Rodgers, a Miami Dolphins linebacker, was charged with spouse assault. Rodgers allegedly punched and kicked his wife and assaulted her male companion, apparently because he believed they were having an affair.

In professional basketball, Glenn Robinson, a star with the Milwaukee Bucks, was charged in July 2002 with assault, domestic battery, and illegal possession of a firearm in an incident with his former fiancée. A short time later, on September 30, 2002, Kurt Thomas, the New York Knicks center, was arrested for domestic violence and ordered to stay away from his wife. According to Amber Thomas, who had recently filed for divorce, he impulsively attacked her because she could not account for his missing laptop computer. Thomas's angry outbursts during N BA games, in which he has been ejected, fined, and suspended, have earned him a reputation as a hothead.

Also in September 2002, former New York Knicks forward Sly Williams was sentenced to five years in prison for kidnapping and sexual assault. Prosecutors charged that a year earlier he had held a woman captive for nearly twenty-four hours while he raped her and threatened her with a knife. Williams allegedly raped the same woman again four months later.

Major League Baseball has also had its share of recent domestic violence cases. In August 1999, while pitching for the Colorado Rockies, Pedro Astacio was accused of assaulting his estranged wife. Astacio initially pleaded guilty to third-degree assault, but when he learned that such a conviction could lead to his being deported to his native Dominican Republic, he changed his plea to not guilty. In a deal with prosecutors, he later pleaded to a reduced charge of misdemeanor domestic violence and avoided deportation.

Bobby Chouinard, a pitcher with the Arizona Diamondbacks, was charged with spousal assault in December 1999. His wife claimed that he hit her during an argument and also terrorized her by holding a loaded gun to her head. Chouinard pleaded guilty to aggravated assault and was given a one-year sentence that was tailored so he could serve three months in prison in each of the next four years during the off-season, which would allow him to continue his baseball career. Soon afterward he was released by the Diamondbacks and signed on with the Colorado Rockies.

Armando Benitez, the ace relief pitcher for the New York Mets, was twice accused of domestic violence in early 2001. In both cases the charges were dismissed for insufficient evidence. In other cases, Baltimore Orioles star pitcher Scott Erickson was accused of assaulting his girlfriend in July 2002 and Kirby Puckett, a Minnesota Twins Hall of Famer, was charged with criminal sexual misconduct for groping a woman in a restaurant in September 2002.

Possible Solutions

Violent behavior toward women among athletes at both the college and professional levels is a significant problem. Dave Meggyesy, a former professional football linebacker who subsequently worked with the NFL Players' Association, points out the early sense of specialness and entitlement many athletes experience as one cause of their abuse of women: "If a person at a fairly young age is identified as special, as many athletes are, and there are no consequences of living outside the rule structure, then it's fairly predictable there will be problems."[88]

When an athlete is accused of assaulting women, the sports star typically downplays its seriousness. Sportswriter Gary Shelton summarizes the predictable cover-ups that athletes offer, such as "It's a private matter," "It's just miscommunication," "It's a family situation," or "Things have been blown out of proportion."[89] Frequently the story is indeed blown out of proportion by zealous sports columnists, but there is usually at least some truth to the accusation, and it is a cop-out to soft-pedal the serious nature of these incidents.

The four major sports leagues long ago instituted policies to discipline players for using illegal drugs and gambling, but only recently have they begun to consider similar sanctions for violence toward women. The message to athletes has been, "If you are self-destructive (using drugs or gambling), you will be punished; but if you are destructive toward others, it will be overlooked." The time is overdue for the sports establishment to levy penalties for domestic violence. As Jeff Benedict has pointed out, both the NCAA and the professional sports leagues impose sanctions for gambling, illegal drugs, and using steroids, and these standards need to be expanded to include violent crimes against women.

Historically, disciplinary action has rested with each league's commissioner, under the broad "detrimental to the integrity of the game" clause in the players' contracts. In practice, however, commissioners

Athletes and Violence toward Women

have limited their power to fine, suspend, or expel players primarily to gambling or illegal use of drugs. Various players have been sanctioned under this arbitrary power of a commissioner. The eight Chicago White Sox baseball players were banned for life by Kenesaw Mountain Landis for fixing the 1919 World Series even though they were acquitted in a court of law. Leo Durocher was suspended by Happy Chandler for "conduct detrimental to baseball." Dennis McLain was suspended by Bowie Kuhn for bookmaking. Pete Rose was banned for life by Bart Giamatti for betting on baseball. Steve Howe was suspended six times for illegal drug use. In professional basketball Jack Molinas was banned for life by Maurice Podoloff for gambling, and Micheal Ray Richardson was given a lifetime ban by David Stern for three drug violations. In professional football, Frank Filchock and Merle Hapes were suspended by Bert Bell for failing to report a bribe offer. Lance Rentzel was suspended by Pete Rozelle for drug possession after two prior convictions for indecent exposure, and Rozelle also suspended Art Schlichter for gambling. To the best of my knowledge, the only case in which a player was sanctioned in connection with criminal violence toward women occurred in 1990, at the discretion of Paul Tagliabue, when Philadelphia Eagles lineman Kevin Allen was denied reentry to the NFL after serving a thirty-three-month prison term for rape.

In 1998 in drafting a collective bargaining agreement with the players, the NFL took the lead in establishing a policy in which all criminal convictions will be treated in accordance with the league's drug policy. The provision mandates suspension for a conviction or guilty plea for violent crimes. This personal conduct policy, as it has come to be called, has led to several disciplinary actions for violent crimes against women.

Among those players sanctioned is Mario Bates, who pleaded guilty to misdemeanor charges of slapping his girlfriend in the face three times. He was fined $2,000, sentenced to two years' probation, and ordered to attend a domestic nonviolence program. Under the league's new policy, Bates was suspended for one game in 2000. Denard Walker of the Tennessee Titans was suspended for two games in 2000 after charges that he assaulted his girlfriend, who was the mother of his nineteen-month-old son. He was placed on probation after he pleaded guilty in response to Rhonda Chesser's claim that he threatened her, pushed her, and tried to strangle her.

In 2001 Victor Riley of the Kansas City Chiefs was accused of ramming his car into another vehicle containing his wife and infant daughter. He was charged with aggravated assault and child endangerment. As an alternative to prison, Riley entered a diversion program to learn to deal with his anger, and in accordance with the league's policy, he was given a one-game suspension.

Leon Searcy of the Baltimore Ravens also received a one-game suspension in 2001 for a misdemeanor domestic violence arrest and entered a pretrial diversion program.

By imposing these punishments, the NFL is sending a message about the unacceptability of off-field misconduct such as domestic violence. According to a study by the *Harvard Law Review*, the aim of this type of nontolerance policy would be to emphasize that players must control themselves and take responsibility for their actions.[90] The other major sports leagues have yet to develop the equivalent of the NFL's personal conduct policy.

In recent years there has been a surge of efforts to educate athletes about the problem of violence toward women. For example, at the University of Oklahoma, which has had its share of reported incidents, athletes must attend a seminar on date rape. Other universities too are increasingly requiring athletes to attend behavior workshops. Another forward step occurred in 1997 when a coalition of 216 schools agreed to establish a standard of conduct toward women in which any athlete convicted of a violent crime against women would face a one-year suspension. A second conviction would result in permanent expulsion from the team. This is a move in the right direction, but it unfortunately doesn't apply to the many situations in which abusers avoid conviction because their victims back away from pressing charges.

Kathy Redmond, who allegedly was twice raped by football player Christian Peter while attending the University of Nebraska, heads an organization aimed at curtailing athletes' violent behavior toward women. Redmond calls for the fans to voice their outrage directly to the teams or schools involved. She implores readers, "If a college athlete commits a crime, call the college president and ask him to revoke the athlete's scholarship. . . . [P]lease remember that a single public outcry can and has caused a team to get rid of a player with a criminal past."[91] These protests help draw attention to the unacceptability of athletes' abusive behavior toward women.

All the major sports leagues should implement a policy that disciplines abusers of women. Penalties must extend beyond fines to include suspension and expulsion, depending on the crime. Sportswriter Mike Freeman has proposed a plan for professional sports leagues. In Freeman's proposal, "an initial conviction for violence against a woman, domestic or otherwise, or a plea bargain involving such a crime, would result in a year-long suspension without pay. Seems excessive? Consider that a first-time steroid abuser in the NFL is suspended for four games. A second conviction or guilty plea for domestic violence would result in a lifetime ban from the sport."[92] Such a plan, which would need to be part of each league's collective bargaining agreement, would also contain an appeal clause.

There may be built-in resistance to professional teams' endorsing such a program, since a player's suspension or banishment may hurt the success of the club. But one could reasonably argue that a policy that places disciplinary action for violence against women on a par with drug or gambling offenses would be in the best interest of the leagues by presenting a positive image of the game.

8. Athletes and Murder

The Americans are certainly hero worshipers and
always take their heroes from the criminal classes.

Oscar Wilde

The ultimate fall from the pedestal of fame occurs when a high-profile athlete is involved in a murder case. In addition to developing an attitude of entitlement and lack of accountability, many athletes come from a socioeconomic background in which they have seen violence as a way of resolving conflict. It has been estimated that 65 percent of all NFL players have been exposed to domestic violence during their formative years.[1] This approach to conflict stays inside them regardless of how elevated they become as sports heroes.

These background factors may account to some extent for cases of extreme violence, including murder. Football star Rae Carruth was convicted of plotting the murder of his pregnant girlfriend. Baltimore Ravens hero Ray Lewis was tried for the murder of two men after a Super Bowl celebration. St. Louis Rams defensive star Darryl Henley was convicted in a murder-for-hire plot while in prison for drug trafficking. Seattle Seahawks wide receiver Brian Blades was charged with manslaughter in the death of his cousin, Charles Blades. Former New England Patriot Raymond Clayborn was charged with attempting to murder his ex-wife and her boyfriend. Former New Jersey Nets basketball star Jayson Williams was accused of manslaughter in the death of his limousine driver. Baseball players César Cedeño and Julio Machado were convicted of murder. Their stories and others will be examined in this chapter.

Murders of Athletes' Wives and Girlfriends

In its extreme form, domestic violence can escalate to murder. At what point do the factors that motivate domestic violence culminate in murder?

Because so much has been written about the O. J. Simpson murder case, it is not necessary to summarize it here. It is worth emphasizing, however, that in the passionate public reactions that debated Simpson's guilt or innocence, the prosecutor's premise was that "the affable public face of the star athlete hid a controlling spouse, who tried to dominate his wife and who killed her when he failed." [2] In her opening remarks at the trial, prosecutor Marcia Clark proclaimed that "the evidence will show that on June 12th, 1994, after a violent relationship in which the defendant beat her, humiliated her, and controlled her, after he took her youth, her freedom, and her self-respect, just as she tried to break free, Orenthal James Simpson took her very life in what amounted to his final and his ultimate act of control." [3] Prosecutor Christopher Darden added, "She left him. She was no longer in his control. He was obsessed with her. He could not stand to lose her. And so he killed her." [4] The prosecutors also brought in as evidence the 911 tapes that documented a history of domestic violence.

Although O. J. Simpson was acquitted, the prosecution had formulated his alleged actions in terms of the psychological profile of the athlete who has been conditioned to expect others to comply with his needs and wishes and who may sometimes resort to violent solutions to conflict.

In December 1999 Rae Carruth, a twenty-six-year-old wide receiver for the Carolina Panthers, became the first active professional athlete to face a capital murder charge, in the violent death of his pregnant girlfriend, Cherica Adams. Carruth, like many other NFL players, came from a stormy background. His father abandoned the family soon after his birth, and his mother, after remarrying and getting divorced, ultimately raised him and his sister alone in a Sacramento, California, neighborhood that was infested with drugs and crime. Rae was popular in high school and later excelled as a wide receiver at the University of Colorado. In 1997 he was selected as a first-round draft pick by the Carolina Panthers and received a four-year contract worth $3.7 million. At about the time he turned professional, Carruth was hit with a paternity suit and was ordered to pay $3,500 a month in child support.

He was an outstanding player in his rookie season, but he was sidelined by a broken foot in the 1998 season and by a sprained ankle in 1999.

On November 16, during his injury-plagued 1999 season, twenty-one-year-old Cherica Adams, who was pregnant with Carruth's child, was shot while driving her car. Just before the shooting, Carruth and Adams had gone to the movies and afterward agreed to meet at Adams's apartment. They drove separate cars, and Cherica was shot four times when a car pulled up alongside her. Miraculously, she was not killed and was able to call 911 on her cell phone. In that call she allegedly accused Carruth of being involved in the attack. While desperately pleading for help, she told the 911 operator, "He was driving in front of me and stopped in the road and a car pulled up beside me and he blocked the front and never came back."[5]

Their son, Chancellor, was delivered ten weeks early by emergency cesarean section. Tragically, Chancellor had suffered permanent brain damage causing cerebral palsy and was developmentally disabled.

Nine days later Rae Carruth was arrested along with three others and charged with conspiracy to commit first-degree murder, attempted murder, and shooting into an occupied vehicle. Cherica Adams slipped into a coma, and Carruth, who was free on bail, agreed to turn himself in if either Cherica or Chancellor died. When Cherica died one month later and the charges were upgraded to first-degree murder, Carruth panicked and fled; he was found the next day hiding in the trunk of a friend's car in Tennessee.

Carruth was brought to trial, and the prosecution asserted that he had planned the assault and had enlisted his three codefendants, Van Brett Watkins, Michael Eugene Kennedy, and Stanley Drew Abraham, to carry out the attack on Adams. The defense attorney portrayed Carruth as a "warm, caring, humble, self-deprecating personality," but the prosecution argued that he arranged the shooting because Adams wouldn't get an abortion and he didn't want to be shackled with support payments for another child.

At the very least Carruth, who had no criminal record, had used poor judgment in associating with criminals. Watkins, who admitted firing the shots, was reputed to be a drug dealer and career criminal, and Kennedy, who confessed to driving the ambush car and testified that Carruth had hired Watkins to kill Adams, had a history of arrests on weapons charges and for drug dealing. The fourth defendant, Stanley Drew Abraham, was Kennedy's best friend but had no criminal record. As the case proceeded, Watkins, the triggerman, accepted a plea bargain in which he would be spared the death penalty in exchange for testifying against Carruth. Watkins pleaded guilty to second-degree murder, testified that Carruth had paid him to murder Adams, and received a forty-year prison sentence.

On January 20, 2001, Rae Carruth was acquitted of first-degree murder, but he was convicted of conspiracy to commit murder, shooting into an occupied vehicle, and using an instrument with the intent to destroy an unborn child. He was sentenced to a minimum prison term of eighteen years and eleven months. The defense had unconvincingly argued for Carruth's innocence on the grounds that the codefendants were pursuing Carruth after he had refused to finance a large drug deal and that Watkins had impulsively shot Adams when she made an obscene gesture toward him.

In defense of her son, Theodry Carruth appeared on Court TV and 20/20 to protest his innocence and proclaim that the jury had convicted him precipitously with minimal evidence. Carruth's mother argued that he had been excessively punished as a backlash from the O. J. Simpson case.

It is difficult to fathom how a promising athlete with no criminal record could allow himself to plan the murder of a girlfriend. One theory is that Carruth could not tolerate feeling taken advantage of by Adams, particularly while his career was plagued by injury. Codefendant Michael Kennedy noted in his testimony that Carruth had been upset over his teammates' teasing him about Adams: "They were ridiculing him and picking at him because she was a stripper and a gold digger, and she was trying to juice him for money."[6] We might speculate that his ankle injury, which sidelined him and raised doubts about his career, threatened his identity as a star athlete and increased his need to assert control in their relationship. The prospect of child support payments may have led him to take desperate measures.

The Carruth murder case reflects an extreme solution to a common problem. Numerous high-profile athletes (e.g., Steve Garvey, Vance Johnson, Larry Johnson) have been hit with multiple paternity suits resulting in overlapping child support commitments. Star athletes experience the additional responsibility that goes with being sought after by women who see affiliation with a celebrity as a way of elevating their status and self-esteem. Some may be lax about protecting themselves from abuse and about birth control. The athlete, who is in a position of power, needs to set limits and take more responsibility for the consequences. This can be difficult for athletes who have been anointed as special and have come to expect impunity. Unfortunately, the mindset of the celebrated athlete is all too often, "If she wants to get herself pregnant, that's her problem. I'm used to getting my needs met without having to consider hers." As a result, the combination of some women who might welcome getting pregnant by a celebrity athlete and the irresponsibility prevalent among certain professional athletes, creates a situation in which athletes' fathering children out of wedlock has become all too common.

In addition to Rae Carruth, there have been several other cases involving athletes who were charged with murder or attempted murder of a wife or girlfriend. Themes of jealousy, retaliation, and domestic violence escalating to impulsive rage have been central in precipitating these incidents.

In February 2001 Ralph Cherry, a former NFL player with the Washington Redskins and Detroit Lions, was convicted a second time of strangling his estranged wife. The thirty-seven-year-old player was charged with first-degree murder after his wife, Jerri, was found dead at their home in December 1998. Prosecutors maintained that Cherry became violent after learning that his wife had filed for divorce. He was found guilty and sentenced to life imprisonment, but the conviction was overturned when a judge determined that jurors had been discussing the case before court deliberations. As a result, Cherry was given a second trial but was quickly convicted again; this time he was given a thirty-year sentence. A petition to rehear the Cherry's case was denied in 2002.

Former New England Patriots defensive back Raymond Clayborn was arrested for attempted murder in 1992. Clayborn allegedly found his estranged wife, Cynthia, in bed with another man and attacked them. The aggrieved Clayborn supposedly chased the man from the bedroom to the kitchen, where he picked up a knife and threw it at him. At his trial his wife testified that Clayborn also put a knife to her throat and threatened her. A jury cleared Clayborn of attempted murder but convicted him on an assault charge of kicking and punching his wife's boyfriend.

Attempted murder charges have also tainted college football. Jonathan Beauregard, age twenty-two, an offensive lineman for California State University, Northridge, was arrested on August 29, 1994, in the shooting of his former girlfriend and her male companion. Dunyella

Smith was wounded in the hip and Van Thompson was shot in the chest and arm as they sat in a car outside a San Bernadino bar. Both testified that Beauregard was the triggerman. Smith claimed that Beauregard was the father of her child and that he could not accept the breakup of their relationship. But a jury failed to reach a verdict, and though they deadlocked nine to three in favor of conviction, several jurors later said Smith had not been a credible witness. Beauregard was tried again, and another deadlock occurred. This time the jury voted eleven to one in favor of acquittal and another mistrial was declared.

Earlier in 1994 Troy Smith, a former University of Louisville basketball player, was sentenced to five to twenty-five years in prison for the murder of Kelly Dwyer. Smith allegedly pushed Dwyer down during an argument, and the twenty-year-old mother of his infant son died later that day from severe head injuries. Smith, who pleaded guilty to involuntary manslaughter, served only one year of his sentence and was then freed on probation.

Another 1994 homicide centered on Derrick Riley, a basketball player for Fresno State and Pacific College in the mid-1980s. Riley, age twenty-nine, was accused of murder for suffocating his wife, Diana, who was eight and a half months pregnant with their second child, after her body was found floating in a California aqueduct on February 5, 1994. Riley's defense attorney attempted to get the charges against the former player reduced to manslaughter on the grounds that Riley had not intended to kill his wife. That motion was denied, and Riley was convicted of second-degree murder of his wife and unborn child and sentenced to thirty years to life in prison.

Latoyonda Promise Mose, a former San Diego State University track star, was charged with murder in the June 15, 2002, slaying of her live-in boyfriend, Allen Hardy. Promise, as she was most widely known, claimed she had accidentally plunged a kitchen knife into Hardy's chest after he beat her during a fight. The twenty-three-year-old Mose, who was once the top five-hundred-meter high school runner in the United States, maintained they had been arguing over Hardy's claiming to be single. It was determined in court that Hardy had a history of domestic violence, and Mose's defense attorney portrayed her as a battered woman. Mose pleaded guilty to involuntary manslaughter and was given a one-year jail sentence. As far as I can ascertain, this is the only case on record in which a female athlete has been accused of murder.

It is somewhat surprising that there have not been similar incidents in which female athletes respond violently to battering.

Early Cases of Murder by Athletes

Athletes' being involved in murder is not new. In the early years of Major League Baseball at least three players were implicated in murders.

Charles "Pacer" Smith pitched for the Cincinnati Red Stockings during the first two years of the National League's existence in 1876 and 1877. Nearly twenty years later Smith shot and killed his five-year-old daughter and seventeen-year-old sister-in-law and tried to shoot his wife. Smith was hanged on November 28, 1895. This event stands as the only execution on record of a Major League player. According to *Sporting Life* magazine, "the tragedy was the culmination of several years of domestic infidelity, coupled with a career of drunkenness and immorality on the part of Smith."[7]

On January 19, 1900, Marty Bergen, the regular catcher for the Boston Braves at the end of the nineteenth century, killed his wife and two young children with savage blows with an ax. The twenty-nine-year-old player then cut his throat with a razor. It was noted that Bergen had a history of depression. He also had broken a hip in the previous season, threatening to end his career, which may well have exacerbated his depression.

John Clarkson is seldom remembered as an outstanding major leaguer in the 1880s and 1890s, but he compiled some amazing pitching records. In 1885, at a time when pitchers were not coddled and given four days of rest between games, Clarkson won an astonishing fifty-three games while playing for the Chicago Cubs. Equally incredible by today's standards is that he started seventy games, completed sixty-eight, and pitched 623 innings that year. Four years later the rubber-armed Clarkson, then with the Boston Braves, repeated his herculean feat with forty-nine wins, seventy-two starts, sixty-eight completed games, and 620 innings pitched. After retiring in 1894, Clarkson reportedly slashed his wife to death with a razor.[8] He died in 1909 and was posthumously elected to the Hall of Fame in 1963.

Murders by Baseball Players

Hank Thompson was the third black man to play in the Major Leagues. He was signed by the St. Louis Browns in 1947 shortly after Jackie Robinson had broken the color barrier. He did not perform well, and the Browns released him after his first season. The next year, while out of Major League Baseball, Thompson killed an acquaintance who threatened him with a knife in a barroom encounter. Fortunately for Thompson, the murder was ruled a justifiable homicide, and the case was dismissed. Thompson was then picked up by the Giants and was an integral part of their championship teams in 1951 and 1954. After leaving the game he turned to crime and was arrested several times for armed robbery. He was sentenced to ten years in a Texas prison in 1963, and he died of a stroke at age forty-three soon after he was paroled in 1969.

Mike "Pinky" Higgins excelled in a fourteen-year career as third baseman with three American League teams in the 1930s and 1940s. In 1938 he set a long-standing record in getting twelve consecutive base hits. After retiring as a player, he went on to become a manager and then a scout. While working as a scout for the Houston Astros in 1968, Higgins was charged with negligent homicide and driving under the influence of alcohol in connection with an accident in which one man was killed and several others were injured. Higgins pleaded guilty and was sentenced to four years' hard labor in a Louisiana prison. He was paroled on March 20, 1969, after serving only two months, and one day later he died of a heart attack at age fifty-nine. Between his conviction and his sentencing Higgins had suffered two heart attacks, so the stress of this ordeal may have contributed to his untimely death.

César Cedeño was hyped as the next Willie Mays when he reached the majors with the Houston Astros in 1970 at age nineteen, and for the next several years he was a bright star. His setback occurred on December 11, 1973, when the woman he was spending the night with in a motel in his native Santo Domingo was killed. Cedeño was arrested for voluntary manslaughter, but the charges were later reduced to involuntary manslaughter when evidence revealed that the woman had accidentally shot herself in the head while handling the revolver. He was convicted and let off with a fine of only $100. Cedeño returned to the Astros in time for the next spring training, and he continued to play in the big leagues for another thirteen years, but his productivity diminished and the flame of his predicted greatness flickered. After his retirement he was arrested several more times for assault.

Julio Machado, a journeyman relief pitcher with the New York Mets and Milwaukee Brewers, saw his life change in a flash on December

8, 1991, with the death of a twenty-three-year-old woman. Machado, twenty-six, was spending the off season in his native Venezuela when he got into a traffic accident that turned into violence. After a brief dispute with the driver of the other car, Machado pulled out a 9-mm and fired two shots. One killed Edicta Vasquez, an innocent passenger. The ballplayer claimed he thought he was about to be robbed. Machado reached an out-of-court settlement, agreeing to pay the victim's parents $38,000. Nevertheless he was tried for unintentional murder and illegal possession of a handgun; he was convicted in 1996 and sentenced to twelve years in a Venezuelan prison.

Murders by Football Players

Barely two months after the shooting of Rae Carruth's girlfriend, Cherica Adams, the NFL's image was further tarnished when another superstar was charged with murder. Ray Lewis, the Baltimore Ravens All-Pro linebacker, was implicated with two friends in the killing of Jacinth Baker and Richard Lollar in a street brawl. The incident took place outside Cobalt, an Atlanta nightclub, after the Super Bowl on January 30, 2000. When first questioned by the police, Lewis was vague and evasive, causing the deputy chief to conclude that "Ray Lewis has not cooperated at all, other than to provide misleading statements and outright lies."[9] Lewis and his codefendants, Reginald Oakley and Joseph Sweeting, were charged with murder, and if convicted the twenty-four-year-old player faced life in prison or the death penalty.

Lewis was no stranger to charges of violence. In 1994 and 1995, while he was a student athlete at the University of Miami, two women, who reportedly were pregnant with his children, accused him of assaulting them. He was again accused of battering a woman in 1999. These earlier incidents were not so different from many star athletes' violent entanglements, but murder was another story altogether.

The prosecutors alleged that Lewis took part in the fight in which Baker and Lollar were fatally stabbed three times in the heart and chest. They built their case around the statements of Duane Fassett, Lewis's limousine driver, who asserted that he saw Lewis punch someone during the fracas. Although no witness claimed to have seen Lewis wielding a weapon, under Georgia law a person can be convicted of felony murder if he is found to have committed a related crime, such as assault, that led to a victim's death. Lewis's defense attorney contended that the star player was "simply in the wrong place at the wrong time" and that during the fight he was "acting as a peacemaker trying to pull people away." He acknowledged that Lewis had left the scene of the crime and had lied to the police about his relationship with his codefendants, but he asserted that it was for fear his career would be damaged, not because he had stabbed anyone.

During the investigation a security guard, Keven Brown, told authorities he had witnessed the attacks and that Ray Lewis was not involved. At the murder trial Duane Fassett, the limousine driver, backed away from his earlier statements that he had seen Lewis throw a punch and had overheard Oakley and Sweeting admit to the stabbings. As a result the prosecutor's case fell apart, and Lewis pleaded guilty to a misdemeanor charge of obstruction of justice. He was given one year's probation and then testified against Oakley and Sweeting, who nevertheless were acquitted.

After the trial the commissioner fined Lewis $250,000, the largest fine ever levied on an NFL player that was not related to substance abuse. With the case behind him, Lewis went on to have an outstanding season, leading the Baltimore Ravens to a Super Bowl championship, and he was named the NFL's defensive player of the year. Before the January 2001 Super Bowl, Lewis bitterly complained that he had been unfairly targeted in the killings because he was a sports star. He told the media, "Don't be mad at me because I was on center stage. The person you should be mad at was [District Attorney] Paul Howard [and] the mayor of Atlanta, the people who never said one time we're going to find out who killed these two. They said we're going to get Ray Lewis . . . The real truth is that this was never about those two kids dead in the street. This is about Ray Lewis."[10]

Lewis was widely excoriated by the press for portraying himself as the innocent victim of overly zealous political forces. Amid all the hype that characteristically precedes a Super Bowl game, Jay Greenberg, a reporter for the New York Post, concluded, "The game that Ray Lewis says is the only reason he is here has never seemed less worth playing when one of its stars proves to be nothing but trash piled upon the pedestal we absurdly place him upon."[11]

The entire melee outside the Cobalt nightclub took only a few minutes. Two young men were killed, and the perpetrators remain unpunished. The impact of the incident on Ray Lewis and his image may continue to haunt him for many years to come. Although he was exonerated of murder, the case highlights the fragile ground our sports heroes tread.

Another football player who faced charges of attempted murder because he was in the wrong place at the wrong time was Riley Washington, a University of Nebraska wingback. In Lincoln, Nebraska, on August 4, 1995, twenty-two-year-old Jermaine Cole was shot outside a convenience store. Cole, who had been fighting with another Nebraska player, claimed that Washington came up and declared "Your life is gone" as he shot him in the side.

Cole was not seriously injured in the attack, but Washington was arrested and charged with attempted second-degree murder and using a gun to commit a felony. He claimed he was an innocent bystander who fled when he heard gunshots. Riley Washington, who comes from a very poor family, spent thirteen days in jail before friends were able to accumulate $10,000 for his bail. Washington was a key player on a powerful college football team, and his beleaguered coach, Tom Osborne, came to his defense. Osborne announced that he believed Washington was innocent and took the controversial position of reinstating him to the team while he was awaiting trial. At the trial Washington's defense attorneys effectively challenged the credibility of witnesses, and he was found innocent.

A series of self-destructive choices that culminated in a conviction for murder conspiracy truncated the promising career of professional football star Darryl Henley and wrecked his life. Henley was an All-American at UCLA and was drafted by the Los Angeles Rams in 1989, where he became an outstanding cornerback. In 1993, at the prime age of twenty-six, he and four others were accused of operating a nationwide drug network. His downfall began in July 1993 when a former Rams cheerleader, Tracy Donaho, was arrested for carrying twelve kilos of cocaine in a suitcase on a flight to Atlanta. Donaho implicated Henley and claimed he had paid her to carry suitcases of cocaine around the country.

In March 1995 Henley and his codefendants were convicted of drug conspiracy and faced a minimum of ten years in prison. But Henley's problems were only beginning. He sought a new trial on the grounds that one of the jurors had solicited a bribe in exchange for a "not guilty" vote. To make matters worse, another juror purportedly had been biased

Athletes and Murder

to convict Henley because of racial prejudice. But rather than ordering a new trial, Judge Gary Taylor ruled that the evidence against Henley outweighed the juror's racial bias.

Henley was so enraged that while he was in jail awaiting his sentencing he enlisted his younger brother, Eric, and a prison guard to arrange a heroin deal to finance a hit man to murder both Judge Taylor and Tracy Donaho, who had testified against him. Henley's crimes had now escalated from drug trafficking to a murder-for-hire plot. He pleaded guilty to both charges, and in March 11, 1997, he was sentenced to forty-one years in a maximum security prison.

Neither Henley nor the prosecution could present a plausible reason why a star athlete, who seemed to have it all, would make these reckless decisions that led to his precipitous fall. According to Jim Ward, a former Stanford track star who befriended Henley, "The young athletes learn early on that the rules are different for them. Darryl always felt no price would be paid." [12] Thus Ward believes that many athletes become conditioned by our hero-worshiping culture to believe they can act special, entitled, and arrogant. Henley acknowledged how easy it is for young athletes to get caught in "the limousine life [and] . . . the sensuous world of women, booze, drugs and fast talking agents [which] starts in college." [13] He seems deeply repentant for the mistakes he made and seeks to warn the next generation of young athletes about the temptations they will encounter.

Another football star, Brian Blades, a wide receiver for the Seattle Seahawks, was charged with manslaughter while he was an active NFL player. The mishap occurred at Blades's home on July 5, 1995, when a cousin, Charles Blades, was fatally shot as he attempted to intercede in a dispute between Brian and his brother, Bennie Blades, a defensive back for the Detroit Lions. During the course of the evening there had been considerable drinking, and Bennie and Brian began to argue. In the midst of the argument Brian brought out his .38-caliber semiautomatic handgun, and during a struggle the gun fired accidentally, fatally shooting Charles Blades.

Brian Blades initially pleaded no contest to the manslaughter charges, but later he changed his plea to not guilty. In a jury trial he was found guilty and faced up to ten years in jail. However, after the verdict the presiding judge, Susan Lebow, supported a defense motion that Blades had not acted with culpable negligence in his cousin's death and ruled that the prosecutors had not proved that Brian used his gun recklessly or negligently. She determined that the case did not merit being brought to a jury. Judge Lebow's ruling amounted to a directed acquittal for the thirty-year-old player.

Blades returned to the Seahawks, where he continued to sparkle as a professional football player during his eleven-year career. The prosecutors contested Judge Lebow's ruling, but sixteen months after the trial an appeals court upheld his acquittal.

In July 2002 Blades was arrested again on charges of resisting arrest with violence and disorderly intoxication stemming from a barroom brawl. In this case he avoided time in prison by accepting a plea bargain for two years' probation.

Boxer Henry Tillman

A moment of rage may have sparked the violent reaction of boxer Henry Tillman, a former Olympic gold medalist, who was accused of shooting two men outside a nightclub near Los Angeles International Airport on January 10, 1996. Tillman, who won his heavyweight medal in the 1984 Olympic Games, had a confrontation with Lauri Meadows in the club; later, while she was flirting with two men who were sitting in a car, Tillman allegedly knocked her down, then leaned into the car and shot Leon Milton and Kevin Anderson. Milton, who survived chest wounds, contended that the incident was precipitated by an earlier "stare-down" between Tillman and the two victims. The situation's macho overtones quickly led to violence. Tillman supposedly chased the car when Milton sped away and fired more shots. At some point Anderson was shot in the eye, and two days later he had a stroke and died.

Tillman was charged with murder and attempted murder, and the prosecutor portrayed him as an athlete who "thinks he's bigger than life and above the law."[14] According to prosecutor Michael Duarte, "Tillman's arrogance . . . allowed him 'to commit a crime in front of a lot of people, thinking that nobody would say or do a thing.' "[15]

A mistrial was declared when the judge learned that Duarte had not fully disclosed the criminal record of a police informant who was to testify against Tillman. But Tillman was not destined to gain his freedom. In February 2001 a second trial resulted in a conviction, and the thirty-nine-year-old Tillman was sentenced to six years in prison. Because he had been in jail since the shootings in 1996, he was required to serve only one additional year.

In his youth Tillman had been rescued from a California youth home by a boxing coach who admired his talent. As an adult he had faced other criminal charges. At the time of the shooting he was about to begin serving thirty-two months in prison for credit card fraud.

Murders by Basketball Players

A charge of manslaughter was brought against former N BA star Jayson Williams in the shooting of Costas "Gus" Christofi on February 14, 2002. Williams, thirty-four, was acclaimed for his superb rebounding ability when he played for the Nets and the Seventy-sixers in the 1990s. He was forced into retirement in 1999 when he hurt his leg in a collision with a teammate on the court, and he was working as a basketball commentator for N BC at the time of the incident.

Christofi, a limousine driver Williams had hired to transport friends from a charity event back to his New Jersey estate, was shot in the chest and died in the bedroom of Williams's mansion. It appeared to be an accident; Williams was "playfully twirling a shotgun while giving a tour of his mansion when the weapon went off."[16]

One of the factors that made this case unusual was the apparent cover-up efforts. Christofi's death was initially reported as a suicide, but when forensic evidence suggested otherwise, Williams was accused of the killing. A Sports Illustrated article reported that Williams had tampered with evidence by attempting to place Christofi's palm print and fingerprints on the shotgun, and that he also discarded his bloody clothes before meeting the police.

On investigation, the charges against Williams were upgraded from reckless manslaughter to include tampering with evidence, conspiracy to obstruct justice, and witness tampering. The prosecutors claimed the shooting had occurred during a night of heavy drinking, that Williams's blood alcohol limit was above the legal limit for intoxication, that he had reportedly cursed and humiliated Christofi earlier in the evening, that he had positioned the shotgun in the victim's hand to make it look like a suicide, and that he had told the other guests who were present to lie about the circumstances. If convicted on all charges, Williams faced up to fifty-five years in prison.

Jayson Williams had been accused of violent behavior several times.

In 1992 he was charged with smashing a beer mug over a man's head during a barroom brawl. Two years later he was accused of firing a semiautomatic pistol at a truck in the Meadowlands arena parking lot, and in the same year three teenagers filed a lawsuit against Williams and his teammate Derrick Coleman for allegedly beating them up when the youths taunted them after a Nets playoff loss. In his autobiography the basketball star relates his earlier troubles to "a lot of beers and barroom brawls and some scrapes with the law and too many fights and some yelling matches with coaches and a bunch of headlines."[17]

Williams was known for his generosity, but he also seemed to have a darker side that triggered aggressive outbursts. The grandiose self-image typical of many of today's athletes is reflected in his boast, "I'm the king of New Jersey."

After a fifteen-week trial Williams was acquitted of aggravated manslaughter, illegal possession of a gun, and pointing it at Christofi—the most serious of the charges against him. But he was convicted on cover-up charges, and the jury deadlocked on the charge of reckless manslaughter.

The Christofi family filed a wrongful death civil lawsuit, and a settlement was reached in which Williams agreed to pay an undisclosed sum in compensation.

Death from Child Abuse

A particularly chilling murder case centered on Jeremiah Parker, a former New York Giants defensive end. Parker and Touleah Kelly, his live-in girlfriend, were accused of aggravated manslaughter, child endangerment, and child cruelty and neglect in the death of Kelly's four-year-old son. Elijah Kelly died on May 14, 2001, two days after Parker found him motionless on the bedroom floor of the apartment he shared with Touleah. An autopsy indicated that the child died from blunt force injuries to the head sustained over a period of time.

In this horrific case of apparent extreme child abuse, Parker and Kelly each contended that the other was responsible for the prolonged mistreatment that led to Elijah's death. Prosecutors maintained that Parker had tried to hide signs of his abuse by covering marks on the wall made by the electrical cords and belts he used to hit the boy. Court documents indicated that Parker admitted disciplining Elijah by making him "stand shivering in front of a fan."[18] Kelly described to investigators how she had once found the child in a freezer covered with water, a punishment administered by Parker. The authorities did indeed find a child's handprint inside the freezer, according to the court papers. Kelly claimed that Parker had "socked" her son in the head, and that he had also punched her, burned her face with a cigar, and attempted to smother her with a pillow.

Touleah Kelly accepted a plea bargain in January 2003 in which she would plead guilty to manslaughter and child endangerment and receive a seven-year prison sentence. Jeremiah Parker, who played in four games for the Giants in 2000, rejected a similar deal for seven years of jail time, with eligibility for parole in eighteen months. He opted to go to trial and was convicted of endangering the welfare of a child, for which he received a ten-year prison sentence. He was acquitted of the more serious charge of aggravated manslaughter, which could have carried up to thirty years in jail.

Athletes as Murder Victims

There are also a number of incidents on record in which athletes have been murder victims. According to baseball historian Dan Gutman, between 1885 and 1988 thirty-seven Major League players were murdered, including six who were playing ball within a year of their untimely deaths.[19]

Lyman Bostock was the last active Major League Baseball player to be killed. Bostock, who was compared to Pete Rose by his manager, Gene Mauch, was in his fourth year in the majors when he was gunned down on September 23, 1978. After a game in Chicago, the California Angels outfielder visited an uncle in the area. Later that evening Bostock was riding in a car with his uncle and two women who were the uncle's godchildren. The ballplayer was in the back seat with one of the women when her husband pulled up alongside the car, cut them off, and fired a shotgun at the back window. In an enraged husband's attempt to gun down his wife, Bostock, who was on the verge of superstardom, became an innocent murder victim.

The most widely publicized case of attempted murder of a baseball player involved Eddie Waitkus. A nineteen-year-old Chicago woman, Ruth Ann Steinhagen, had become obsessed with the handsome first baseman while he played for the Cubs. Waitkus was then traded to the Philadelphia Phillies, and when the team played in Chicago on June

14, 1949, Steinhagen took a room at the hotel where the players were staying. She sent Waitkus a note inviting him to her room late in the evening, and when he took her up on it she shot him in the chest with a rifle. Although the bullet nearly pierced his heart, Waitkus miraculously recovered and continued his career for another five years. Steinhagen, charged with intent to murder, was diagnosed as psychotic, sent to a mental hospital, and discharged three years later. The obsessive love angle fascinated the public, and the event became a central feature in Bernard Malamud's novel The Natural, which was made into a movie.

Recently, murder has also touched football players. In July 1999 former NFL star Demetrius Du Bose was shot twelve times—five times in the back—by two policemen after he allegedly grabbed one officer's weapon and lunged at them. Du Bose was a captain on the Notre Dame team, where he starred from 1989 to 1992, and then he played for four seasons with the Tampa Bay Buccaneers. The police officers were absolved of any wrongdoing when a federal jury ruled that their actions were justified.

On the college level, Brandon Hall, a University of Minnesota football player, was killed during a violent encounter between a group of players and three men near a Minneapolis bar. The tragedy occurred on September 2, 2002, shortly after Brandon had played in his first college game. He was with a group of teammates when another player told them he had been robbed by three men. When the group chased the robbers, nineteen-year-old Brandon Hall was fatally shot.

I described earlier how Jack Molinas, a former NBA star and the mastermind of the college basketball scandal of 1961, was murdered in what was most likely a gang-related slaying (see chapter 5). An even more bizarre murder mystery involving an NBA star is the recent disappearance of Brian Williams. Williams, who in 1998 changed his name to Bison Dele, had played with five NBA teams during eight seasons, including a stint with the Chicago Bulls and Michael Jordan during their 1997 championship season. In 1999 he walked away from $35 million remaining on his long-term contract with the Detroit Pistons in order to "explore the world." While in the NBA Dele (Williams) was diagnosed with clinical depression and reportedly had made a suicidal gesture by driving an antique car into a telephone pole at a low speed.

In July 2002 Dele and two companions were declared missing and presumed dead after they vanished from his catamaran, which was sailing from Tahiti to Honolulu. His brother Kevin (Miles Dabord), was traveling with the group on Dele's boat, and he was suspected of killing them. According to a *Los Angeles Times* article, Dabord confided to a girlfriend that a struggle on the boat, started by his brother, had led to the death of Dele and the other two passengers. [20]

During the investigation Dabord made a suicide attempt that left him in a coma with severe brain damage. He was not expected to recover, and the facts in this episode will never be known.

Murder of Athletes by Terrorists

The only politically motivated murder of athletes occurred at the 1972 Summer Olympics in Munich, Germany. On September 5 five Arab terrorists climbed a fence into the lightly guarded compound where twenty-six Israeli athletes were staying. The terrorists were joined by three confederates inside the Olympic village, and they attacked the Israeli quarters. Two Israelis were killed, and nine others were taken hostage.

The attackers identified themselves as members of Black September, a Palestinian terrorist group, and demanded that two hundred Arab prisoners in Israel be released. The Israeli government, under Prime Minister Golda Meir, refused to capitulate to these demands, and intense negotiation ensued. After many hours an agreement was reached that the terrorists and the hostages would be taken from the Olympic Village by helicopters to a nearby airport, where a plane would fly them to Cairo.

The German authorities agreed to provide passage out of Germany, but at the same time they concocted a plan to free the hostages. They decided that a rescue operation was imperative because they believed a flight to Egypt would have meant certain death for the Israeli athletes. The hostages, who were blindfolded, bound hand and foot, and roped together, were placed on the helicopters. At this point German sharpshooters attempted to free them. A gunfight ensued, and five terrorists and all nine hostages were killed. News reports said one of the helicopters holding the hostages was blown up by a grenade thrown in by a terrorist, and the other hostages were shot. Three of the terrorists were captured during the shoot-out and were charged with kidnapping and murder.

In response to the savage attack, the Olympic Games were suspended, but they resumed one day later in what many observers felt was an insensitive decision. The incident, the most violent assault ever inflicted on athletes, has come to be known as the Munich Massacre.

In considering these cases of athletes and murder we might ask what underlies these heroes' lapses in judgment. It seems insufficient to categorize all these cases as impulsive acts of violence. We need to consider how privilege and a sense of specialness induce some athletes to believe they can operate outside the law with impunity and to lack appropriate fear of the consequences.

What message is our hero-worshiping culture sending to these athletes?

9. Violence between Athletes

It will do no good to search for villains or heroes or saints
or devils because there were none; there were only victims.

Dalton Trumbo

Athletes are trained to be aggressive on the playing field, and, indeed, an
optimal level of aggression frequently fuels success. Our sports heroes
are generally able to compartmentalize this trait—to turn it off after the
game and reignite it for the next game. For some athletes there may be a
fine line between aggression within the appropriate boundaries of their
sport and violent behavior. Sometimes intense competition sparks intentional or unintentional eruptions toward opposing players or teammates and even between players and their coaches. These eruptions may
cause life-threatening injuries to others and may destroy an athlete's
own career.

Some athletes are quickly dethroned from their pedestals for attacking another player. For example, professional football star Jack Tatum's
image was badly tarnished when he never apologized for the hit that
paralyzed Darryl Stingley. Basketball star Kermit Washington was vilified for decades after "the punch" that severely damaged Rudy Tomjanovich. And Latrell Sprewell's violent response toward his critical
coach, P. J. Carlesimo, created a cadre of taunting fans, clouded his
future offensive heroics, and blighted his stardom.

Baseball

Bench-clearing brawls are commonplace in baseball when a batter is
hit by an errant pitch and charges the mound. Generally there is a lot of
pushing and shoving, but only occasionally are there serious injuries.
Carl Furillo of the Brooklyn Dodgers backed into a batting title in 1953
when his little finger was broken during a melee between the Dodgers
and their archrivals the New York Giants. The incident occurred in early
September, and Furillo, who was leading the league in hitting, was able

to withstand challengers while sitting on the bench for the rest of the season.

The Dodgers and Giants have shared the most intense rivalry in baseball history, and their players engaged in another memorable exchange after they were transplanted to the West Coast. While batting against Sandy Koufax in a crucial game on August 22, 1965, Giants pitcher Juan Marichal suddenly smashed Dodgers catcher John Roseboro over the head with his bat several times. Blood gushed as Roseboro fell, and his teammates tried to attack Marichal. Roseboro had been returning Koufax's pitches by zipping the ball perilously close to Marichal's ear as he stood at the plate, probably to retaliate for Marichal's hitting a Dodgers batter earlier in the game. When Marichal protested almost being pegged by Roseboro, the catcher took off his mask, and Marichal claimed he thought Roseboro planned to hit him with it. Marichal was suspended for eight games by National League president Warren Giles, who characterized his violent act as "unprovoked," "obnoxious," and "repugnant." Fortunately Roseboro's injury was less serious than it seemed at first, and he was sidelined for only three games. He later sued Marichal for $110,000 on assault charges and settled out of court for $7,500. Marichal became an increasingly intimidating pitcher as he went on to amass 243 lifetime victories, and in 1983 he was elected to the Hall of Fame.

One of baseball's all-time bad boys was the tumultuous Billy Martin. During his combative career as player and manager, he got into fistfights with Jimmy Piersall, Clint Courtney, Jim Brewer, Dave Boswell, and Ed Whitson. The most serious incident was the fight with Brewer in August 1960. While pitching for the Cubs, Brewer threw a brushback pitch at Martin, and the feisty Martin responded by throwing his bat toward the pitcher's mound. The players exchanged words, and Martin landed a punch that fractured the orbit of Brewer's right eye. It took three operations to repair the damage. Brewer later filed a lawsuit against Martin, and after a jury trial Martin was held liable for $25,000 in damages.

Like the Roseboro-Marichal episode, some of the worst violence in baseball has taken place around home plate. One infamous incident on July 4, 1932, involved the legendary Yankees Hall of Fame catcher Bill Dickey and Carl Reynolds, a Washington Senators outfielder.

Dickey, who was not known as a fighter, took umbrage when Reyn-

Violence between Athletes

olds barreled into him instead of sliding while scoring on a squeeze play. The infuriated Dickey decked Reynolds with a punch that broke his jaw and put him out of commission for seven weeks. For his aggressive response, Dickey was suspended for thirty days and fined $1,000 in what was at that time one of the stiffest penalties ever assessed on a Major League player.

Another celebrated collision at home plate involved Pete Rose and Cleveland Indians catcher Ray Fosse at the end of the 1970 All-Star Game. Fosse was blocking the plate, trying to keep Rose from scoring the winning run in the twelfth inning of a tie game. Instead of sliding home, which would have been the traditional maneuver as Fosse awaited the relay throw, Rose ran into Fosse and hit the vulnerable catcher with his left shoulder. Fosse accepted it as a clean hit, but it was later determined that he had suffered a separated shoulder, damaging his later productivity as a hitter.

Rose defended himself on the grounds that playing hard was the only way he knew: "I just want to get to that plate as quickly as I can. Besides, nobody told me they changed it to girls' softball between third and home."[1] Rose claimed he learned his fiery approach to the game from his father's coaching, and throughout his career he may have been motivated by a perpetual need to gain his father's approval. Like Ty Cobb, whose long-standing record for most career base hits he eclipsed, Rose seemed to maintain a fierce competitive drive because he believed an idolized father would admire his rough style of play.

It is ironic that in the major sports leagues baseball, which has the least direct body contact, has had the only death caused on the playing field. On August 10, 1920, Ray Chapman, the Cleveland Indians shortstop, was fatally beaned by New York Yankees pitcher Carl Mays. Chapman collapsed at the plate, was helped up by his teammates, then staggered and collapsed again as he was being led off the field. The blow had fractured his skull, and at the hospital he lost consciousness. Emergency surgery was performed on his brain, but the twenty-nine-year-old player died the next morning.

Mays had a reputation for his brush-back pitches, and in fact he had led the league in batsmen hit in a previous season. Many observers thus believed Mays had deliberately thrown at Chapman. Others maintained that Chapman had frozen in the batter's box and was slow to move away from the pitch, which hit his left temple with such a loud crack that spectators thought the ball had hit his bat. Indeed, Mays fielded it as it careened toward him and threw it to first base. Chapman himself, before being rushed to the hospital, tried to defend Mays: "I'm all right. Tell Mays not to worry." [2] Chapman had married earlier in the year, and his wife was pregnant at the time of his death. In a sad postscript, their daughter died at age one, and eight years after Ray's sudden death Kathleen Chapman committed suicide by drinking cleaning fluid.

Whether the beaning was intentional or unintentional, the tragedy and the suspicions surrounding it were undoubtedly stressful for Mays. We might expect that such circumstances might make a professional athlete's career unravel. He could develop a fear of throwing too close to another hitter, or his concentration could suffer because of the accusations against him. Instead, Mays demonstrated amazing resilience. In his next game he pitched a shutout, and in the next season he compiled a 27-9 record. Under severe stress some athletes rise to the occasion and adaptively compartmentalize their feelings, while others allow the stress to interfere with their performance.

In addition to the violence between ballplayers, some baseball players have had highly aggressive encounters with umpires, sportswriters, and fans. John Rocker threatened a reporter because he felt he was misrepresented in a December 1999 *Sports Illustrated* story that portrayed him as an loudmouthed bigot. The uproar that followed the article and Rocker's physical challenge to the writer may have distracted Rocker and contributed to his premature ineffectiveness as a Major League pitcher.

This was not the first incident of its kind. Back in 1964 Bo Belinsky, a flashy pitcher with the California Angels who had made headlines two years earlier by pitching a no-hitter in only his fourth big league game, slugged newspaper reporter Braven Dyer. Belinsky believed he had been mistreated in a piece Dyer wrote and threatened to assault the reporter. Dyer, a former star football player who was now sixty-four, refused to be intimidated by the boisterous Belinsky and went to the player's room for a confrontation. The aging Dyer was no match for the twenty-seven-year-old Belinsky; he required six stitches under his ear and suffered double vision after the pitcher knocked him out. Belinsky, who had been struggling to regain his pitching form, was released by the Angels after this ugly incident.

Billy Martin, who always seemed ready to settle a score with his fists, engaged in a brawl with Reno sportswriter Ray Hagar in 1978. Hagar filed a lawsuit against Martin for assault, and they later settled out of court.

For more than a century players and managers have been combative toward umpires when decisions go against them. It is common for players to be ejected from a game for arguing too vehemently or crossing the line of verbal abuse. Managers are sometimes banished for bumping the umpire or kicking dirt on him during a confrontation. A different kind of umpire abuse occurred toward the end of the 1996 regular season when Roberto Alomar of the Baltimore Orioles became enraged over a controversial call and spit on umpire John Hirschbeck. In spite of his shameful action Alomar was allowed in postseason play, though he was suspended for the first five games of the next season. Umpires throughout the league felt the penalty was too lenient and backed Hirschbeck in demanding that Alomar be banished from the forthcoming playoffs. They also threatened a strike to protest the ruling, but a federal court injunction prevented it. The fans also condemned Alomar's outrageous gesture and subjected him to jeering taunts for years to come.

Babe Ruth, the Sultan of Swat, once managed to abuse both an umpire and a fan in the same game. While playing against the Washington Senators on May 26, 1922, Ruth tried to stretch a single into a double and was called out by the umpire. He was enraged by the call and threw dirt in the umpire's face. Ruth was ejected from the game, and on his way out he charged into the stands to attack a fan who had been heckling him. The Babe was fined, suspended, and stripped of his new appointment as Yankee captain.

In recent years fans have become more and more aggressive in harassing players during a game. Some fans have even run onto the field before being ostentatiously restrained by security guards or tackled by a player. There is little doubt that fan violence is on the rise, and it takes such forms as throwing objects at players and infringing on a player's personal space. In a Dodgers-Cubs game in 2000, Dodgers pitcher Chad Kreuter was sitting in the bullpen when a fan reached out from the stands and snatched Kreuter's cap, appeared to hit him, and ran away. Kreuter, joined by his teammates, jumped into the stands to chase the culprit, and a melee broke out between players and fans.

One of the most notorious incidents of violence between a player and a fan involved the legendary Ty Cobb. Claude Leuker had been heckling the players during a game on May 15, 1912. The abuse escalated, and when Leuker called him a "half-nigger," Cobb, who was reputed to be a racist, ran into the stands and assaulted the fan. Leuker, who had recently lost his left hand and most of his right in an accident, was not trying to provoke a physical confrontation. Nevertheless his insults enraged Cobb, who punched him several times, knocked him down, and repeatedly kicked him. When an observer screamed, "Don't kick him, he has no hands!" Cobb answered, "I don't care if he has no feet."[3]

Hockey

Violence between players is a long-standing tradition in the National Hockey League (NHL). Fighting is admired, and many hockey brawls have led to accidental as well as intentional injuries. Junior skaters are trained to develop the rough-and-tumble side of the game. Players learn early on that rule violations and illegitimate tactics often increase one's value to the team. The culture of professional hockey dictates that very aggressive, and sometimes violent, play is rewarded by coaches and management.

Sociologist Edmund Vaz notes that "a rule violating normative system is a structural part of the larger hockey system. Illegitimate tactics (including various forms of violence) are considered technical skills for achieving team success, and are the standards for the evaluation and recruitment of players."[4] Vaz's study of violence in hockey reveals that being branded a "fighter" does not impede a player's career; on the contrary, it helps it. Penalizing players for illegitimate tactics does not seem to affect the success of a team. As the Vaz study points out, "The data reveals that the highest ranked teams in the National Hockey League are often the most heavily penalized, which means that the system of penalizing individual players does not seriously jeopardize a team's chances of success."[5] Thus violence toward other players, as measured by penalty minutes accumulated, produces winning hockey. Vaz maintains that rule violation is the norm in hockey and is condoned, supported, and reinforced throughout the system. He concludes "[that] the violation of rules is widespread, expected conduct on the ice, and that varying forms of infraction receive moral support throughout the system, i.e., players, officials, and others are favorably disposed towards the conduct."[6] In their defense, NHL authorities maintain that they

Violence between Athletes

have been unfairly accused of condoning and even promoting violence because fights on the ice sell tickets.

It seems likely that in the Canadian hockey system, where most of the future NHL professionals are developed, young players are programmed to become violent on the ice. Gordon Bloom, a sports psychology researcher at McGill University in Montreal, asserts that there is an increase in violent tactics among amateur minor league players as they identify with their professional brethren. Bloom draws on earlier research by Vaz indicating that "the structure of the Canadian hockey system was designed so that players who were unable or unwilling to deal with ongoing violent tactics were progressively weeded out or dropped out . . . and that by the age of 14, hockey players had learned that such qualities as toughness and recklessness were essential to progress through the minor hockey system."[7]

In 1996 Graham James, a Major Junior coach, was convicted of serial sexual assaults on Sheldon Kennedy, a junior player. In the aftermath of the scandal, the Canadian Hockey League launched an investigation into the practices within Major Junior hockey. According to Jeff Mac-Gregor, a writer with *Sports Illustrated*, the investigation was widely criticized as a sham, but it further exposed "the systematized violence of junior hockey and the intractable code of silence surrounding it."[8]

But hockey violence sells tickets, and many fans are known to come to the games hoping they will get to see violent encounters. Researchers Gordon Bloom and Michael Smith have developed what they refer to as "cultural spillover theory," which contends that to the extent that sports violence is condoned within our culture, it sets the stage for players to engage in violence off the field. In a study comparing 601 minor hockey players with a similar sample of nonplayers, these researchers found that "hockey players over the age of 17 who were playing in highly competitive select/competitive leagues were prone to a spillover-of-violence effect."[9]

Several cases of hockey violence have resulted in legal intervention. In a 1969 NHL exhibition game, Ted Green of the Boston Bruins, noted for his aggressive style of play, punched Wayne Maki, a St. Louis Blues player, in the face. Maki retaliated by slashing Green on the head with his stick. The blow leveled Green, who fell and hit his head on the ice. This fight occurred in an era when players did not wear helmets, and either Maki's stick to his head or the impact with the ice fractured Green's skull. It took three operations to save his life. The left side of his body was paralyzed, and it was unlikely he would ever play again. The game was played in Ottawa, and Canadian authorities filed assault charges against both players. In separate cases both athletes were acquitted. Ted Green made a remarkable comeback and helped the Bruins win the 1972 Stanley Cup.

In 1975 Dave Forbes, while skating for the Boston Bruins, became the first professional athlete playing in the United States to be indicted for a crime during play. During a game on January 4, 1975, Forbes high-sticked Detroit Red Wings star Henry Boucha. The blow inflicted an eye injury that needed surgery, and Boucha, who had been Rookie of the Year in the 1972–73 season, was forced to retire from the game. Forbes had also banged Boucha's head into the ice. Criminal charges were filed against Forbes, and his trial ended with a hung jury. Boucha filed a separate lawsuit and was awarded $3.5 million in damages.

Dino Ciccarelli had a less fortunate outcome for his stick-swinging incident in 1988. The Minnesota North Stars winger was enraged about being heavily cross-checked by Luke Richardson in a game against the Toronto Maple Leafs; he smashed Richardson in the neck several times with his stick. Ciccarelli was charged with assault and was convicted after the court ruled that hockey players were not above the law. Under a plea bargain, Ciccarelli spent one day in jail.

During an NHL playoff game in 1993, Dale Hunter of the Washington Capitals was suspended for twenty-one games for viciously blindsiding the New York Islanders' Pierre Turgeon. Turgeon was celebrating after scoring the winning goal when Hunter stalked him and delivered a powerful check that left Turgeon with a separated shoulder and out of the remaining playoff games. For the unprovoked attack Hunter received what was at the time the longest suspension in the league's history.

This infamous record was eclipsed seven years later by Marty McSorley of the Boston Bruins, who was suspended for twenty-three games after severely injuring Donald Brashear of the Vancouver Canucks. The attack occurred on February 21, 2000, with only three seconds left in the game. McSorley swung his stick with both hands and hit Brashear in the right temple. Brashear fell backward, cracked his head on the ice, and was knocked unconscious. He suffered a concussion and memory lapses and was sidelined for several weeks.

McSorley already had a history of on-ice violence and six previous suspensions. Apparently the hit on Brashear was the culmination of a series of rough exchanges between the two players. Early in the game the pair had scuffled, and Brashear got the best of that fight. Later in the first period McSorley tried to initiate another brawl, but Brashear simply skated away. At some point Brashear skated in front of the Bruins bench and "flexed" in front of the opposing team. This perceived taunt appears to have enraged McSorley, who sought to retaliate as time ran out at the end of the game. In view of the severity of Brashear's injury, it seems that McSorley was overreacting to the provocation. In reflecting on the episode one month later, Brashear felt that a harsher punishment was warranted: "He really tried to injure me . . . I could have died. I don't think this guy should be playing in the league anymore."[10] McSorley was put on trial for criminal assault and testified that he had not intended to slash Brashear in the head but was only trying to hit him in the shoulder to initiate another fight. His explanation did not impress the presiding judge, who declared, "Brashear was struck as intended. [McSorley] slashed for the head. A child, swinging as at a tee-ball, would not miss. A housekeeper swinging a carpet-beater would not miss. An NHL player would never, ever miss."[11] McSorley was found guilty of assault with a weapon, and under the law he could have faced up to eighteen months in jail. Instead he was sentenced to eighteen months' probation.

In a March 9, 2004, game Todd Bertuzzi, an All-Star forward with the Vancouver Canucks, sucker punched the Colorado Avalanche's Steve Moore and then drove his head into the ice. Moore was hospitalized with a broken neck, a concussion, and deep facial cuts. The brutal unprovoked assault by the 245-pound Bertuzzi appeared to be in retaliation for an incident a month earlier in which Moore had struck a teammate of Bertuzzi's, sidelining him for three games with a concussion. The NHL suspended Bertuzzi for the rest of the season and the playoffs, and his eligibility for future reinstatement was to be determined by Commissioner Gary Bettman. Bertuzzi made a tearful apology expressing his remorse for "what happened out there," but he fell short of taking full responsibility for his egregious actions.

It seems likely that in his quest for revenge Bertuzzi lost control and went far over the line. In a sport where fighting is condoned, it is amazing that serious attacks do not happen more frequently. The professional hockey culture stimulates such encounters. Will a player have to die before violence is curtailed in the NHL? In that momentary rush of aggression Todd Bertuzzi surely did not intend to kill Steve Moore—but he could have.

It is natural for young players to emulate their major league heroes. Canada's Major Junior system is the primary training ground for future United States NHL players. The system is composed of three leagues, which draft promising prospects as teenagers from the regional or divisional minors. The three leagues are subdivisions of the Canadian Hockey League (CHL), and it is estimated that 65 percent of NHL players emerge from the Major Junior system.

Violent exchanges occur regularly in these games, in line with the tradition of fighting among established professional hockey players as skaters vie to demonstrate their dominance. It is widely believed that their coaches encourage these players to be superaggressive to forge ahead in the system.

One of the most violent episodes took place between two nineteen-year-olds during an April 17, 1998, playoff game of the Ontario Hockey League (one of the three divisions of the CHL). The incident, which received international attention, put the names of previously little known teams on the map of ice hockey. Jesse Boulerice played for the Plymouth Whalers, and Andrew Long played for the Guelph Storm.

Early in the first period of the game Boulerice cross-checked Long and swung his stick into Long's face. It was estimated that the stick, swung with both hands, was traveling at fifty to seventy-five miles an hour when it hit Andrew Long's face. Long suffered convulsions and had injuries to his nose, nasal cavity, and cheekbone. The vicious blow knocked him unconscious, and he also had a concussion, either from the force of the attack or from hitting his head on the ice when he fell. After regaining consciousness, Long was disoriented and agitated for some time, symptoms often associated with head trauma. Sportswriter Jeff MacGregor noted that "had the stick landed a hand's width higher or lower, Andrew might have been killed . . . [and] what is most surprising about the Jesse Boulerice–Andrew Long matter is not that it happened, but that it doesn't happen more often."[12]

In the aftermath, Boulerice was suspended for one year by the Ontario Hockey League, which was an insignificant punishment since he was expected to play the following season in the American Hockey

Violence between Athletes

League (AHL) as the next rung in the ladder on the way to the pros. The AHL levied a token penalty by banning Boulerice for the first month of the next season.

Boulerice, who had had no history of trouble with the law, was charged with "assault to do great bodily harm less than murder," a felony charge that carried a maximum ten-year prison term if he was convicted. He avoided a prison sentence by pleading no contest to the reduced charge of aggravated assault, and he received ninety days' probation. He also made a public apology to Long.

Boulerice resumed his rough style of play and was later signed by the Philadelphia Flyers for the 2001–2 NHL season and the Carolina Hurricanes for 2002–3.

As a result of the violent contact that often occurs in professional hockey games, players are frequently sidelined with concussions. Some players even have multiple concussions over an extended career. Head trauma and its related symptoms are serious, but such consequences are too readily accepted as a part of the game by the NHL and its participants. When Pat La Fontaine, a five-time All-Star, sustained his sixth concussion (caused by a freakish collision with a teammate) in March 1998, it was the fifty-sixth concussion suffered by an active player in that season alone. Among the injured was superstar Eric Lindros, who missed a month after sustaining the second concussion in his career. Brett Lindros, Eric's younger brother, had been forced into early retirement in the 1995 season when he sustained two concussions within eight days. Eric Lindros continued to be a dominant NHL player, but by January 2004 he had sustained his eighth career concussion.

La Fontaine stands out as the model of the gutsy NHL hero who sustained repeated concussions during his fifteen-year career and each time fearlessly came back to the game. La Fontaine had been injury-free during his first 450 NHL games when he received his first concussion from a powerful body check by defenseman James Patrick during an Islanders-Rangers playoff game on April 5, 1990. His fifth concussion came from a ferocious hit from Pittsburgh Penguins defenseman François Leroux in an October 1996 encounter in which he crashed headfirst onto the ice without his helmet. Like many concussion victims, La Fontaine was debilitated with an array of recurrent symptoms including migraine headaches, depression, mood swings, nausea, and dizziness. He reluctantly retired at age thirty-three, after the 1997–98 season, when a neurologist told him that if he continued playing he would be putting himself "beyond minimal risk." After many years of bouncing back, it was getting harder each time. Under the threat of lasting neurological damage, La Fontaine decided to call it quits.

Football

While hockey has a more consistent array of fights that sometimes lead to injuries, there is little question that football is an even more violent sport, and the toll of serious or life-threatening injuries is at times staggering. It has been estimated that each NFL team can expect to have an average of seventeen players sidelined with significant injuries each season.[13] When bodies weighing 250 to 300 pounds or more are crashing into each other during each play of a game, damage is inevitable. Concussions are among the more dangerous consequences. Harry Carson, a former New York Giants star linebacker who has researched the effects of concussions in professional football, has succinctly argued, "People say it's a contact sport. It's not; it's a collision sport."[14] When Mike Webster, the Pittsburgh Steelers Hall of Fame center, died in a coronary care unit at age fifty, the *New York Times* stressed that Webster had suffered some brain damage from numerous concussions during his career.[15]

Quarterbacks are particularly susceptible to concussion. Ron Jaworski claims to have received as many as thirty-five concussions during his seventeen-year NFL career. The careers of Troy Aikman, Steve Young, and Chris Miller were also prematurely ended by postconcussion syndrome.

One of the more memorable images from the early years of television coverage of football is the blindsiding of Giants halfback Frank Gifford by Philadelphia Eagles defenseman Chuck Bednarik in a crucial game on November 20, 1960. Gifford was hit as he ran downfield reaching for a long pass, and he was knocked out with a concussion that kept him out of football for more than a year.

After a player suffers a concussion he often wants to get back in the lineup as quickly as possible. In doing so he is putting himself at risk for what is now recognized as postconcussion syndrome, symptoms that occur when there is a second concussion before the first one has fully healed. Green Bay Packers tackle Tony Mandarich missed the entire 1992 season because of postconcussion syndrome. Another casualty

Violence between Athletes

was running back Merril Hoge, who was forced into retirement in 1994 after suffering four concussions within five weeks while playing for the Chicago Bears. According to Jeffrey Margolis, Hoge's postconcussion syndrome left him with periodic painful headaches, memory loss, and occasional difficulty in recognizing his own family.[16] Both Merril Hoge and Frank Gifford later became prominent television football announcers.

Al Toon, the second-leading pass catcher in New York Jets history, was forced out of football in 1992 at age twenty-nine because of postconcussion syndrome. Toon had received nine concussions during his eight-year NFL career. His residual symptoms included vertigo, headaches, nausea, aphasia (difficulty using or understanding words), and short-term memory loss. Toon's situation demonstrates the typical pattern in which a player is increasingly vulnerable to concussions and each time the recovery takes longer.

In November 2003 Wayne Chrebet, another prominent Jets receiver, was sidelined for the rest of the season after recovering more slowly from what was believed to be his sixth career concussion. When he practiced in the Jets minicamp five months later, Chrebet described a lingering "hangover" characterized by headaches, blurred vision, and hypersensitivity to noise and light, some of the serious long-term effects of this type of sports injury. Chrebet suffered another concussion in the last game of the 2004 regular season, and it seemed likely that he would be forced into retirement.

Players ranging from junior high school age to the professional level have suffered more permanent injuries from collisions on the football field. A tragic example involves Marc Buoniconti, whose father, Nick Buoniconti, had starred with the great Miami Dolphins of the 1970s. While he was playing in a game at the Citadel on October 26, 1985, Marc's spinal cord was severely damaged when he tackled the opposing team's running back. His arms and legs were paralyzed, and he has been confined to a wheelchair ever since. In a flash his future had been transformed from potential stardom to permanent disability. Marc Buoniconti has handled his affliction in a most courageous way by heading the Miami Project, a foundation whose mission is to find a cure for paralysis. Though the Buoniconti tragedy was not caused by a vicious blow from a rival player, it highlights how the violence in football can end a career and even a life at any moment. Buoniconti was the best known of many younger players to suffer a paralyzing injury. According to Dr. Fred Mueller, who has studied catastrophic sports injury, between 1977 and 1990 there were 142 such injuries, and all of the injured college and high school players became quadriplegics.[17]

Seven years before the Buoniconti incident, in an NFL preseason game on August 12, 1978, Darryl Stingley, a New England Patriots wide receiver, became a quadriplegic. Stingley collided head to head with Oakland Raiders defensive back Jack Tatum when he ran a slant pattern and was reaching for an overthrown pass. The injury fractured Stingley's fourth and fifth vertebrae (in effect, a broken neck) and left him permanently paralyzed. Tatum had a reputation as a rough player, and in many quarters the blow was described as "one of the most brutal hits in NFL history."[18] Other observers characterized it as a vicious but clean tackle; nevertheless Tatum was roundly criticized for his actions as well as for not apologizing to Stingley.

Tatum responded to being vilified by writing a best-selling book, *They Call Me Assassin*, in which he claimed he hit Stingley "because of what the owners expect of me when they give me a paycheck."[19] Tatum continued his career and was criticized for never contacting the incapacitated Stingley. Tatum maintains that his attempts were rebuffed. In 1996 a meeting finally was arranged for them to discuss the fateful incident eighteen years earlier. It was promoted as a reconciliation prompted by Tatum's unresolved remorse, and it was to be taped and later aired by Fox TV. Stingley agreed to a proposal by which Fox would show an 800 number on the screen so fans could contribute to his charitable organization that helps Chicago youths. Shortly before the scheduled event, Stingley learned that it was timed to coincide with the release of Tatum's new book, in which he again discussed the collision. Stingley canceled the show because he felt Tatum was manipulating him to get publicity for his book. A bitter and disillusioned Stingley declared, "I asked myself, why after 18 years is Tatum coming back for this reconciliation? I just figured it was something he had to deal with and get over. Nothing was ever said about a book, and it bothers me to even talk about it because the last time, they used a quote from me about Tatum in ads for the book."[20]

In our compassion for the victim, we often overlook the traumatic effect on the aggressor who causes a sports injury that turns out to be far more serious than he may have intended. Characteristically, the injured

Violence between Athletes

player receives widespread concern and sympathy and the aggressor is maligned. I am not suggesting that Jack Tatum suffered the same personal damage as Darryl Stingley, but at some level Tatum's life was also drastically changed by the paralysis he caused and the subsequent public outcry. At one point Tatum asked the NFL pension fund for benefits related to his "mental anguish" over the blow that made Stingley a quadriplegic. We can only wonder what issues Carl Mays struggled with after his fatal beaning of Ray Chapman. In the more recent McSorley-Brashear hockey episode, McSorley quickly stated, "I'm still in shock at what I did. . . . I apologize to Donald Brashear and all the fans who had to watch that. I embarrassed my hockey team. . . . I got way too carried away. It was a real dumb play."[21]

The next major freak accident that led to paralysis occurred on November 19, 1991. Mike Utley of the Detroit Lions, a six-foot-six-inch, 290-pound guard, sustained a career-ending spinal cord injury while pass blocking David Rocker of the Los Angeles Rams. The two collided, and Rocker fell on Utley, who lost his balance and crashed onto the artificial turf. Utley fractured his sixth cervical vertebra, leaving him paralyzed below the chest. A lawyer representing Utley charged that the Pontiac Silverdome's artificial turf was in "dangerous and defective condition" and caused the player's injury, but medical experts maintained that the same damage could have happened on a soft turf field.

Just one year after the Utley tragedy another NFL player became paralyzed in a collision on the field. On November 29, 1992, Dennis Byrd, the New York Jets defensive end, became partially paralyzed after colliding with teammate Scott Mersereau as they converged from opposite sides while attempting to sack Kansas City Chiefs quarterback Dave Krieg. Byrd fractured his fifth cervical vertebra, the equivalent of a broken neck. As he lay motionless on the turf for seven minutes, the 266-pound player was terrified to realize he could not move his legs. He kept asking the doctors and trainers, "Am I going to be paralyzed?" Byrd underwent spinal surgery three days later, and he was fortunate to walk again after extensive rehabilitation.

In the days after this freakish incident, questions were raised within the NFL about whether the injury was avoidable. It was suggested that the twenty-six-year-old Byrd might have improperly used his helmet in a tactic called spearing, causing his headfirst impact. Spearing is using the helmet as the point of attack, and players are routinely trained to tackle with their heads up to minimize the likelihood of injury.

While Dennis Byrd's recovery was still unknown, it was inappropriate to question his part in his injury. Byrd's impairment was a reminder of the life-threatening dangers associated with football collisions, but it did little to penetrate the pervasive denial among players. To survive in football, you must believe that though a paralyzing injury may happen occasionally, it won't happen to you.

Basketball

The most serious incident of violence between players in the NBA was the Rudy Tomjanovich–Kermit Washington encounter on December 9, 1977. Washington, a six-foot-eight-inch, 222-pound defensive star with the Los Angeles Lakers, was tangling with the Houston Rockets' Kevin Kunnert, who he claimed was elbowing him. When Tomjanovich, a four-time All-Star with the Rockets, raced down the court to break up the fight, he got slammed.

Washington's fist exploded into Tomjanovich's face—or Tomjanovich's face crashed into Washington's fist, depending on your perspective. According to noted sportswriter John Feinstein, "The punch dislodged Tomjanovich's skull and nearly killed him . . . the force from Washington's right hand catapulted Tomjanovich backward. He landed squarely on his back, his head bouncing off the floor . . . and then as he lost consciousness rolled over into a fetal position." [22] The blow left Tomjanovich disfigured, and it was uncertain whether he could ever play again. He required five surgeries for facial reconstruction, but miraculously he came back and regained his earlier prowess during the next season.

Washington was fined $10,000 and given a sixty-day suspension for his part in the altercation. By all accounts he had not intended to deliver a malicious hit but had reacted reflexively when he sensed an opposing player coming at him from behind. He did not put his hands up to defend himself from an attack; instead, he lashed out against what he perceived as a menace. From Washington's perspective the punch was instinctive self-defense. His reaction may have been exacerbated by his childhood history of being pinned and beaten and by a fight in the previous NBA season when another player jumped him from behind.

The angle of the blow caused the worst possible damage to Tom-

Violence between Athletes

janovich. As Feinstein described it, "The damage the punch inflicted was an absolute fluke. Washington's strength played a part, but the devastating effect arose from an awful confluence of factors that led to the punch landing exactly where it did with both puncher and punchee supplying momentum. If the punch had landed in a slightly different way, it would have been nothing more than a footnote."[23]

Washington expressed remorse about the assault, and he was reinstated in February 1978. Both players went on to have several more productive seasons. Tomjanovich and the Rockets sued the Los Angeles Lakers, the first time an NBA player had ever sued another player or another team, and a jury awarded Tomjanovich $3.25 million in damages, more than he had requested in the lawsuit. To avoid an extended appeal, the two sides settled for $2 million.

Both players have had to deal with substantial psychological upheaval. Tomjanovich initially suffered the anguish of hearing that there was no guarantee he would ever play again. Later, when he was praised for his talent or designated an All-Star, he was never sure the recognition was not motivated by sympathy. He was also left with post-traumatic stress disorder and recurrently dreamed he was dying. He later developed a problem with alcohol, and when he was drinking he sometimes had panic attacks.

The two players became defined in the public eye as the puncher and the punchee. An embittered Washington resents being remembered primarily for "the punch," which overshadows everything else in his life. Although he was the assailant, Washington has also been severely damaged. In a sense he too was a victim. He has had to deal with public opinion characterizing him as a villain who maliciously mauled Rudy Tomjanovich. He must have felt deeply misunderstood and unfairly portrayed for a regrettable reflexive response to a player's swooping on him from behind. In the well-known flight-or-fight response, a person who feels threatened either runs away or attacks. Washington attacked and has been genuinely remorseful ever since. From his perspective he had never intended to hurt Tomjanovich and has been unfairly persecuted by the media and the fans. His position is understandable; the videotape of the punch has been shown repeatedly on television whenever there is a violent incident in sports. After the attack he also received numerous death threats.

Kermit Washington has lived ever since with people's thinking of him as a thug, and he wants to be recognized for more than those brief seconds in 1977. In a letter to the *New York Times* twenty-three years later, Washington vented his feelings about the repercussions of that violent moment. He describes how, in the years after his retirement from the NBA, "I have applied for various coaching jobs from high school to the pro level, but have always been turned down because no one wanted to be associated with my reputation. My name stood for violence and bad publicity. . . . Everything I've ever accomplished in life is overshadowed by this incident. No one stops to ask me about my charities or the work I do in the community. . . . All people are ever going to remember me for was this one blemish. . . . How do I change the way people look at me every time there's a violent act in sports?"[24]

One can experience and express various levels of remorse for a violent act. I believe that Kermit Washington is truly remorseful, has endured considerable animosity, and deserves more compassion from the media and the public. It is unfortunate that no matter how much Rudy Tomjanovich and Kermit Washington might wish to reconcile and move on, they continue to be remembered primarily for their violent encounter.

As in other major league sports, basketball players have been known to react violently to fans, referees, coaches, and even cameramen during games. Vernon Maxwell of the Houston Rockets was suspended for ten games and fined $20,000 for running into the stands and punching a heckling fan during a game against Portland on February 6, 1995. On April 10, 1996, Nick Van Exel of the Los Angeles Lakers, in a fit of pique after being ejected from a game, went after the diminutive referee, Ron Garretson, and shoved him into the scorer's table. The league levied a seven-game suspension for his violent outburst. Van Exel was an outstanding player in college, but he had been accused of assaulting a teammate as well as physically abusing his girlfriend; and according to *Sports Illustrated* he had acquired a reputation as a "bad seed."[25] Many teams passed over him in the draft, and in response to the incident with Garretson some NBA executives said they were surprised it had taken three years for this violent side of Van Exel to emerge.[26]

Dennis Rodman stands out as a player who chronically stepped over the line of violent engagement. The NBA file on Rodman lists multiple suspensions and fines for head-butting opposing players and referees. His record includes a one-game suspension and a $7,500 fine for butting Stacey King (December 18, 1993), a one-game suspension and

Violence between Athletes

a $5,000 fine for butting John Stockton (March 3, 1994), a suspension from a playoff game and a $10,000 fine for kneeing Stockton in another game (May 2, 1994), and a six-game suspension and a $20,000 fine for butting referee Ted Bernhardt (March 18, 1996). Since he was being paid up to $9 million a year, these fines hardly put a dent in his pocketbook; moreover, Rodman seemed to relish his "bad boy" image.

Rodman's most egregious episode occurred during a game against the Minnesota Timberwolves on January 16, 1997. After twisting his ankle when he tripped over a row of courtside photographers, Rodman vented his rage by kicking one of the cameramen, Eugene Otis, in the groin. Otis was taken by stretcher to a hospital, where he was treated and released. An unapologetic Rodman maintained that Otis exaggerated the seriousness of his injury, but he eventually agreed to pay the cameraman $200,000. The NBA hit Rodman with an eleven-game suspension and a $25,000 fine.

This was the harshest suspension the NBA had meted out for a non-drug violation since the Kermit Washington case twenty years earlier. Many players in the NBA supported Rodman, arguing that the penalty was excessive, and the players' association filed a grievance on his behalf. Some even declared that Commissioner David Stern treats the superstars less harshly than the other stars. In the words of the Knicks' Charles Oakley, "The league picks on certain guys. You don't see superstars get suspended that long. . . . Charles Barkley does the same stuff. He spit on people, kicked people, gets away with murder. There's definitely superstar treatment in this league." [27] And many eyebrows had been raised about the lenient treatment of Michael Jordan amid allegations of gambling.

At the other end of the spectrum are those who feel that Rodman's penalty was too soft. Given his chronic crossing the line and his "bad as I wanna be" attitude, a stronger message may be needed to deter his violent outbursts.

It is also a sad commentary on our culture that Dennis Rodman's outrageous actions appeal to some fans, who admire him as an independent, rebellious antihero. Such people are apt to imitate their heroes' acting-out.

A new level of violence in the NBA was reached on December 1, 1997, when twenty-seven-year-old Latrell Sprewell, the leading scorer and three-time All-Star of the Golden State Warriors, choked the team's coach, P. J. Carlesimo, during a practice session as his teammates looked on. Sprewell was kicked out of the practice, but he returned fifteen minutes later and again choked his coach and threatened to kill him.

Sprewell had previously had some violent outbursts during games. Two years earlier he had been is a fight with teammate Jerome Kersey, and when things escalated he came back and threatened Kersey with a two-by-four and said he would go get a gun. He also had attacked another teammate, Byron Houston. In addition, Sprewell, like Dennis Rodman, had been less than compliant with authority figures. The most widely publicized incident was when he was pulled over for speeding by a police officer of Japanese descent. The officer claimed that Sprewell was abusive and called him racial epithets. P. J. Carlesimo had a reputation as a very demanding coach whose needling and abrasive style grated on some players. It is likely the two had been on a collision course for some time. The choking episode was precipitated by Carlesimo's ordering Sprewell to make better passes during a drill. A shouting match followed, and then Sprewell lost it.

The Warriors responded by voiding the remaining $24 million on Sprewell's four-year contract on the grounds that he had violated the Uniform Player Contract, which states that players must "conform to standards of good citizenship and good moral character" and prohibits "engaging in acts of moral turpitude." In addition, the NBA suspended him for a full year, the longest penalty ever handed out for a nondrug violation. (Ron Tarpley and Richard Dumas had been banned for life for violating the league's substance abuse policy.) Commissioner David Stern determined that Sprewell's coming back to confront his coach again was "the defining aspect of the case, because it was premeditated." In evaluating the altercation, a New York Times editorial, trying to be evenhanded, portrayed Sprewell as a thug and Carlesimo as a provocative bully. The players' union took umbrage at the severity of the suspension and intimated that league officials were using this incident to remedy the tarnished image of the NBA, which had recently been plagued by the violent behavior of several revered star players, including Rodman, Allen Iverson, and Charles Barkley. If the league had been waiting to show that it would not tolerate violence and other deviant behavior, it now had its chance.

Sprewell's agent derided the suspension as "an abuse of the Commissioner's power," and some players thought Carlesimo had provoked the attack. The union also accumulated testimony from several players who claimed to have undergone repeated verbal abuse by Carlesimo.

A few days later Sprewell showed little remorse when he publicly apologized for the incident—but not to the coach, whom he lambasted for ongoing verbal abuse that drove him over the line. From his perspective the attack was at least partially justified because he had been bullied, criticized, and provoked by Carlesimo, who did not back off when Sprewell shouted, "Don't come up on me."

The case is reminiscent of a similar incident in March 1977 when a Texas Rangers baseball player, Lenny Randle, punched his manager, Frank Lucchesi, three times, fracturing his cheekbone and injuring his back. Randle was fined $10,000 and suspended for thirty days by the team. But for Randle, in contrast to Sprewell, it was a onetime aberration and he seemed genuinely contrite. The manager did file a civil suit, and he received $30,000 in an out-of-court settlement. He also saw to it that Randle was traded to the New York Mets, where he subsequently flourished.

Walt Frazier, a former NBA superstar, wrote an op-ed piece in the *New York Times* in which he viewed the Sprewell-Carlesimo situation as a prime example of what had gone awry in professional sports. Frazier points to "the astronomical salaries, the media hoopla, the iconization of players by fans, the special treatment accorded superstars by management"[28] as contributing to the black eye sustained by professional sports leagues, and he pleads for the sports world to recover its values.

The incident also reflects a larger sociological issue in this country— a breakdown of respect for standards, rules, and laws. The respect for authority among some sports figures has continued to erode as their salaries have escalated along with their egos. It has reached a point where their sense of entitlement and grandiosity prompt certain athletes to demand that their team's management fire a coach they don't get along with if they are to stay with the team. In the past a player might request a trade if he was unhappy, but now he might insist that the coach—the symbol of leadership—be dismissed.

Sprewell assembled a legal team, including Johnnie Cochran of O. J. Simpson fame, to file a lawsuit against the Warriors and the NBA. His suit was dismissed as "worthless," and he was required to pay the NBA's court costs. Sprewell had contended that racial prejudice entered into his excessive punishment, since shortly before his episode a white player, Tom Chambers, had punched a Phoenix Suns assistant coach and had received no suspension. Arbitration reduced his suspension by five months, covering sixty-eight games and a loss of $6.4 million in salary. Sprewell was traded to the New York Knicks before the 1998–99 season. He became a leading scorer, but he got in trouble for coming late to practice sessions and had a brief suspension for failing to report an injury promptly.

In an interview a year later, Sprewell still showed little remorse when he acknowledged that what he did was wrong but said he had been pushed over the edge. At his reinstatement he again apologized for the attack, although he couldn't bring himself to apologize directly to Carlesimo. He said he was a caring person and not someone with an attitude problem as he has been portrayed by the media. He also recognized that, as in the Tomjanovich-Washington affair, the incident would never be behind him in the public's mind.

Sprewell's attack is indefensible, even though Carlesimo's coaching style likely was abrasive and abusive, but it does seem that the penalty was extreme in the context of other incidents. Perhaps the NBA did capitalize on the assault to crack down on violence throughout the league and send a message about setting limits and controlling thuggery.

The violent outbursts in professional basketball may also be filtering down to the college and high school levels. In a January 1999 San Antonio High School game, eighteen-year-old Tony Limon threw an elbow in Brent Holmes's face, causing a concussion and a broken nose that needed surgery. Limon was convicted of aggravated assault with serious bodily injury and after pleading no contest was given a five-year prison term. It is probable that he received such a stiff sentence because he was already serving four years' probation for an attempted burglary just one month earlier. Limon claimed that his coach, Gary Durbon, encouraged his aggressive play and right after the assault had commented, "It's about time someone drew blood." Many fans want to see fights between players, and some coaches admire players who employ intimidating tactics. It appears that Tony Limon was rewarded with more playing time as he became increasingly aggressive on the court.

Perhaps reflecting more widespread violence within basketball, this case was the first instance of a high school athlete's being charged in a

Violence between Athletes

criminal action for a sports-related encounter. Tony Limon served one year in jail and then was paroled.

In surveying the violent episodes between athletes we should distinguish those actions that happen in the heat of battle—impulsive aggression—from premeditated aggression as well as differentiating repetitive and aberrational aggression. The damage inflicted by Kermit Washington and Jack Tatum can be classified as impulsive aggression, whereas the assaults by Marty McSorley and Latrell Sprewell were premeditated. Dennis Rodman and Billy Martin were repeat offenders, in contrast to Juan Marichal and Lenny Randle, whose violence was an aberration. In all of these incidents the line between hero and villain becomes somewhat blurred, and even assaulters like Carl Mays, Kermit Washington, and Latrell Sprewell become victims of their own aggression in that they will perennially be remembered for their blows.

Violence in sports mirrors our violent society. Professional sports leagues need to take firmer control by applying stiffer sanctions to those who are violent toward players, coaches, fans, and others. The leagues thus need to do a better job of policing themselves and withstanding the pressure to be lenient toward those superstars who cross the line.

10. Athletes' Mental Health Problems

His was one of the tragic lives that spot the game's history—brilliance
lost in alcohol, drugs, or mental illness.
  Neil Sullivan, *The Diamond in the Bronx*

Being a gifted athlete does not exempt a person from mental health
problems. Stardom is often accompanied by stress that creates or exac-
erbates psychological disturbances. Moreover, the distorted self-image
that many athletes acquire can lead to serious lapses in judgment off the
field, sometimes with dire consequences. The Rae Carruth murder case,
the Denny McLain drug and racketeering conviction, and the Pete Rose
gambling scandal stand out as examples. Most athletes find it extremely
difficult to accept mental illness. Depression, anxiety, bipolar disorder,
and paranoia, to name a few syndromes, carry a stigma. Elite athletes
are programmed to be strong and in control.

When Kobe Bryant was charged with rape in July 2003, it shocked
the sports world because of Bryant's squeaky clean image. While other
sports heroes were known to be less than pillars of the community,
Kobe was portrayed as the All-American clean-cut superstar who was
destined to become the next Michael Jordan. His image had been carefully crafted, and many people who yearn for their heroes to remain
heroes did not want to believe Bryant could be capable of a serious
crime. I believe Allen Iverson supplied an accurate perspective: "He's
a human being. The media made Kobe Bryant. The media made him
squeaky clean. I don't know nobody squeaky clean. I never met a man
in my life who is squeaky clean."[1] In other words, everyone has flaws or
dark sectors in their personality that can be activated in certain circumstances.

Most psychotherapists agree that mental health ranges along a con-
tinuum from very healthy to very disturbed. Even the most well ad-
justed individuals may have encapsulated pockets of pathology, and
some severely disturbed people appear to function normally. For ex-

ample, we no longer view schizophrenic patients as being psychotic twenty-four hours a day. This was brought home to me while I was a psychologist in training on a chronic schizophrenia unit of a state mental hospital. There was a lovely middle-aged woman who was perpetually engaged with hallucinations and delusions in which her persecutors were berating her. Every day she would battle her imagined tormenters in stormy arguments, but whenever I passed through her area she would compose herself and connect with me in a socially appropriate way. Then, as soon as I walked out of range, she would resume the interrupted dialogue with her persecutors.

In contrast, some individuals by all appearances lead healthy, normal lives, but significant areas of pathology may coexist alongside their well-adjusted presentation. A classic example of this dichotomy was depicted in the 2003 documentary film *Capturing the Friedmans*. Arnold Friedman is a devoted husband, father, and schoolteacher in suburban Great Neck, New York, who is convicted of sexually abusing a series of young boys who came to him for computer lessons.

Certain athletes may be especially prone to antisocial behavior because of the distorted self-images they have acquired. Although they function well in most circumstances, they may indulge their libidinal desires without evaluating the risks to their careers and to their lives. They may hold a skewed belief that being among "the chosen" exempts them from retribution. This belief is reinforced by a sports culture in which coaches, schools, and major league team management, whose emphasis is on winning, downplay the off-field infractions of athlete-heroes.

Among the most egregious examples of such antisocial lapses are the sexual exhibitionism cases of Edward Bouchee and Lance Rentzel. These episodes drew public opprobrium because they involved a psychological assault on others. Bouchee was the regular first baseman for the Philadelphia Phillies when he was arrested in January 1958 for exposing himself to a six-year-old girl. Apparently this was not an isolated incident. Bouchee acknowledged four similar experiences with girls ranging from ten to eighteen. The twenty-five-year-old player was treated leniently by the legal system. He was placed on three years' probation, got psychiatric treatment, and returned to play Major League Baseball later that season. The long-term traumatic effect on the victims remains unknown.

According to psychoanalytic theorists, sexual exhibitionism is meant to compensate for a subjective loss of self-esteem. The individual is indirectly bolstered by thinking that someone else is looking at him with surprise, admiration, and awe. The fleeting reaction of the spectator reassures the exhibitionist that he has something worthwhile, which makes him feel whole, complete, and desirable. This process contains a considerable element of magical thinking, since in reality the startled spectator is generally repelled and frightened. The exhibitionist needs the reaction of an audience to make him feel intact and OK. The perpetrator's aim is not sexual gratification but rather the restoration of psychological equilibrium. He feels as if he has lost an essential part of himself and seeks to restore a feeling of well-being by exposing his genitals. According to traditional mental health theory, the sexual exhibitionist "unconsciously says to his audience, 'Reassure me that I have a penis by reacting to the sight of it.' Inner doubt impels the individual to call upon objects as witnesses."[2]

Lance Rentzel was a full-fledged sports hero as a wide receiver with the Dallas Cowboys when he was charged with indecent exposure on November 19, 1970. Rentzel seemed to have it all. In the previous season he had led the N FL in average yards per reception and total touchdowns. He was also married to the beautiful entertainer Joey Heatherton. Apparently he exposed himself to a ten-year-old girl whose father happened to be an attorney and insisted on pressing charges. Rentzel was indicted on a felony charge and could have been sentenced to two to fifteen years if convicted. In April 1971 he pleaded guilty to indecent exposure, and an agreement was reached in which he was sentenced to five years' probation along with continuing psychiatric treatment.

Rentzel had a history of sexual exhibitionism involving young children. Four years earlier, while playing with the Minnesota Vikings, he allegedly exposed himself to two young girls. In that case he pleaded guilty to disorderly conduct and was ordered to seek psychiatric counseling in lieu of a sentence.

In 1972, after many years of therapy, Rentzel wrote about these events in an autobiography, *When All the Laughter Died in Sorrow*. His psychiatrist believed it would be therapeutic for him to express in words his understanding of the forces that propelled the self-destructive exhibitionism that ruined his career. He described how through therapy he came to

Athletes' Mental Health Problems

recognize that "the act was more magical than sexual, a ritual to restore that all important sense of power that the defeats of life had temporarily destroyed." [3] He claimed that there was no sexual gratification in his exhibitionistic acting-out, but rather a distorted attempt to bolster his ego after he experienced setbacks in football. His rationale was that his self-doubts drove him to an outlet that made him feel more manly— the nonsexual aspect of the act restored a firmer sense of himself. In Rentzel's words, it provided a "vital reassurance" (at a time when he was depressed and struggling with a "deep feeling of failure" about his playing and his marriage), even though it involved a suspension of "all reason, all judgement, all forethought." [4]

In discussing an exposure incident in St. Paul, Minnesota, in 1966, before his psychiatric treatment, he portrays a classic profile of how a pattern of acting-out can become entrenched with no insight into the underlying internal forces that drive it. He recalls how "on this day, for some reason, I needed someone to play with me in a childish game I was making up. Look at me, look at me. Look at what I've got. I sat in the car and they [two girls] came over and I exposed myself. It took maybe 10 seconds, then I drove off, strangely relieved." [5] In this account Rentzel describes a suspension of reason and a denial of the consequences to himself and the impact on the girls.

Rentzel's psychiatrist, Dr. Louis J. West, maintained that "his psychiatric disorder is less an affliction than it is an impairment of maturation in a rather small area of his personality." [6] Nevertheless, the expression of this dimension of his personality was undoubtedly a prominent factor in the premature end of both his football career and his marriage. In the storm of the Dallas scandal Joey Heatherton initially stood by him, but according to Rentzel "she finally left him, not because of his 'crime,' but because of his 'Let's have some laughs and forget it' attitude afterwards." [7] This suggests that Rentzel was conspicuously deficient in empathy toward those his actions affected.

Still regarded as a prominent football player, he was traded to the Los Angeles Rams before the 1971 season, but he never regained his high level of performance, and after 1974 he was out of the NFL at age thirty-one. His inability to take his situation seriously was reflected in further self-destructive acts. While he was still on NFL probation related to the second charge of indecent exposure, Rentzel was convicted of marijuana possession in 1973, and Commissioner Pete Rozelle suspended him for "conduct detrimental to pro football." He was reinstated after one year, but at that point his career was a shambles.

Sexual exhibitionism is an especially injurious disorder because it can inflict substantial psychological damage on the victim. It is an emotional assault on other people, often children. As such, these cases inspire great public contempt. A professional athlete who is convicted of these charges quickly loses his status as a sports hero, and he also becomes a victim of his own behavior. Not surprisingly, Lance Rentzel was subjected to an unrelenting torrent of hostile reactions from an unforgiving public. In his book he describes how he was frequently taunted in restaurants and by fans during games, received hate mail and nasty phone calls, and was demeaned by late-night television show hosts. This was the price he paid for failing to control his antisocial impulses.

Sometimes athletes become the target of other people's pathology. This was apparent when baseball star Eddie Waitkus was shot by a deranged young woman who was caught up in obsessive love for him. Aspiring young athletes in gymnastics, tennis, and hockey who are sent away from home to develop their skills in training programs are at risk for sexual abuse by predatory coaches. Teenagers who admire their coaches and are eager to advance are especially vulnerable. According to a survey conducted in 1995 by Sports Canada, which oversees amateur sports, 20 percent of the respondents from various national teams acknowledged sexual involvement with their coaches. Moreover, almost half of these amateur players said they had been subjected to forced sexual intercourse, in some cases before age sixteen.

In a stunning case, hockey player Sheldon Kennedy, who fulfilled the dream of every junior player by making it to the NHL, revealed that he had been sexually abused regularly for six years while he was under the tutelage of Graham James in the Canadian junior hockey system. The talented Kennedy, who later played for the Boston Bruins, Detroit Red Wings, and Calgary Flames, was sent at age fourteen to train with James, who was one of the most successful junior league coaches in western Canada. According to Kennedy the sexual abuse began on his first night with James, and it occurred more than 350 times. As an adult Kennedy later brought charges against James, and he described the anguish and helplessness he experienced as the object of the coach's predatory assaults. "You do not have a clue what to do. You tell your

Athletes' Mental Health Problems

mom and she makes you come home. You tell your friends and they will just portray you as a gay guy. It is just a very scary thing. . . . He was just a very smart, manipulative man. It was the position of power he was in." [8] At the time Kennedy, who was raised without a father, undoubtedly was overwhelmed, confused, and easily influenced by Graham James. Kennedy also said he believed this problem was widespread and asserted that "other coaches and officials in junior hockey must have known what his coach was doing, but did nothing to stop him." [9]

At James's trial another current NHL player, whose name was withheld by court order, testified that he also had been repeatedly sexually assaulted by the coach. On January 2, 1997, Graham James pleaded guilty to two counts of sexual assault for offenses on two teenage players under his supervision between 1984 and 1994. He was sentenced to three and a half years in jail and ten years' probation.

The case generated a wider study into sexual abuse by junior hockey coaches. The investigation revealed that Brian Shaw, a coach, general manager, and later chairman of the Western Hockey League board of governors had seduced young players for thirty years before he died in 1993. Other discoveries included a Quebec coach who pleaded guilty to sexual assault on minors and was given a five-month prison sentence and another junior coach in Quebec who was fired after admitting he had groped two boys. In the wake of the Graham James–Sheldon Kennedy scandal, the Canadian Hockey League began to look into coach-screening programs as a step toward controlling this problem, which may be even more prevalent than has been recognized. We can only wonder why it took them so long. The James case also warned parents of young athletes to be more vigilant about the dangers and less blindly trusting about the atmosphere they send their kids into. Greater parental involvement may deter sexual abuse.

Graham James served less than two years of his prison term and was then given a modified form of parole. At a court hearing he issued an apology in which he seemed to feel remorse and to acknowledge the broader impact of his crimes: "I brought unwelcome suspicion on conscientious coaches everywhere. I betrayed my role as a guardian of the game." [10] Sheldon Kennedy, who was present at the hearing, seemed unmoved by the apology and later said, "I'll never feel sorry and I'll never forgive Graham James. I hope he understands what he did and the damage that he's done." [11]

Graham James was banned for life from coaching hockey in Canada, but he subsequently was hired in Spain as an assistant coach for the Spanish national team.

Anxiety Reactions

Although we wish that our sports heroes would always play like supermen, they sometimes experience a meltdown of their skills. At times a star, even after he has won athletic prominence, persistently falters. Although there may be an apparent physical basis for this underperformance, the problem might really be a mental block. In professional golf a top professional player occasionally falls into a sustained pattern of being unable to putt effectively. Golfers refer to this syndrome as "yips," "a nervous disorder that can destroy a player's ability to putt, turning the stroke into a twitching or jerking movement."[12]

In professional basketball, superstar Shaquille O'Neal has become infamous for his poor foul shots. This circumscribed underperformance has plagued O'Neal for several seasons.

Chuck Knoblauch, late in his career as a second baseman for the New York Yankees, became intermittently inept at routine throws to first base. As the problem persisted, it appeared to become a psychological block—expecting another miscue makes it more likely to happen. Failure feeds on itself, reinforces anxiety, and becomes a conditioned response.

This type of performance interference is called "social anxiety disorder." Mental health experts have pointed out that "there may be a vicious cycle of anticipatory anxiety leading to fearful cognition and anxiety symptoms in the feared situation, which leads to actual or perceived poor performance in the feared situations, which leads to embarrassment and increased anticipatory anxiety about the feared situations, and so on . . . the individual fears that he or she will act in a way that will be humiliating or embarrassing."[13]

After a while a player dreads each ground ball hit toward him for fear he will further embarrass himself. Knoblauch never overcame this affliction, and the problem was resolved by shifting him to a regular outfield position. Steve Sax, another prominent second baseman, suffered the same meltdown while playing for the Los Angeles Dodgers. After being named Rookie of the Year in 1982, Sax inexplicably lost his ability to make the simple toss to first base. As he became preoccupied

Athletes' Mental Health Problems

with the problem, it got worse, and he made an astounding thirty errors the following season. This type of mental block, which has affected many established Major League players, has been named "Steve Sax disease."

Sax himself overcame this problem through visualization techniques. Others have not been as fortunate. One theory holds that the anxiety created by the expectation of sustained performance at the Major League level leads to a breakdown in physical functioning. New York Mets psychiatrist Allan Lans explains, "It's stage fright. When you have stage fright, what are you afraid of? Embarrassing yourself. And when you get nervous, what do you do? You embarrass yourself. It's a cycle."[14]

Several pitchers have been especially prone to mental blocks that have wrecked their careers. In 1958 Von McDaniel was an eighteen-year-old phenomenon with the St. Louis Cardinals who found quick success, then suddenly lost his mechanics. Within a year he was demoted and never again was able to compete on the Major League level. Perhaps the adulation and pressure to produce overwhelmed him. His brother Lindy, who enjoyed a long big league career, described Von's downfall: "He lost his coordination and mechanics. There was no real explanation. Some people thought it was psychological. . . . They sent Von down to the minors, but he couldn't get anyone out. He kept sinking further and further until he couldn't pitch anymore. It depressed him for years after he left baseball. But he couldn't talk about it."[15]

A similar scenario surrounded Rick Ankiel, the twenty-one-year-old St. Louis Cardinals pitcher who self-destructed during the 2000 playoffs. The talented Ankiel, who had previously been acclaimed High School Player of the Year and then Minor League Player of the Year, was expected to be a dominant player. As a rookie he achieved instant success, but in three playoff games he walked eleven batters and threw nine wild pitches in only four innings. During the season he had to cope with the emotional turmoil of his father's being sent to federal prison on drug charges as well as his parents' divorce, but it didn't seem to affect his stellar pitching performance. The added pressure of the playoffs may have caused his collapse. The humiliation and embarrassment of unraveling also affected him deeply, and so far he has been unable to regain his earlier form, let alone fulfill the great expectations laid on him.

Post-traumatic Stress Disorder

Another mental block plagues athletes who are struck down at the height of their career. Monica Seles was among the highest-ranked professional tennis players when she was stabbed by a fan during a match in 1993. Although her wounds healed completely, Seles never regained her prominence. It was as if the trauma laid a lasting cloud over her competitive skills. Similarly, Herb Score was heralded as the next Bob Feller when he came to the Cleveland Indians camp in 1955. He had had two outstanding seasons when he was struck in the eye by a line drive during a game in 1957. It took a year for Score to fully recover from the injury, but he was unable to regain his effectiveness and was out of baseball by age thirty.

Current psychiatric knowledge suggests that both Seles and Score suffered from post-traumatic stress disorder: "The person has been exposed to a traumatic event in which both of the following were present: 1) the person experienced, witnessed, or was confronted with an event or events that involved actual or threatened death or serious injury, or a threat to the physical integrity of self or others, 2) the person's response involved intense fear, helplessness, or horror." [16] Thus trauma often breeds unmanageable fear. We can speculate that fear became lodged deep in the minds of both Monica Seles and Herb Score, an ongoing impediment to superior performance.

Bipolar Disorder

The sports world has been conspicuously slow to adopt an enlightened attitude about athletes who become dysfunctional because of mental health problems. While problems with alcohol and drugs are commonplace and are treated with compassion by teammates, mental illness is poorly understood, regarded as alien and weak, and often responded to with "Get over it!"

There has been a long, winding road of breakthroughs and setbacks in accepting mental problems as a legitimate illness. More and more athletes are speaking out about their battles with depression, bipolar disorder, and anxiety, and this is gradually creating a more tolerant and understanding climate. Yet progress has lagged.

It is more than fifty years since we first learned about the mental illness of Jimmy Piersall, the flamboyant Boston Red Sox outfielder. In 1952, during his rookie season, Piersall was confined to a mental hos-

Athletes' Mental Health Problems

pital and treated with electroconvulsive shock therapy for what in those days was called a nervous breakdown. Before his breakdown Piersall had demonstrated emotionally volatile and irrational behavior numerous times, on and off the field. Initially he was perceived simply as a high-strung prankster; only belatedly did the Red Sox grasp that his bizarre actions were a product of mental disturbance.

A central feature in Piersall's background was his abrupt separation from his mother, who was hospitalized with a mental breakdown when he was seven years old. She returned after six months, then a year later she suffered a relapse and was hospitalized again. Piersall was close to his mother, and these absences left him with a profound insecurity. In his best-selling autobiography *Fear Strikes Out*, which later became a hit movie, he described how he became riddled with apprehension, constantly worried that something bad was about to happen.[17] When he reached the Major League, the pressure to succeed seemed to exacerbate his insecurity, and he developed paranoid thinking, ascribing malevolent motives to the Red Sox organization for not giving him more playing time as a rookie. His irrational thinking coalesced around the belief that management's plan to convert him into a shortstop was an elaborate plot to make him fail so they could get rid of him. In the tortured mind of a disturbed person, these overwhelming fears and beliefs seem very real.

In truth Piersall was plagued with manic-depressive illness, or what is currently called bipolar disorder, characterized by severe mood swings. Phases of euphoria, excitability, and hyperactivity may alternate with periods of bleakness and despair. His zany clowning during ball games probably reflected his manic state. Among his more outrageous stunts were doing a hula dance in the outfield while a pitcher warmed up, squirting home plate with a water pistol after being called out on strikes, and thumbing a ride on the jeep bringing relief pitchers from the bullpen. The fans loved it, and he became a great crowd pleaser, but his antics became a distraction to the team, and they eventually got him to accept hospitalization. He was released after six weeks of successful treatment, then returned to the Red Sox and played for seventeen Major League seasons with five teams without further episodes.

Piersall's public account of his struggle with mental illness paved the way for a greater understanding that such afflictions can beset our sports heroes. But future generations of athletes and fans have not remained consistently tolerant.

When Barret Robbins, the All-Pro center with the Oakland Raiders, succumbed to a bipolar episode and disappeared on the eve of the 2003 Super Bowl game, he was condemned by his teammates and fans for irresponsible behavior. The Raiders went into the game as favorites to win the coveted Super Bowl, and they were trounced by the Tampa Bay Buccaneers 48–21. In their disappointment, some of the players pointed to the distraction as contributing to their loss. They resented Robbins for letting the team down, and their lack of empathy about his mental illness was epitomized by teammate Mo Collins, who snapped, "Whatever rock he came up from, he can stay there as far as I'm concerned."[18] Fortunately, as explanations about his mental illness emerged during the following weeks, many of the players gradually became more compassionate, and Robbins was welcomed back to the Raiders for the next season.

Robbins, a twenty-nine-year-old, 320-pound lineman, had been diagnosed as bipolar in 1997 but had reportedly stopped taking the medication that kept his erratic behavior in check. According to Cartier Dise, a friend who had been partying with Robbins, a bout of heavy drinking the night before the Super Bowl had left him despondent and suicidal. Dise described to the press how Robbins had fallen into the black hole of depression: "He was crying and totally depressed about his life and the pressure he was under. . . . He was talking about killing himself, saying he was disappointing people and he had a lot of people to support financially and he was letting them all down."[19] Raiders coach Bill Callahan added that Robbins had been incoherent and didn't know where he was. He was hospitalized in San Diego, where he spent the next thirty days in treatment.

Studies indicate that as many as 20 percent of people with bipolar disorder eventually commit suicide.[20] Dimitrius Underwood, a young NFL defensive end with great promise, is afflicted with bipolar disorder and has attempted to kill himself. Underwood, a deeply religious man who was torn between professional football and the ministry, joined the Minnesota Vikings in 1999 as a first-round draft pick with a five-year contract for $5.3 million. The twenty-two-year-old player, six-foot-six and 270 pounds, disappeared from training camp on the first day of practice. He was soon cut by the Vikings and signed on with the Miami

Athletes' Mental Health Problems

Dolphins, but one month later he slashed his throat with a kitchen knife. Underwood had been injured in a preseason game and missed the first two Dolphins games. The day before his suicide attempt he also was arrested for failing to pay child support, and these two events may have helped precipitate his impulsive gesture. Although it seems likely that his effort to kill himself was related to his bipolar disorder, his mother, an ordained minister, put a curious spin on the episode by suggesting that Dimitrius's suicide attempt and strange behavior were attributable to his being influenced by "a cult that's posing as a church."

Underwood recovered from his wound, was dropped by the Dolphins, and signed on with the Dallas Cowboys. A little over a year later, on January 7, 2001, he again tried to kill himself by running into traffic on a busy highway in Florida, saying he "wanted to go to Jesus." Later that year the troubled player was also accused in a lawsuit of sexually assaulting a woman in the team hotel when the Cowboys were in Oakland for a game on October 7, 2001. In 2003 he was committed to a state hospital after he was deemed not mentally competent to stand trial on charges of assaulting and robbing a disabled man in a wheelchair. It appears that through his actions Dimitrius Underwood is pleading for proper treatment that will help him gain control over his erratic and impulsive behavior.

Depression

According to a U.S. Surgeon General's report in 2001, almost 8 percent of the adult population is afflicted by disorders that involve disruptions in the brain's chemistry. Depression accounts for a large proportion of these disorders. The frequency of such disorders among athletes probably mirrors that found in the general population, although it may be even higher because of the stress of maintaining outstanding performance. Stress and heredity are thought to be the greatest risk factors for depression.

Many elite athletes find it hard to accept mental illness when it strikes them. They are expected to be strong, and in many quarters mental problems are still viewed as weakness. A glimmer of progress is that sports stars are starting to speak openly about these problems. The roster includes NFL heroes Ricky Williams and Alonzo Spellman, NBA players Kendall Gill and Jason Caffey, and the celebrated jockey Julie Krone.

Professional athletes with mental health problems not only must overcome their own defense mechanism of denial but need to struggle with a sports establishment that remains uninformed and unaccepting of their disorders. Ricky Williams, a Miami Dolphins superstar who has battled social anxiety disorder, maintains that "there's a physical prejudice in sports. When it's a broken bone the teams will do everything in their power to make sure it's okay. When it's a broken soul, it's like a weakness." [21] Williams says that his coach's reaction to his psychological problem when he played for the New Orleans Saints was, in effect, "Stop being a baby and just play football." [22] Terry Bradshaw, a Pittsburgh Steelers Hall of Fame quarterback and a popular television broadcaster, who has experienced his own postretirement bouts with depression, concurs: "That's how it is in football. We're supposed to be big, tough guys. You have depression? Shoot, that's not depression. That's weakness." [23] And Russ Johnson, an infielder in the New York Mets, who has been diagnosed with depression, describes the ongoing stigma: "Blow out your knee, get into trouble with the law, fail a drug test, and the team will help you back. Suffer a mental or emotional injury, and it's a big mark against you." [24]

A high-profile case of depression was that of Pete Harnisch, an established pitcher with the New York Mets. Feeling the pressure to perform successfully after shoulder surgery and two losing seasons, during the 1997 spring training preseason Harnisch became plagued with signs of depression, including severe insomnia, light-headedness, social withdrawal, and loss of appetite. At first he kept his problems to himself and tried to talk himself out of them, but his symptoms only worsened. As the team's leading pitcher he was given the opening day assignment, and he lost the game.

When he confided in the team's managers that he had symptoms, such as not sleeping for five days, that interfered with effective functioning, they initially attributed his problems to nicotine withdrawal or Lyme disease and only belatedly considered depression. Harnisch claimed that manager Bobby Valentine was insensitive and called him "gutless" in front of the other players.

Over the next several months Harnisch lost forty pounds as he plummeted into despair. It is not clear to what extent his depression was caused by the pressures of a comeback season, by nicotine withdrawal, or by heredity (he has a family history of depression), but once he was

Athletes' Mental Health Problems

correctly diagnosed and treated with an antidepressant and psychother-apy, he overcame depression. After being sidelined for six months, he resumed his career. He was unable to reestablish rapport with Valen-tine, who denied making the "gutless" accusation, and he was traded to the Milwaukee Brewers and later the Cincinnati Reds, with whom he successfully continued playing at the Major League level until 2003.

Depression sometimes emerges as a by-product of head trauma dur-ing games. Players in high-contact sports like hockey and football are especially vulnerable. Pat La Fontaine, a Buffalo Sabres hockey All-Star, developed symptoms of depression in 1996 after being diagnosed with postconcussion syndrome. One of his most pronounced symptoms was a sudden lack of enthusiasm for hockey, which alarmed La Fontaine more than any other indicator. Indifference and loss of interest are often a prominent sign of depression.

Not surprisingly, clinical research shows that people who sustain multiple concussions are up to four times more likely to become de-pressed. Some studies have shown that players with repeated head trauma are also at greater risk for developing depression later in life.[25] A prime example is Mike Webster, an offensive lineman who joined the Pittsburgh Steelers in 1974 and helped them win four Super Bowls in his first six seasons. Webster, who played center, suffered numerous big hits during his seventeen-year NFL career. When he died in 2002 at age fifty, it was noted that Webster, who had sometimes been homeless, had not been diagnosed with severe mental deterioration, including depression, until many years after his retirement.[26]

In the general population there is a higher incidence of depression among women than men, and depression is no stranger to female ath-letes. Picabo Street, an Olympic gold medal skier, wrote candidly in her autobiography about her battle with depression after being side-lined by a severe knee injury. Nikki Teasley, a Women's National Bas-ketball Association All-Star, and Julie Krone, a renowned jockey, have spoken openly and nondefensively about their struggles with depres-sion. Krone has even become a spokesperson for the producer of Zoloft, a leading antidepressant medication.

Wendy Williams, an Olympic champion diver, has vividly described her journey with depression. Williams had won a bronze medal in the 1988 Olympics, but shortly before the 1992 games she was forced to retire because of a back injury. She became depressed and even contemplated killing herself by driving off a cliff. One of her most prominent symptoms was that she was often paralyzed by indecision. She recognized that she needed help when she opened her refrigerator and was overwhelmed by deciding what to eat. An antidepressant aided her recovery, and Williams later became a spokesperson on mental illness for the Women's Sports Foundation. She emphasizes the importance of destigmatizing depression: "There is an analogy I like to use. If I was diagnosed with diabetes, I wouldn't see it as a personal weakness. Would I be embarrassed about having diabetes? No. So I learned not to be embarrassed about my depression."[27]

Katrina Price, a professional basketball player, was less fortunate in dealing with her depression. Price was a reserve guard with the Philadelphia Page of the American Basketball League when the league folded in December 1998. One month later Katrina, who was despondent about her prospects, called to tell her sister how depressed she was. Her sister assured her that their large family of nine sisters would help her through her despondency, but it was too late. After the phone call Katrina killed herself with a twelve-gauge shotgun. She was twenty-three.

While professional athletes have gradually become more accepting of mental illness, by and large they are still loath to consider that in many cases it may be related to early mistreatment or emotional neglect by caregivers or other environmental failures. It seems that it is acceptable to treat problems such as depression and social anxiety disorder with medication, but there is often strong resistance to probing the psychological sources of the disorder. The need for psychotherapy continues to be seen as shameful.

Ty Cobb's Mental Illness

Ty Cobb, the first player to be elected to the baseball Hall of Fame, chosen for his legendary accomplishments on the field, reportedly was highly disturbed during his entire lengthy career. According to Al Stump, his biographer, Cobb suffered from delusions of persecution and had been psychotic throughout his playing days.[28] His lack of impulse control was flagrant, his rage was easily triggered, and whenever he felt mistreated he would overreact, often violently, as if his very existence were being threatened. Historian Harold Seymour portrays Cobb as a tragic hero "who did not so much play baseball as wage it, for to him it was a war. . . . He fought his own teammates. . . . He battled the management, the fans and everyone in the world who crossed him." [29] In his readiness to do battle, Cobb became notorious for sharpening his spikes before games so he could wound opposing ballplayers, whom he considered his enemies.

Al Stump, who lived with Cobb while collaborating on his biography toward the end of his life, depicts Cobb as a paranoid schizophrenic when functioning at his worst and describes what we would currently refer to as a narcissistic personality disorder when he was at his best. [30] The outside world saw him as a despicable human being, but we must also recognize that he must have lived in a constant state of inner torment.

in 1905, at age eighteen, Cobb had experienced an unusual trauma that significantly shaped his personality just as he was breaking into the major leagues. In a bizarre accident his mother, who was only fifteen when Ty was born, killed his father with a shotgun, mistaking him for an intruder. It has been speculated that Cobb's father, a saintly man who was highly respected in the community, suspected his wife of infidelity and, after leaving for a trip, crept through his wife's bedroom window to check his suspicion. Cobb maintained that he worshiped his father, who has been described in his biography as powerful and dominant, and he claimed that his life-and-death approach to baseball was a tribute to his devoted father. The trauma of his father's murder plagued Cobb for the rest of his life and seemed to trigger a perpetual burning drive to excel and to indirectly avenge his father. Harold Seymour concluded that "throughout his life Cobb appears to have been obsessed by the dreadful circumstances surrounding the death of his revered father . . . it was a tragedy that preyed on his mind and apparently exacerbated his disturbed personality." [31] Stump has pointed out earlier signs of Ty's "uncontrollable temper." For example, he was briefly suspended from school at age ten when he physically attacked a classmate for making an error in a spelling bee. [32] It seems safe to infer that a low tolerance for frustration, poor impulse control, and a readiness to act out aggressively were present from an early age, and these tendencies were intensified after his mother killed his father. It is likely that he could not express his rage directly toward his mother, so he displaced it onto others who got in his way, frustrated his wishes, or made him feel mistreated. In Cobb's own words, "I had to fight all my life to survive. They were all against me . . . but I beat the bastards and left them in the ditch."[33] It is also likely that in some respects Cobb became an extreme version of his authoritarian, strict father, a kind of caricature often seen in offspring who identify with the more prominent aspects of a parent's personality.

Cobb's status as a hero is derived largely from his enormous success as a hitter. His lifetime batting average of .367 is the highest of anyone who has ever played Major League Baseball, and it is a record that probably will never be broken. In contrast to most of the other sports stars discussed in this chapter, whose mental health problems interfered with their athletic performance, Cobb's megalomania and paranoid orientation seemed to fuel a fierce determination that heightened his ability to excel.

He was able to get away with much of his violent behavior because of his celebrity status. (He once threatened a butcher with a gun for being disrespectful to his wife, he pummeled a disabled fan who had heckled him, and according to biographer Al Stump, he had even killed a man who had tried to mug him.) It was a classic case of Cobb the man thinking and acting as if his baseball feats made him a god.

Nevertheless, he suffered profound emotional and interpersonal difficulties. Constantly battling his demons, warding off perceived attacks, and unable to be sensitive to the needs of others, Ty Cobb lived a lonely and combative existence. Only a few people from the world of baseball attended his funeral.

Suicide

There has been a long-standing debate among mental health experts about whether suicide attempts are an expression of mental illness. Does one have to be mentally ill to perform such an extreme act? The answer is inconclusive, but except for terminally ill patients and those who are intent on controlling their own destiny, suicide generally reflects an absence or a failure of coping mechanisms. It is estimated that people diagnosed with bipolar disorder are ten to twenty times as likely to commit suicide as the general population. Those with untreated depression are also at higher risk for suicide.

A pronounced loss of self-esteem with little hope of regaining it and an attempt to relieve unbearable internal pressure—an escape from what is experienced as overwhelming stress—are the leading theories psychoanalysts advance to explain suicide.[34]

Athletes' Mental Health Problems

How does this apply to sports heroes? There is little evidence that those who have been professional athletes commit suicide more often than the general population, but it is easy to see how they might be at greater risk, especially in the transitional years after retirement. As Dan Gutman reports in *Baseball Babylon*,[35] Loren Coleman, who researched suicide among Major League Baseball players, found that more than half of the players who killed themselves did so within ten years of their retirement. Considering that most leave the game before age forty, this is a significant statistic. Moreover, the highest risk period appears to be soon after leaving the game (there are at least seven known suicides within one year), which reflects their enormous adjustment problems.

A prominent example of how the loss of self-esteem and the need to relieve unbearable internal pressure can precipitate suicide is seen in the death of California Angels pitcher Donnie Moore. In a 1986 playoff game Moore was within one strike of leading his team into the World Series when he yielded a home run that led to his team's loss and ultimate elimination from the playoffs. In the aftermath he became depressed and obsessed with his failure, and he never regained his effectiveness as a pitcher. Three years later, after being dropped by Major League Baseball and undergoing a stormy marital separation, Moore shot his wife (she survived) and then blew his brains out in front of his ten-year-old son.

Hugh Casey, one of the most famous early relief pitchers in baseball with the Brooklyn Dodgers, also took his own life in a violent way in stressful circumstances. In 1951, his first year out of baseball, Casey, thirty-eight, had struggled to deal with a heart ailment, estrangement from his wife, and a tax lien filed against him. Even more compellingly, he was humiliated and despairing over a paternity suit judgment against him. Just seconds before he killed himself by firing a shotgun into his neck, Casey called his wife and said, "I am completely innocent of those charges. . . . I can't eat or sleep since going through all the embarrassment. And I had to drag you through it too, but I swear with a dying oath that I am innocent."[36]

It is important to consider the cultural context in which Hugh Casey committed suicide. Today it is commonplace for professional athletes to deal with paternity suits without shame. If DNA testing confirms fatherhood, then the athlete is held responsible. In the 1950s, before DNA testing, such allegations were difficult to disprove, and a judicial judgment, as in Casey's case, meant disgrace. By today's standards, when we routinely see headlines about athletes accused in paternity suits and in sexual assaults on women, it is unlikely that "embarrassment" would have driven Casey to suicide.

Willard Hershberger stands out as the only active player in Major League history to commit suicide. Hershberger was a backup catcher for the Cincinnati Reds during their championship season in 1940 when he inexplicably slashed his throat. His suicide stunned the baseball world, but in retrospect there had been warnings. Hershberger had been depressed over his recent play and blamed himself for the loss of a tough game. He had also been losing weight, suffered from insomnia and headaches, and had even confided to his manager that he had previously attempted suicide. Hershberger's father had killed himself eleven years earlier, and this family history undoubtedly put him at greater risk for suicide, as a response to internal stress and a loss of self-esteem that made him feel like a failure.

An impulsive suicide of an active professional football player occurred on December 14, 1993. Jeff Alm, a Houston Oilers defensive tackle, was driving with a friend at 3:00 a.m. when his car crashed on a Houston freeway overpass. Alm was driving, and his best friend was thrown from the car and killed. The twenty-five-year-old player was overwhelmed by the tragedy—he grabbed a shotgun from the trunk and shot himself in the head. In contrast to the Willard Hershberger situation, in Alm's case there were no warning signs. Alm was legally drunk and speeding at the time of the accident, and he may have felt responsible for his friend's death. It seems likely that guilt and self-loathing, plus the influence of alcohol, led to the rash decision to kill himself.

The suicides of two other NFL players illustrate the precipitous decline that may occur on retirement from the game. Jim Duncan had starred as a cornerback with the Baltimore Colts when they won Super Bowl V in 1970, but his playing fell off dramatically the next season, and after brief stints with the Saints and the Dolphins he was released at age twenty-six. In despair over a broken marriage, a bleeding ulcer, and a huge business failure, he reportedly walked into a police station, grabbed a revolver from a police lieutenant, and shot himself in the head. Shocked by his sudden death, family members questioned the police version of Duncan's shooting, implying that Duncan, who was

Athletes' Mental Health Problems

black, might have become a victim in a racial incident. They were left unsatisfied by an inquest that confirmed he had killed himself. An alternative theory is that Duncan's suicide reflected his inability to cope with multiple personal setbacks after a career in the limelight.

Larry Bethea starred as a defensive lineman for the Dallas Cowboys from 1978 to 1983. He had been a first-round draft pick after being named Most Valuable Player in the Big Ten while playing for Michigan State. When his NFL career floundered, he signed on with the United States Football League, and after two more lackluster seasons he was out of professional football at age twenty-nine. In September 1986 he was charged with assaulting his estranged wife, and during the divorce proceedings he stole his mother's life savings of $64,000. He faced up to twenty years in prison for theft, but he was given only a four-year suspended sentence and two years' probation. Several months later, after being identified as a suspect in two armed robberies of neighborhood convenience stores, Bethea shot himself in the head. His suicide apparently was touched off when his career nosedived and his life spun out of control.

Professional athletes may be at greater risk for suicide (and other forms of mental decompensation) soon after leaving the game, which invariably occurs when they are relatively young. Taking up "normal" life after retirement can be a profound adjustment, and many athletes have trouble ending their careers gracefully. Jim Brown, Sandy Koufax, Joe DiMaggio, and Barry Sanders are among the few superstars who left at the top of their game. Brown, who was dominant in professional football in the 1960s, has pointed out that "an athlete's need to cling to a career that is past due goes beyond a mere love of the game; it says more about an unpreparedness to face a future without sports. . . . To move away from that [sports], not to feel that crowd, not to be able to perform, that's like death."[37]

The loss of recognition, affirmation, and special treatment can lead to depression and other mental health problems. Sports stars also have a very high divorce rate in the year and a half following retirement. Many are at a loss for how to act without their sports identity. When the fickle public abandons them after their retirement, they can be devastated. They need the psychological ability to set new goals and find new ways to feel affirmed. The task is daunting, but the alternative is to become a sports hero as fallen idol.

Epilogue

The prevalence of athletes who are caught up in gambling, drugs or alcohol, violence toward women, murder, violence between players, and mental illness—the primary themes of this book—has been growing rapidly. The cavalcade of new incidents seems endless. Here are a few episodes that have recently made headlines.

January 2003: Dwayne Goodrich, Dallas Cowboys defensive back, was convicted of manslaughter for the hit-and-run deaths of two men who had stopped to help someone in a burning car. Goodrich was sentenced to seven and a half years in prison.

March 2003: Adrian McPherson, a former Florida State University quarterback, was charged with gambling on games he played in. His trial ended in a hung jury and was expected to go to retrial. McPherson was also awaiting trial on charges of grand theft for allegedly receiving $3,500 from a stolen check. He was suspended from the football team. Subsequently he was given thirty months of probation plus community service and required to repay $4,000 in a multifaceted plea bargain.

March 2003: Jim Harrick, the men's basketball coach at the University of Georgia, was suspended in connection with allegations of academic fraud and unethical conduct when it was revealed that three players had been given fraudulent grades in a class taught by his son. Harrick had previously been dismissed for falsifying expense accounts after winning the national title at UCLA in 1995.

April 2003: Zack Randolph, a Portland Trail Blazer reserve forward, was suspended for two games and fined $100,000 for punching teammate Ruben Patterson in the face during a heated practice session.

April 2003: Dennis Weatherby, an Oregon State University cornerback and a leading NFL prospect, was wounded in a random drive-by shooting in a violent neighborhood in California. Weatherby survived and was drafted by the Cincinnati Bengals.

May 2003: Mike Price, newly appointed as football coach at the University of Alabama, was fired for inappropriate behavior: he allegedly partied at a strip club, paid for private dances, and engaged in indiscretions with a woman in his hotel room. Although the penalty seemed excessive, the university president said Price had previously been warned about his conduct.

June 2003: Mike Tyson, former heavyweight boxing champion, was charged with assault and harassment in connection with a brawl in a Brooklyn hotel.

June 2003: Billy Gaines, University of Pittsburgh wide receiver, was legally drunk when he fell from a catwalk in a church and was killed.

June 2003: Jeremiah Parker, former New York Giants defensive end, was acquitted of aggravated manslaughter in the death of his girlfriend's four-year-old son. He was convicted of child endangerment.

July 2003: Kobe Bryant, Los Angeles Lakers superstar, was arrested on charges of sexual assault for an alleged rape in Colorado. The case was eventually dropped.

July 2003: Keith Davis, Dallas Cowboys safety, was wounded in a shooting at a topless nightclub in Dallas.

July 2003: Dwayne Carswell, Denver Broncos tight end, was arrested on charges of battery and domestic violence after allegedly assaulting his girlfriend. Carswell had previously received probation for a similar incident with a former girlfriend.

July 2003: Chris Webber, Sacramento Kings All-Star, was spared a jail sentence for charges that he lied to a grand jury about his affiliation with a former University of Michigan booster who claimed he had given Webber $280,000. In a plea bargain Webber admitted being guilty of criminal contempt.

July 2003: Carlton Dotson, a Baylor University basketball player, was charged with the murder of teammate Patrick Dennehy. Dotson claimed he had been hearing voices and had acted in self-defense. In October 2004 a district judge ruled that Dotson was incompetent to stand trial.

July 2003: Roman Lyashenko, New York Rangers forward, committed suicide while on vacation in Turkey with his mother and sister. He left a note in which he apologized for hanging himself.

August 2003: William Ligue, a fan who with his fifteen-year-old son attacked Kansas City Royals coach Tom Gamboa on the playing field in an unprovoked incident, was given thirty months' probation.

September 2003: Rod Rutherford, University of Pittsburgh starting quarterback, was charged with assaulting a nineteen-year-old woman outside a Pittsburgh nightclub after she refused his advances.

September 2003: Joey Porter, Pittsburgh Steelers Pro Bowl linebacker, was wounded in a drive-by shooting in Denver. He recovered and returned to the starting lineup only three weeks later.

September 2003: Chris Terry, Seattle Seahawks offensive tackle, was suspended by the NFL for four games for violating the league's personal conduct and substance abuse policies.

September 2003: Korey Stringer's widow, Kelci, filed a lawsuit against the NFL charging negligence in of her husband's untimely death in 2001 from heatstroke.

September 2003: Maurice Clarett, the sensational running back who led Ohio State University to the 2002 national championship, was charged with a misdemeanor falsification for lying to the police about the value of items that were stolen from him. Clarett was suspended indefinitely by the university and faced up to six months in prison if convicted. He avoided jail time by pleading guilty to a lesser charge of failing to aid law enforcement.

October 2003: Marcus Williams of the Oakland Raiders filed a lawsuit against teammate Bill Romanowski for injuries sustained in a training camp fight two months earlier. Williams suffered a broken occipital bone when Romanowski punched him in the face.

October 2003: Dany Heatley, a hockey All-Star with the Atlanta Thrashers, was charged with vehicular homicide in connection with the death of teammate Dan Snyder. Heatley allegedly was driving recklessly when his Ferrari went out of control and crashed into a wall. If convicted, he could receive a fifteen-year prison sentence. A trial date is tentatively scheduled for February 2005. Lawyers have been unsuccessful in plea negotiations.

October 2003: Jimmy Smith, Jacksonville Jaguars receiver, was reinstated after sitting out a four-game suspension for violating the NFL's substance abuse policy.

October 2003: Paul Spadafora, former lightweight boxing champion, was arrested for attempted homicide and aggravated assault in the alleged shooting and critical injury of a woman at a gas station near Pittsburgh.

November 2003: Dernell Stenson, a twenty-five-year-old outfielder with the Cincinnati Reds, was murdered in a Phoenix suburb.

November 2003: Mike Anderson, a Denver Broncos fullback who was the NFL's offensive rookie of the year in 2000, was suspended for four games for a repeat violation of the league's substance abuse policy.

November 2003: Four prominent players on the Oakland Raiders— Bill Romanowski, Barret Robbins, Dana Stubblefield, and Chris Cooper—tested positive for TGH, a recently banned steroid.

November 2003: Maurice Taylor, an NBA player with the Houston Rockets, had his suspension for violating the league's substance abuse policy reduced from ten games to six.

November 2003: William Green, the Cleveland Browns' leading rusher, was stabbed in the back, allegedly by his fiancée. Green had previously been suspended for four games for violating the substance abuse policy.

November 2003: Lawrence Taylor's book *Over the Edge* is released; he claims to have provided escort service to opposing teams' star running backs.

December 2003: Ivan Calderon, a former ten-year veteran of Major League Baseball, was shot to death in a store in Puerto Rico.

December 2003: Tennis star Greg Rusedski revealed that he had tested positive for nandrolene in July 2003. Rusedski asserted that the substance was in a supplement provided by ATP trainers, and a hearing on the case was scheduled. He was later cleared of doping charges for lack of evidence.

January 2004: Eric Lindros, New York Rangers hockey star, suffered his eighth career concussion after being flattened by Washington Capitals defenseman Jason Doig.

February 2004: Jamal Lewis, the Baltimore Ravens' star running back, who in 2003 rushed for the second-highest total yardage in a season, was charged with conspiracy to distribute cocaine. Lewis faced ten years to life in prison if convicted. Lewis accepted a plea bargain and received a four-month prison sentence plus two months in a halfway house.

March 2004: The Colorado Avalanche's Steve Moore suffered a broken neck and concussion when he was sucker punched by the Vancouver Canucks' All-Star forward Todd Bertuzzi.

March 2004: Michael Pittman, the Tampa Bay Buccaneers' star running back, pled guilty to felony endangerment after he allegedly rammed another car containing his wife and two-year-old son.

March 2004: Calvin Murphy, an NBA Hall of Famer, was charged with sexually assaulting his five daughters more than ten years earlier.

April 2004: Mike Danton, an NHL player with the St. Louis Blues, was arrested in an alleged murder-for-hire plot. Danton claimed he was afraid the supposed victim would kill him. He accepted a plea bargain and was sentenced to seven and a half years in prison.

May 2004: Jayson Williams, the former New Jersey Nets star, was acquitted of manslaughter but convicted of four counts of coverup in the shooting of limousine driver Costas Christofi.

June 2004: Todd Bertuzzi was charged with assault for attacking Steve Moore on the ice. Bertuzzi pleaded guilty, and in December 2004 he was given one year of probation and eighty hours of community service. He could have received eighteen months in jail.

July 2004: Dany Heatley was indicted on charges of vehicular homicide. Plea negotiations reached a stalemate, and a trial was scheduled for February 2005.

August 2004: Greek sprinters Kostas Kenteris and Katerina Thanou were barred from the Athens Olympics for failing to take drug tests before the Games.

September 2004: Frank Francisco, Texas Rangers pitcher, was suspended for the rest of the season for throwing a chair into the stands and injuring two fans.

October 2004: Ken Caminiti, a former National League Most Valuable Player, died of an overdose of cocaine and opiates.

November 2004: A brawl between the Indiana Pacers and the Detroit Pistons escalated into violence between players and fans.

December 2004: The BALCO steroid scandal intensified.

Among the major stories of 2004 about athletes' misbehavior were the Kobe Bryant sexual assault case, which was dropped; the Jayson Williams murder trial, which ended in a conviction on several counts and required a second trial on additional charges; the growing trend of violence between professional athletes and fans; and the BALCO steroids scandal. All these stories send a message to children that their adored sports heroes may commit illegal, immoral, and violent acts. It is frightening to think that kids may be apt to emulate these antisocial behaviors.

After separate incidents in which baseball players Milton Bradley and Frank Francisco threw dangerous objects into the stands in confrontations with heckling fans, the NBA brawl involving the Indiana Pacers, Detroit Pistons, and a score of spectators resulted in a record suspension for Ron Artest and substantial penalties against teammates Stephen Jackson and Jermaine O'Neal of the Pacers, as well as Ben Wallace of the Pistons.

In the BALCO scandal it was alleged that Olympic star Marion Jones and baseball superheroes Barry Bonds, Jason Giambi, and Gary Sheffield had excelled with the help of performance enhancing drugs.

Major League Baseball is under pressure from the federal government to impose stricter legislation against the use of steroids. Some fans are indifferent to suspicions that their heroes might be breaking long-standing records with the help of drugs; what matters most to them is that they can continue to identify with the herculean accomplishments of their much-needed icons. But other fans are struggling with the uncomfortable realization that many sports heroes must now be seen as tainted rather than sainted.

The incidents cited above are a sample of the self-destructive acts, violent attacks, and gambling offenses committed by present-day sports heroes. Every day there are new other cases that receive media attention. All indications are that this escalating trend is likely to continue even though the major league sports organizations impose suspensions and other penalties for off-field transgressions.

Sanctions can serve as a deterrent, but athletes need to recognize how greatly their values and actions influence their adoring fans. Making team psychologists available to help sports stars deal with their problems may also encourage them to develop a more balanced view of themselves in relation to the world and limit their inclination to act out in destructive ways.

Some people argue that there is nothing new about sports heroes who stumble into self-destructive pathways or are destructive toward others. They maintain that in the past the darker side of our heroes' behavior was hidden by a gentlemen's agreement among sportswriters, who colluded to preserve their pure image and shield the public. While this view may be somewhat accurate, it is also true that the use of illegal substances and other drug-related crimes were not rampant four decades ago; nor would it have been possible to overlook athletes who were accused of murder. Indeed, something has changed in the landscape, and these scandals in the sports world seem to parallel the shift in which tales of corruption have come to permeate our society.

Our hero-worship, which conditions athletes to view themselves as special and entitled to whatever they want, plants the seeds of moral and legal lapses. In addition, the multimillion-dollar contracts and endorsement opportunities showered on our sports stars reinforce their inflated self-image. While suspensions, penalties, and fines will curb some athletes' transgressions, the sports scandals that regularly command our attention will probably continue to bombard us. The genie is out of the bottle, and we risk compiling an ever increasing roster of fallen idols.

On a more positive note, there are some indications that athletes are gradually getting the message—that their destructive behavior hurts them as well as undermining the integrity of the game. Certainly the incidence of gambling scandals has declined significantly. That the major sports leagues are enforcing sanctions against their players' illegal and immoral actions is an important step. Another hopeful sign will be if the majority of fans turn against stars who are found to be using performance enhancing drugs rather than rewarding them for the excitement of record-breaking accomplishments. A more stringent policy against abuse of women is also required to curb the growing epidemic of episodes involving athletes.

Notes

1. The Need for Heroes

1. Peggy Noonan, "Three Presidents: One Lesson," *Wall Street Journal*, February 9, 2001.

2. James T. Farrell, *My Baseball Diary* (Carbondale: Southern Illinois University Press, 1998), 189.

3. Michael Sokolove, *Hustle: The Myth, Life and Lies of Pete Rose* (New York: Simon and Schuster, 1990), 173.

4. Bruce Nash and Allan Zullo, *The Baseball Hall of Shame 3* (New York: Pocket Books, 1987), 52.

5. Nash and Zullo, *Baseball Hall of Shame*, 52.

6. Shaquille O'Neal on *Meet the Press*, February 11, 2001.

7. Alan Schwarz, "In the Spirit of Koufax," *New York Times*, September 9, 2001.

8. Bob Andelman, *Why Men Watch Football* (Lafayette LA: Acadian House, 1993), 4.

9. Andelman, *Why Men Watch Football*, 47.

10. Kate Douglas, "When You Wish upon a Star," *New Scientist* (London) 179, no. 2408 (August 16, 2003): 26.

11. Andelman, *Why Men Watch Football*, 24.

12. Andelman, *Why Men Watch Football*, 45.

13. Andelman, *Why Men Watch Football*, 39.

14. Josh Elliott, "Field of Dreams," *Sports Illustrated*, October 6, 2003, 34.

15. Russell Baker, quoted in Dan Gutman, *Baseball Babylon* (New York: Penguin Books, 1992), 348.

16. Farrell, *My Baseball Diary*, 187, 192.

17. Laurie Nicole Robinson, "Professional Athletes—Held to a Higher Standard and Above the Law," *Indiana Law Journal* 73, no. 5 (1998): 2.

18. Robinson, "Professional Athletes," 2.

19. Roger Angell, *A Pitcher's Story: Innings with David Cone* (New York: Warner Books, 2001), 106.

20. Peter Richmond, "Doc and Darryl," *Gentleman's Quarterly*, July 2001, 164.

21. Richmond, "Doc and Darryl," 166.

22. Richmond, "Doc and Darryl," 167.

23. Interview with Charlie Rose, PBS, February 13, 2001.

24. R. D. Rosen, letter, *New York Times*, August 21, 2001.

25. Lawrence Kudlow and James Cramer, CNBC, December 7, 2004.

26. "Mr. November," *New York Post*, November 1, 2001.

27. Maury Allen, *Where Have You Gone, Joe DiMaggio? The Story of America's Last Hero* (New York: Dutton, 1975).

28. Richard Ben Cramer, *Joe DiMaggio: The Hero's Life* (New York: Simon and Schuster, 2000), 430.

29. Cramer, *Joe DiMaggio*, 430.

30. Ed Linn, *Hitter: The Life and Turmoil of Ted Williams* (New York: Harcourt, Brace, 1993), 30.

31. Press conference, Fenway Park, May 12, 1991, quoted in Linn, *Hitter*.

32. Linn, *Hitter*, 130.

33. Linn, *Hitter*, 125.

34. Linn, *Hitter*, 124–25.

35. Linn, *Hitter*, 125.

2. The Psyche of the Athlete

1. Tom House, *The Jock's Itch* (Chicago: Contemporary Books, 1989).

2. Jim Bouton, personal communication, March 31, 1993.

3. Jim Bouton, personal communication, March 31, 1993.

4. House, *Jock's Itch*, 4.

5. House, *Jock's Itch*, 6.

6. House, *Jock's Itch*, 3.

7. Bill Bradley, *Life on the Run* (New York: Quadrangle Books, 1976), 122.

8. Bradley, *Life on the Run*, 123.

9. Ortiz quoted in Robert Lipsyte, "Spoiled Athletes Have Syndrome All Their Own," *New York Times*, October 7, 2001.

10. Steven M. Ortiz, "When Sport Heroes Stumble: Stress and Coping Responses to Extramarital Relationships among Wives of Professional Athletes," paper presented at the annual meeting of the American Sociological Association, Anaheim CA, August, 2001, 5.

11. Ortiz, "When Sport Heroes Stumble," 3.

12. Ortiz, "When Sport Heroes Stumble," 21.

13. Sokolove, *Hustle*, 183.

14. Sokolove, *Hustle*, 53.

15. Dave Meggyesy, *Out of Their League* (Berkeley CA: Ramparts, 1970), 182.

16. Steven M. Ortiz, *Traveling with the Ball Club: A Code of Conduct for Wives Only* (Greenwich CT: JAI Press, 1997), 237.

17. John Elson, "The Dangerous World of Wannabees," *Time Magazine*, November 25, 1991, 79.

18. Elson, "Dangerous World," 78.

19. Elson, "Dangerous World," 80.

20. House, *Jock's Itch*.

21. House, *Jock's Itch*.

22. David Remnick, "The September Song of Mr. October," in *The Best American Sports Writing of the Century*, ed. David Halberstam (Boston: Houghton Mifflin, 1999), 528.

23. Dennis Rodman, *Bad as I Wanna Be* (New York: Dell Books, 1996), 149.

24. Robinson, "Professional Athletes," 2.

25. William Nack and Lester Munson, "Sports' Dirty Secret," *Sports Illustrated*, July 31, 1995, 62; Jeff Benedict and Don Yaeger, *Pros and Cons: The Criminals Who Play in the NFL* (New York: Warner Books, 1998).

26. Paul Tagliabue, *Face the Nation*, transcript, January 28, 2001.

27. Robinson, "Professional Athletes," 2.

28. Mike Wise, "How Dean Meminger Turned His Life Around," *New York Times*, December 25, 2003.

29. Denny McLain and Mike Nahrstedt, *Strikeout: The Story of Denny McLain* (St. Louis MO: Sporting News, 1998), 15–16.

30. Jim Bouton, "How Baseball Grew a Gambler," *New York Times*, October 26, 1999.

31. Jerry Kramer, *Farewell to Football* (New York: World, 1969), 358–59.

32. Bouton, "How Baseball Grew a Gambler," 28.

33. Bruce Ogilvie, personal communication, November 23, 2001.

34. Reggie Jackson, quoted in Remnick, "September Song," 530.

35. Jim Bouton, *Ball Four* (New York: World, 1970), 106.

36. House, *Jock's Itch*, 127.

37. Stephen M. Weiss, "A Comparison of Maladaptive Behaviors of Athletes and Non-athletes, "*Journal of Psychology* 133, no. 3 (May 1999): 315–22.

38. Bradley, *Life on the Run*, 190.

39. Bob Cousy, quoted in Ira Berkow, "Love of the Game May Be Blind," *New York Times*, March 15, 2001.

3. Baseball Gambling Scandals

1. Eliot Asinof, *Eight Men Out: The Black Sox and the 1919 World Series* (New York: Henry Holt, 1987).

2. Harold Seymour, *Baseball*, vol. 2, *The Golden Age* (New York: Oxford University Press, 1971).

3. Leonard Koppett, *Koppett's Concise History of Major League Baseball* (Philadelphia: Temple University Press, 1998), 143.

4. "Eight White Sox Players Are Indicted on Charges of Fixing 1919 World Series," *New York Times*, September 29, 1920.

5. "Eight White Sox Players Are Indicted."

6. "Eight White Sox Players Are Indicted."

7. Seymour, *Baseball*, 330.

8. Arnold "Chick" Gandil," This Is My Story of the Black Sox Series," *Sports Illustrated*, September 17, 1956, 61–69.

9. Gandil," This Is My Story of the Black Sox Series," 68.

10. Seymour, *Baseball*, 288–89.

11. Louis Effrat, "Chandler Bans Durocher for 1947 Baseball Season," *New York Times*, April 10, 1947.

12. "The Text of Commissioner Kuhn's Statement in McLain Case," *New York Times*, April 2, 1970.

13. George Vecsey, "Baseball Suspends McLain for Ties to Gambling," *New York Times*, February 20, 1970.

14. Robert Lipsyte, "Season's Greetings," *New York Times*, April 9, 1970.

15. Morton Sharnik, "Downfall of a Hero," *Sports Illustrated*, February 23, 1970, 16–21.

16. "Strikeout," *Sporting News*, August 29, 1998, 12.

17. Fred Goodman, "Denny McLain Isn't Sorry," *Gentleman's Quarterly*, March 1998, 202.

18. Sokolove, *Hustle*, 17–18.

19. Sokolove, *Hustle*, 19.

20. Sokolove, *Hustle*, 113.

21. Gutman, *Baseball Babylon*, 200.

22. Gutman, *Baseball Babylon*, 203.

23. Sokolove, *Hustle*, 294.

24. Sokolove, *Hustle*, 292.

25. Craig Neff and Jill Lieber, "Rose's Grim Vigil," *Sports Illustrated*, April 3, 1989, 59.

26. Stanley H. Teitelbaum, letter to the editor, *New York Times*, July 30, 1989.

27. Gutman, *Baseball Babylon*, 204–5.

28. Mike Dodd, "Rose a Long Throw from Returning: Despite a Decade

of Self Promotion, Charlie Hustle's Ban Holds Fast," *USA Today*, August 23, 1999.

29. Joe Queenan, "And Pete Rose Is Still a Jerk," *Gentleman's Quarterly*, May 2000, 155.

30. Fay Vincent, "The Problem with Forgiving Pete Rose," *New York Times*, December 8, 1999.

31. Ken Berger, "Belle Admits to Gambling," *South Coast Today*, February 13, 1997.

4. Football Gambling Scandals

1. Arthur Daley, "Bell Rings the Bell," *New York Times*, April 4, 1947.

2. William Wallace, "Pro Football Ban on Hornung and Karras Lifted after 11 Months," *New York Times*, March 17, 1964.

3. Associated Press, "Hornung and Karras Suspended Indefinitely by Football League for Betting," *New York Times*, April 18, 1963.

4. "Pro Football's Rules," editorial, *New York Times*, April 22, 1963.

5. Arthur Daley, "The Crackdown," *New York Times*, April 19, 1963

6. Wallace, "Pro Football Ban on Hornung and Karras Lifted."

7. Scott MacGregor, "Art Schlichter: Bad Bets and Wasted Talent," *Cincinnati Enquirer*, July 2, 2000.

8. Judith Valente, "A Long Road to Daylight: A Fallen Football Hero Fights to Break Free of the Gambling Addiction That Sacked His Career—and Drove Him to Prison," *People Weekly* 45, no. 2 (January 15, 1996): 86.

9. Ron Reno, "The Dirty Little Secret Behind March Madness," *Citizen Magazine*, March 30, 1999.

10. Reno, " Dirty Little Secret."

11. Gregory Turk, Medill News Service, May 5, 1999.

5. Basketball Gambling Scandals

1. "Three Get Prison Term in Basketball Fix," *New York Times*, April 26, 1952.

2. "Baseball Hailed by Hoover of FBI," *New York Times*, February 5, 1945.

3. Arthur Daley, "Court Scandal," *New York Times*, January 31, 1945.

4. Arthur Daley, "The Newest Sports Hero," *New York Times*, January 6, 1949.

5. "Roth Regretful, Cautions Others," *New York Times*, February 20, 1951.

6. Ira Berkow, "Scandal, the Unwanted Scar of Triumph," *New York Times*, March 29, 1996.

7. Charley Rosen, *Scandals of '51* (New York: Seven Stories Press, 1978), 129.

8. Rosen, *Scandals of '51*, 134.

9. Rosen, *Scandals of '51*, 159.

10. Rosen, *Scandals of '51*, 202.

11. Rosen, *Scandals of '51*, 220.

12. Rosen, *Scandals of '51*, 220.

13. Rosen, *Scandals of '51*, 182.

14. Alfred E. Clark, "Judge in Fix Case Condemns Kentucky Teams and Coach," *New York Times*, April 30, 1952.

15. Clark, " Judge in Fix Case Condemns Kentucky Teams and Coach."

16. "Sports Bill Signed by Dewey," *New York Times*, March 22, 1951.

17. "The Cancer of Sports," editorial, *New York Times*, February 20, 1951.

18. Tim Cohane, "Behind the Basketball Scandal," *Look*, February 13, 1962, 87.

19. Cohane, "Behind the Basketball Scandal," 92.

20. Cohane, "Behind the Basketball Scandal," 92.

21. Jimmy Breslin, "The Fix Was On," *Saturday Evening Post*, February 23, 1963, 18.

22. Breslin, "Fix Was On," 18.

23. Cohane, "Behind the Basketball Scandal," 87.

24. Charley Rosen, *The Wizard of Odds* (New York: Seven Stories Press, 2001), 53.

25. "Molinas's Past Sifted for Clues," *New York Times*, August 6, 1975.

26. Rosen, *Wizard of Odds*, 417.

27. "A Stain on the Game: Another Point-Shaving Scandal Rocks College Basketball," *Sports Illustrated*, CNNSI.com, March 27, 1998,

28. Mike Vietti, *Kansas State Collegian*, August 31, 1998.

29. Armen Keteyian, Harvey Araton, and Martin Dardis, *Money Players: Inside the New NBA* (New York; Pocket Books, 1997), 9.

6. Self-Destructive Athletes

1. Benedict and Yaeger, *Pros and Cons*, ix.

2. Stephen S. Dubner, "Life Is a Contact Sport," *New York Times Magazine*, August 18, 2002, 23.

3. John Mossman, "Coach, QB Say Arrest 'No Distraction,' " Associated Press, November 1, 2000.

4. Sally Jenkins, "A Dream within a Dream: Celtics Pick Bias," *Washington Post*, June 18, 1986.

5. William Gildea and Dave Sell, "Driesell: ACC's Best Ever," *Washington Post*, June 20, 1986.

6. Gildea and Sell, "Driesell."

7. Tom Verducci, "Totally Juiced," *Sports Illustrated*, June 3, 2002, 44.

8. Verducci, "Totally Juiced," 36.

9. Steve Courson and Lee R. Schreiber, *False Glory, Steelers, and Steroids: The Steve Courson Story* (Stamford CT: Longmeadow Press, 1991).

10. Courson and Schreiber, *False Glory*, 115.

11. Buster Olney, "It's Time for Players to Police Themselves," *New York Times*, June 3, 2002.

12. George W. Bush, State of the Union address, January 20, 2004.

13. D. Keller and G. L. Todd, "How Cocaine Kills Athletes," *International Journal of Cardiology* 44, no. 1 (1994): 19–28.

14. Ron Suskind, "Deadly Silence," *Wall Street Journal*, March 9, 1995.

15. Steve DiMeglio, "Opinions Mixed on Ephedra Use in Baseball," *USA Today Sports Weekly*, February 26, 2003, 5.

16. Bobby Ojeda, "Extreme Baseball," *New York Times*, February 23, 2003.

17. Bob Nightengale, "Beaning Up Is Rooted in Clubhouses," *USA Today Sports Weekly*, March 5, 2003, 11.

18. William Rhoden, "Faustian Pact: Performance for Health," *New York Times*, November 16, 2002.

19. George Gipe, *The Great American Sports Book* (New York: Doubleday, 1978), 330.

20. Jon Entine, *Taboo: Why Black Athletes Dominate Sports and Why We're Afraid to Talk about It* (New York: Public Affairs, 2000), 231.

21. Entine, *Taboo*, 273.

22. Entine, *Taboo*, 328.

23. Entine, *Taboo*, 328.

24. Dave Anderson, "The Meaning of Responsibility," *New York Times*, January 2, 1986.

25. Roy S. Johnson, "For Richardson, Another Chance," *New York Times*, January 16, 1986.

26. George Veesey, "The Bottom Line," *New York Times*, February 26, 1986.

27. Gutman, *Baseball Babylon*.

28. Lawrence Taylor and David Falkner, *LT: Living on the Edge* (New York: Times Books, 1987), 4.

29. Taylor and Falkner, *LT*, 120.

30. Taylor and Falkner, *LT*, 155.

31. Taylor and Falkner, *LT*, 14.

32. Ira Berkow, "Taylor's Dangerous Game," *New York Times*, August 30, 1988.

33. Berkow, "Taylor's Dangerous Game."

34. "Strawberry Gets More Jail Time and Is Ordered to Get Treatment," *New York Times*, November 10, 2000.

35. Steve Popper, "Mason's Arrest Adds to the Hornets' Troubles," *New York Times*, February 27, 2000.

36. Carrie Seidman, "Furlow of Utah Jazz Dies in Crash in Ohio," *New York Times*, May 24, 1980.

37. Claire Smith, "A touch of Normalcy, a Courageous Appearance," *New York Times*, March 25, 1993.

38. Jeff Pearlman, "At Full Blast: Shooting Outrageously from the Lip, Braves Closer John Rocker Bangs Away at His Favorite Targets," *Sports Illustrated*, December 22, 1999, 60.

39. Murray Chass, "Campanis Is Out: Racial Remarks Cited by Dodgers," *New York Times*, April 9, 1987.

40. David Grann, "Baseball without Metaphor," *New York Times Magazine*, September 1, 2002, 41.

41. Michael Rubinkam, "Judge Dismisses All but One Charge against Iverson," Associated Press, July 30, 2002.

42. "Iverson Says He Fears the Police and Might Leave Philadelphia," *New York Times*, November 20, 2002.

43. Kristen Lans, "Muscle vs. Aesthetics," *George Street Journal* 22, no. 21 (1998), www.brown.edu.

44. Lans, *Muscle vs. Aesthetics*.

45. "Drug Wars," *Tennis Magazine*, October 2002, 19.

46. Andrew Taber, "Roid Rage," *Health and Body*, November 18, 1999.

47. Grant Wahl, L. Jon Wertheim, and George Dohrmann, "Passion Plays," *Sports Illustrated*, September 10, 2001, 62.

48. Wahl, Wertheim, and Dohrmann, " Passion Plays," 63.

7. Athletes and Violence toward Women

1. Jeffrey A. Margolis, *Violence in Sports* (Berkeley Heights NJ: Enslow, 1999), 70.

2. Gutman, *Baseball Babylon*, 34.

3. Todd W. Crosset, Jeffrey R. Benedict, and Mark A. McDonald, "Male Student-Athletes Reported for Sexual Assault," *Journal of Sports and Social Issues* 19, no. 2 (1995): 126.

4. Jeff Benedict, *Public Heroes, Private Felons* (Boston: Northeastern University Press, 1997), ix.

5. Margolis, *Violence in Sports*, 68.

6. Robinson, "Professional Athletes," 5.

7. Robinson, "Professional Athletes," 9.

8. Robinson, "Professional Athletes," 10.

9. Paul Levy, "Studies Find More Violence by Athletes," *Minneapolis Star Tribune*, January 9, 1996.

10. Lisa Faye Kaplan, "Gang Rape: Why Are Athletes Suspect?" *Gannett News Service*, May 21, 1990.

11. Robert Leach, "Violence and Sports," *American Journal of Sports Medicine*, September 19, 1997.

12. Levy, "Studies Find More Violence by Athletes."

13. Levy, "Studies Find More Violence by Athletes."

14. David Holmstrom, "Do Aggressive Sports Produce Violent Men?" *Christian Science Monitor*, October 16, 1995.

15. Mike Freeman, "Commissioner Defends the Off-Field Behavior of Players," *New York Times*, January 27, 2001.

16. Paul Levy, "Studies Find More Violence by Athletes."

17. Nack and Munson, "Sports' Dirty Secret," 69.

18. Howard Manly, "Pro Football: Reasons Are as Inexplicable as the Violence," *Boston Globe*, February 6, 2000.

19. Manly, "Pro Football."

20. "Athletes and Violence," *Ask E. Jean*, America Today Television, November 20, 1995.

21. Jean, "Athletes and Violence."

22. Jean, "Athletes and Violence."

23. Jean, "Athletes and Violence."

24. "Violent Incidents Involving Professional Athletes," *Rivera Live*, February 3, 2000.

25. Holmstrom, "Do Aggressive Sports Produce Violent Men?"

26. Julie Cart, "Special Report: Crime and Sports '95; Sex and Violence," *Los Angeles Times*, December 27, 1995.

27. "Violent Incidents Involving Professional Athletes."

28. Margolis, *Violence in Sports*, 74.

29. Amy Worden, "Women Often Targets of Athletes," apbnews.com, January 25, 2000.

30. Benedict, *Public Heroes, Private Felons*, 77.

31. Benedict, *Public Heroes, Private Felons*, 215.

32. Robinson, "Professional Athletes," 3.

33. Cart, "Special Report," 1.

34. Robinson, "Professional Athletes," 4.

35. Robinson, "Professional Athletes," 4–5.

36. Robert Lipsyte, "Many Create the Climate for Violence," *New York Times*, June 18, 1995.

37. Cart, "Special Report," 4.

38. Vance Johnson, *The Vance: The Beginning and the End* (Dubuque IA: Kendall/Hunt, 1994), 77.

39. Johnson, *Vance*, 81.

40. Johnson, *Vance*, back cover.

41. Mike Vaccaro, "Peter Wasn't About to Quit," *Newark Star Ledger*, November 1, 1999.

42. Benedict, *Public Heroes, Private Felons*, 122–23.

43. Tom Osborne, *On Solid Ground* (Lincoln: Nebraska Book Publishing, 1996), 92–93.

44. Joe Lambe, "Phillips Sued for Assault," *Kansas City Star*, September 4, 1996.

45. Lambe, "Phillips Sued for Assault."

46. Michael Farber, "Coach and Jury," *Sports Illustrated*, September 25, 1995.

47. Farber, "Coach and Jury."

48. Osborne, *On Solid Ground*, 149–50.

49. Osborne, *On Solid Ground*, 151.

50. "Phillips to Stand Trial," CNNSI.com, June 27, 2000.

51. Philip Shenon, "Gastineau Ordered to Assist at Rikers," *New York Times*, November 21, 1984.

52. Judy Battista, "Contrite Gastineau Pays Visit to the Jets," *New York Times*, August 7, 2002.

53. "Unnecessary Roughness," Forty-eight Hours Investigates, CBS NEWS.com, April 5, 2002.

54. Benedict, *Public Heroes, Private Felons*, 83–100.

55. Benedict, *Public Heroes, Private Felons*, 89.

56. Benedict, *Public Heroes, Private Felons*, 86.

57. Michael A. Messner and Donald F. Sabo, *Sex, Violence, and Power in Sports: Rethinking Masculinity* (Freedom CA: Crossing Press, 1994), 53.

58. Messner and Sabo, *Sex, Violence, and Power in Sports*, 53.

59. Messner and Sabo, *Sex, Violence, and Power in Sports*, 53.

60. Johnson, *Vance*, 103.

61. Charlie Nobles, "Spike's Wife Details a Pattern of Violence," *New York Times*, August 29, 1995.

62. Mike Freeman and Steve Strunsky, "The Violent Life of Tito Wooten," *New York Times*, February 27, 1998.

63. Nack and Munson, "Sports' Dirty Secret," 64–65.

64. Nack and Munson, "Sports' Dirty Secret," 65.

65. Benedict, *Public Heroes, Private Felons*, 205.

66. Benedict and Yaeger, *Pros and Cons*, 185.

67. Benedict, *Public Heroes, Private Felons*, 210.

68. *Oprah Winfrey Show*, January 24, 2003.

69. Deborah Sontag, "Fierce Entanglements," *New York Times Magazine*, November 17, 2002, 55.

70. Benedict, *Public Heroes, Private Felons*, 206.

71. Nack and Munson, "Sports' Dirty Secret," 67.

72. Nack and Munson, "Sports' Dirty Secret," 66.

73. Nack and Munson, "Sports' Dirty Secret," 67.

74. Nack and Munson, "Sports' Dirty Secret," 70.

75. Nack and Munson, "Sports' Dirty Secret," 74.

76. Rachel Shuster, "Domestic Abuse No Stranger to Sports," *USA Today*, October 4, 1994.

77. "Wilkinson Pleads Innocent to Domestic Violence Charge," *USA Today*, September 15, 1995.

78. Charles Thompson, *Down and Dirty: The Life and Crimes of Oklahoma Football* (New York: Carroll and Graf, 1990).

79. Robert Lipsyte, "Violence, Redemption, and the Cost of Sports," *New York Times*, October 17, 1997.

80. Messner and Sabo, *Sex, Violence, and Power in Sports*, 62.

81. Greg Garrison and Randy Roberts, *Heavy Justice: The State of Indiana vs. Michael G. Tyson* (Reading MA: Addison-Wesley, 1994), 163.

82. Benedict, *Public Heroes, Private Felons*, 156.

83. Timothy Smith, "A Dream Destroyed," *New York Times*, July 5, 1998.

84. Smith, "Dream Destroyed."

85. Benedict and Yaeger, *Pros and Cons*, 263.

86. Jim Edwards, "Baseball's Al Martin Faces Bigamy Probe," Associated Press, April 24, 2000.

87. Edwards, "Baseball's Al Martin Faces Bigamy Probe."

88. Geoff Calkins, "Athletes and Domestic Violence," *Fort Lauderdale Sun-Sentinel*, October 17, 1995.

89. Gary Shelton, "Don't Let Abusers Off the Hook," *St. Petersburg Times*, July 25, 2002.

90. "Out of Bounds: Professional Sports Leagues and Domestic Violence," *Harvard Law Review* 109, no. 5 (1996): 1052.

91. Kathy Redmond, "It Is Time to Protect Students and Not Just College Athletes," *New York Times*, October 19, 1997.

92. Mike Freeman, "Fix Needed for Epidemic of Violence," *New York Times*, July 26, 2002.

8. Athletes and Murder

1. Benedict and Yaeger, *Pros and Cons*, 185.

2. Jim Newton and Andrea Ford, "Prosecutors Tell Tale of 'Other' Simpson Trial," *Los Angeles Times*, January 25, 1995.

3. Newton and Ford, "Prosecutors Tell Tale."

4. Newton and Ford, "Prosecutors Tell Tale."

5. "Jury Hears the 911 Tape, Deathbed Notes in First Day of Testimony," Court TV Online, November 20, 2000.

6. "Carruth Co-defendant Still on Hot Seat," Court TV Online, November 27, 2000.

7. Gutman, *Baseball Babylon*, 68.

8. "The Sports Felon Hall of Fame," Maximonline.com/sports, article 4459, January 2002.

9. "Text of Lewis' Statement to Police," *Atlanta Journal-Constitution*, February 16, 2000.

10. Adrian Wojnarowski, "Ranting Raven," *Bergen (NJ) Record*, January 24, 2001.

11. Jay Greenberg, "This Superstar Raven Is Also a Pathetic Disgrace," *New York Post*, January 24, 2001.

12. Gordon Forbes, "Henley Hoping to Spare Others a Life Behind Bars," *USA Today*, December 8, 2000.

13. Forbes, "Henley Hoping to Spare Others."

14. Ann W. O'Neill, "Tillman Killed in Arrogance, Prosecutor Says," *Los Angeles Times*, January 29, 2000.

15. O'Neill, "Tillman Killed in Arrogance."

16. Sheila Hotchkin, "Ex-NBA Star Williams Surrenders to Police," Associated Press, February 25, 2002.

17. Hotchkin, "Ex-NBA Star Williams Surrenders."

18. "Prosecutors: Ex Giant Parker Tried to Hide Signs of Abuse," sportingnews.com, June 30, 2001.

19. Gutman, *Baseball Babylon*, 65.

20. Mike Wise, "Dele and Dabord: The Twisting Trail of Two Brothers," *New York Times*, September 22, 2002.

9. Violence between Athletes

1. "Pete Rose and the Collision at Home Plate," The Baseball Page.com, May 2, 2004.

2. Gutman, *Baseball Babylon*, 74.

3. Gutman, *Baseball Babylon*, 292.

4. Edmund Vaz, "Institutionalized Rule Violation in Professional Hockey: Perspectives and Control Systems," in *Sport Sociology: Contemporary Themes*, ed. Andrew Yiannakis, Thomas D. McIntyre, Merrill J. Melnick, and Dale Hart (Dubuque IA: Kendall/Hunt, 1987), 252.

5. Vaz, "Institutionalized Rule Violation," 255.

6. Vaz, "Institutionalized Rule Violation," 253.

7. Gordon A. Bloom, "The Implications of Violence and Aggression in Hockey, "Better Hockey.com, October 16, 2002.

8. Jeff MacGregor, "Less Than Murder," *Sports Illustrated*, March 22, 1999, 103.

9. Gordon A. Bloom and Michael Smith, "Hockey Violence: A Test of Cultural Spillover Theory," *Sociology of Sport Journal* 13 (1996): 65–77.

10. "Suspension Not Enough, Brashear Says," ESPN.com, March 17, 2000.

11. "McSorley Found Guilty of Assault, Avoids Jail Time," CNNSI.com, October 7, 2000.

12. MacGregor, "Less Than Murder," 114.

13. Peter King, "The Unfortunate 500," *Sports Illustrated*, December 7, 1992, 23.

14. Joe Mandak, "Webster Remembered as a Man Who Valued Family," *Detroit News*, September 28, 2002.

15. Mike Freeman and Linda Villarosa, "The Perils of Pro Football Follow Some into Retirement," *New York Times*, September 26, 2002.

16. Margolis, *Violence in Sports*, 22.

17. Robert McG. Thomas Jr., "Lineman for Lions Is Paralyzed Below Chest," *New York Times*, November 20, 1991.

18. Langston Wertz Jr., "Stingley Draws Inspiration from Father," *Charlotte Observer*, April 11, 2003.

19. Jack Tatum, *They Call Me Assassin* (New York: Everest House, 1979).

20. Will McDonough, "Invitation from 'Assassin' Actually Was an Ambush," *Boston Globe*, October 18, 1996.

21. "McSorley Suspended Indefinitely for Slashing Brashear," CNNSI.com, February 23, 2000.

22. John Feinstein, *The Punch* (Boston: Little, Brown, 2002), 49.

23. Feinstein, *Punch*, 255.

24. Kermit Washington, "A Sudden, Violent Moment That Still Haunts a Life," *New York Times*, May 14, 2000.

25. Jack McCallum and Don Yaeger, "I Know He's Gone Off Before," *Sports Illustrated*, April 29, 1996, 37.

26. McCallum and Yaeger, "I Know He's Gone Off Before."

27. Mike Wise, "Two Knicks View Penalty as Too Severe," *New York Times*, January 18, 1999.

28. Walt Frazier, "When Athletes Run Amok," *New York Times*, December 6, 1997.

10. Athletes' Mental Health Problems

1. Allen Iverson, interviewed on ESPN Sports Center, August 18, 2003.

2. Otto Fenichel, *The Psychoanalytic Theory of Neurosis* (New York: W. W. Norton, 1945), 345.

3. Lance Rentzel, *When All the Laughter Died in Sorrow* (New York: Saturday Review Press, 1972), 254.

4. Rentzel, *When All the Laughter Died*, 204.

5. Rentzel, *When All the Laughter Died*, 118.

6. Rentzel, *When All the Laughter Died*, 265.

7. Pete Anthelm, review of *When All the Laughter Died in Sorrow*, by Lance Rentzel, *New York Times*, January 7, 1973.

8. George Vescey, "Questions for Parents of Athletes," *New York Times*, January 10, 1997.

9. Anthony DePalma, "Sex Abuse Jolts Canada's Revered Pastime: Hockey," *New York Times*, January 16, 1997.

10. Rick Mofina, "Coach in Abuse Case Given Parole in Canada," *New York Times*, October 22, 1998.

11. Mofina, "Coach in Abuse Case Given Parole."

12. Jay Morelli and Jim Reichert, *The Original Golf School Way* (New York: Schoolhouse Press, 2001), 124.

13. American Psychiatric Association, *Diagnostic and Statistical Manual of Mental Disorders*, 4th ed. (Washington DC: American Psychiatric Association, 1994), 412, 416.

14. Gutman, *Baseball Babylon*, 244.

15. Pat Jordan, "A Mound of Troubles," *New York Times Magazine*, February 11, 2001, 58.

16. APA, *Diagnostic and Statistical Manual*, 412, 416.

17. Jimmy Piersall and Al Hirshberg, *Fear Strikes Out: The Jim Piersall Story* (1955; Lincoln: University of Nebraska Press, 1999).

18. L. Jon Wertheim, "Prisoners of Depression," *Sports Illustrated*, September 8, 2003, 74.

19. "His Coach Says Robbins Was Acting Incoherently," *New York Times*, January 30, 2003.

20. Lisa Olsen, "Depression Disorders Encompass Superstars," *New York Daily News*, February 18, 2003.

21. Wertheim, "Prisoners of Depression," 74.

22. Wertheim, "Prisoners of Depression," 74.

23. Wertheim, "Prisoners of Depression," 74.

24. Wertheim, "Prisoners of Depression," 72.

25. Mike Freeman and Linda Villarosa, "The Perils of Pro Football Follow Some into Retirement," *New York Times*, September 26, 2002.

26. Freeman and Villarosa, "Perils of Pro Football."

27. Richard Lustberg. "Fearsome Opponent," PsychologyofSports.com, March 10, 2003.

28. Al Stump, *Cobb: A Biography* (Chapel Hill NC: Algonquin Books, 1994), 27.

29. Harold Seymour, *Baseball: The Golden Age* (New York: Oxford University Press, 1971), 107.

30. Stump, *Cobb*, 298.

31. Seymour, *Baseball*, 110.

32. Stump, *Cobb*, 35.

33. Seymour, *Baseball*, 111.

34. Fenichel,*Psychoanalytic Theory of Neurosis*, 400–401.

35. Gutman, *Baseball Babylon*, 244.

36. "Casey, Ex Dodger, Is Atlanta Suicide," *New York Times*, July 4, 1951.

37. William Rhoden, "Some Stars Don't Know How to Quit," *New York Times*, March 2, 2002.

Index

Canadian Hockey League (CHL), 203, 206–7, 225
Canisius College, 89
Canseco, José, 107, 127, 138
Capriati, Jennifer, 134–35
Capturing the Friedmans, 221
Carlesimo, P. J., 197, 216–18
Carolina Hurricanes, 126, 207
Carolina Panthers, 179
Carruth, Rae, 142, 178, 179–82, 186, 220
Carruth, Theodry, 181
Carson, Harry, 4, 143–44, 208
Carswell, Dwayne, 241
Casey, Hugh, 237–38
Cedeño, César, 178, 185
Center for Compulsive Gambling, 66
Center for the Study of Sports in Society, 139, 146
Chamberlain, Wilt, 3, 148
Chambers, Tom, 218
Chandler, A. B. "Happy," 44–46, 175
Chapman, Kathleen, 200
Chapman, Ray, 199–200
Charlotte Hornets, 124
Chase, Hal, 42–43, 100
Cherry, Ralph, 182
Chesser, Rhonda, 175
Chianakas, Mike, 79–80
Chiasson, Steve, 126
Chicago Bears, 58, 172, 209
Chicago Bulls, 99, 155, 194
Chicago Cubs, 56, 115, 184, 193, 201
Chicago White Sox, 138, 175. *See also* Black Sox scandal
children: abuse of, 151, 154–55, 157, 221–24, 241, 244; emulating athletes, 110, 245; groomed to become professional athletes, 17–20, 29, 64–65, 90, 154; murder of, 192–93; sports heroes and, 1–3, 24; witnessing domestic violence, 144–46, 158, 160, 167, 178
Chmura, Mark, 25, 138, 141, 142, 172
Chouinard, Bobby, 173

Chrebet, Wayne, 209
Christian, John, 45
Christofi, Costas, 191–92, 244
Chrystal, William, 87, 88
Chung, Connie, 146
Cialdini, Robert, 6
Ciccarelli, Dino, 204
Cicotte, Ed, 33, 35, 36–37, 40–41
Cincinnati Bengals, 66, 162, 164, 169, 241
Cincinnati Reds, 2, 116, 233, 238, 243; gambling scandals and, 33, 50, 52, 53, 55
Cincinnati Red Stockings, 184
Citadel, 209
City College of New York (CCNY), 69, 73, 74–76, 77–78, 82, 84
Clarett, Maurice, 242
Clark, Marcia, 179
Clarkson, John, 184
Clay, Nigel, 164
Clayborn, Raymond, 178, 182
Cleveland Browns, 105, 243
Cleveland Cavaliers, 93
Cleveland Indians, 36, 126, 199, 228
Clinton, Bill, 172
coaches and managers: confrontations with athletes, 201, 215–16, 217; confrontations with fans, 242; crimes committed by, 240; self-destructive, 129–30, 137, 241; sexual abuse of players by, 224–26; violence toward women by, 166
Cobb, Ernie, 92
Cobb, Ty, 8, 14; gambling scandals and, 43, 50, 51; mental illness of, 234–36; self-destructiveness of, 102, 199, 202
cocaine abuse. *See* drug abuse by athletes
Cochran, Johnnie, 217
Cohane, Tim, 89
Cohen, Herb, 75–76, 78
Cole, Jermaine, 188
Coleman, Derrick, 192

Solomon, Harold, 135
Sontag, Deborah, 160
Southern Methodist University, 75
South Pacific, 12
Spadafora, Paul, 243
Speaker, Tris, 43
Spellman, Alonzo, 231
Spiegel, S. Arthur, 52–53
Spikes, Irving, 157, 162
Spikes, Stacey, 157
Spivey, Bill, 83
Sporting Life, 184
Sporting News, 82
Sports Illustrated: coverage of self-destruc-
  tive athletes, 107, 127; coverage of
  violence between athletes, 200, 214;
  coverage of violence by athletes, 137,
  148, 152, 160, 191; gambling scandals
  and, 39, 40, 48, 52, 94
Sprewell, Latrell, 131, 197, 215–18, 219
St. Francis College of Brooklyn, 70
St. John's University, 81, 85, 87, 88
St. Joseph's College, 79, 86
St. Joseph's University, 87
St. Louis Blues, 203, 244
St. Louis Browns, 184
St. Louis Cardinals, 110, 227
St. Louis Rams, 152, 178
St. Louis University, 83
Stabler, Ken, 63–64
Stanky, Eddie, 129
Stanley, Raymond, 88
Stant, Shane, 136–37
Steinbrenner, George, 123
Steinhagen, Ruth Ann, 193–94
Stemmer, Harvey, 59–60, 71–72
Stenson, Dernell, 243
Stern, David, 9, 27, 118, 175, 215
steroids. See performance enhancing
  drugs
Stingley, Darryl, 197, 210
Stockton, John, 215
Stone, Jeff, 171
Stone, Linda, 171

Stossel, John, 127
Strahan, Michael, 143, 153
Strawberry, Darryl, 8–9, 102, 103, 122–
  24, 138, 149, 156
Street, Picabo, 233
Streit, Saul S., 83
Strikeout: The Story of Denny McLain
  (McLain), 48
Stringer, Korey, 113, 115, 242
The Stronger Women Get, the More Men Like
  Football (Nelson), 147
Stubblefield, Dana, 243
Stump, Al, 234–35, 236
sudden death due to drug abuse, 110–14
suicide, 236–39, 242
Sullivan, Neil, 220
Sullivan, Sport, 33–34
Super Bowl, 58, 61, 63, 106, 120, 143–
  44, 178, 186, 187, 230, 233
Suskind, Ron, 112
Sweeney, Jim, 92
Sweeting, Joseph, 186–87
Syracuse University, 67, 77

Tagliabue, Paul, 25, 142, 175
Tampa Bay Buccaneers, 105, 108, 194,
  230, 244
Tarasco, Tony, 107
Tarpley, Ron, 216
Tatum, Jack, 197, 210, 219
tax evasion by athletes, 52–53, 122, 123
Taylor, Gary, 189
Taylor, Lawrence, 102, 103–4, 120–22,
  243–44
Taylor, Maurice, 243
Teasley, Nikki, 233
Teitelbaum, Stanley H., 53–54
Tellem, Art, 56
Tennessee Titans, 175
tennis, 134–35, 228
terrorism, 195–96
Terry, Chris, 242
Test, Edward, 87
Texas Rangers, 119, 217, 245

148, 149–50, 153, 155, 156, 170–72; murder by, 183–84, 193–94; murder of, 178–84; paternity suits and, 181–82, 237–38; sexual promiscuity with athletes, 3–4, 20–25, 123–24, 170; violent toward male athletes, 171–72, 224. *See also* violence toward women

Wooten, Tito, 157–58, 162
Wright, Clyde, 42
Wright, Leroy, 86
Wynn, Jim, 171, 172

Xavier University, 80

Yaeger, Don, 58, 102, 169
Young, George, 121
Young, Steve, 208

Zarowitz, Jerome, 59
Zimmer, Don, 56
Zimmerman, Heine, 42
Zullo, Allan, 3